The
Father
of
Lights

Theology for the Life of the World

Jesus Christ is God come to dwell among humans, to be, to speak, and to act "for the life of the world" (John 6:51). Taking its mandate from the character and mission of God, Christian theology's task is to discern, articulate, and commend visions of flourishing life in light of God's self-revelation in Jesus Christ. The Theology for the Life of the World series features texts that do just that.

Human life is diverse and multifaceted, and so will be the books in this series. Some will focus on one specific aspect of life. Others will elaborate expansive visions of human persons, social life, or the world in relation to God. All will share the conviction that theology is vital to exploring the character of true life in diverse settings and orienting us toward it. No task is greater than for each of us and all of us together to discern and pursue the flourishing of all in God's creation. These books are meant as a contribution to that task.

The
Father
of
Lights

A Theology of Beauty

Junius Johnson

Ꞵ
Baker Academic
a division of Baker Publishing Group
Grand Rapids, Michigan

Published by Baker Academic
a division of Baker Publishing Group
PO Box 6287, Grand Rapids, MI 49516-6287
www.bakeracademic.com

Printed in the United States of America

Library of Congress Cataloging-in-Publication Data
Names: Johnson, Junius, 1976– author.
Title: The Father of lights : a theology of beauty / Junius Johnson.
Description: Grand Rapids, Michigan : Baker Academic, [2020] | Includes bibliographical
    references and index.
Identifiers: LCCN 2020002905 | ISBN 9781540962492 (cloth)
Subjects: LCSH: Aesthetics—Religious aspects—Christianity. | God (Christianity)—Beauty. |
    Philosophical theology.
Classification: LCC BR115.A8 J65 2020 | DDC 261.5/7—dc23
LC record available at https://lccn.loc.gov/2020002905

20 21 22 23 24 25 26   7 6 5 4 3 2 1

Soli Trinitati Gloria
Deus gaudii supermaximi, omnibenefaciens,
vobis sit laus omnium creaturarum,
in vos omnis intentio et desiderium;
in vobis opus hoc et omnes lectores requiescant
saecula usque ad saeculorum.

For my wife, Rebekah,
my partner, friend, and one true love:
your magnificence and grace underlie every page of this book.

For the many ways in which you tirelessly, and too often thanklessly,
remind me of the glory of God, I thank you, and I pray that in this book
you will find some reflection of the glory you have so faithfully
and powerfully reminded me of these many years.

Do you not know? Do you not hear?
  Has it not been told you from the beginning?
  Have you not understood from the foundations
  of the earth?

Isaiah 40:21

Contents

Detailed Contents

Acknowledgments

This book began when I was a teenager and newly converted to the Christian faith. I found that knowledge of the trinitarian God and the magnificent Christ were opening to me all the deep questions I had struggled with in my youthful arrogance. I had at the time as a most faithful and apt companion Rebecca Dennison, a friend who listened to all of my discoveries with a mixture of joy (for what was new to her) and indulgence (for the things she had never not known). But for all the progress I was making, I felt that one question very dear to me was eluding me: the nature of beauty. When I told her this, she responded without hesitation: "Oh. Beauty is what reminds you of God." I fell into her claim as Alice fell into the rabbit hole. In the twenty-five years since that time, I have never ceased to try to find a way to express the simplicity and fecundity of that insight that could in some way do justice to how it became a center around which my life has been ordered. With this book, I at last repay this debt.

More recently, I am indebted to the Anselm Society of Colorado Springs, whose generous invitation to speak to them provided the occasion for the talk that eventually became the first chapter. Likewise I am indebted to the C. S. Lewis Foundation, whose invitation the following summer produced the talk that became the basis for the second chapter.

I received a generous grant from the Yale Center for Faith and Culture, which funded the research leave that allowed me to write the text and provided a forum for discussion of the first chapter (in which connection I am especially grateful to Matthew Croasmun and Adam Eitel for their close reading and perceptive comments). I received ongoing institutional support in various ways from Baylor University, without whose rich community of scholars the writing of this text would have taken much longer.

I would also like to acknowledge the diligent and enthusiastic work of Kaitlyn Morris, who served as my research assistant during the writing of this project. Her tireless energy and thoughtful questions have deepened this project in many ways and have made the writing of it even more of a delight than it already was.

Last, I wish to thank the many individuals who took the time to read the manuscript and give feedback, including students past and present: Kaylie Page, Martha Brundage, Matthew Aughtry, Zachary Watters, Jesse Watters, Ruth Donnelly, Emily Engelhardt, Claire Gostomski, Sarah Jones, Isabel Kazan, Emily Messimore, Duncan Richards, Mary Frances Schorlemer, William Sharkey, William Tarnasky, and Natalie Widdows.

The story that lies in our hearts is not ours alone; it is one and the same story, given to humanity until such time as faith becomes sight. Until that time, what we have are shadows of that story. And this is a comfort: for though shadows cannot be held, they can at least show us the form of the reality.

Our hearts are really wiser than our minds. Our minds look after the shadows, but what the heart holds most dear is nearly always the thing in itself, that which the eyes of the soul recognize in the shadow. At the heart of the shadow lies the thing itself: that which is not best because it is loved by all but rather is loved by all because it is best. There, beneath a veil of myth and legend and science and information, lies the goal of all our longing. To this Three-in-One above all I owe thanks and gratitude.

Introduction

Every good giving and every perfect gift is from on high, coming down from the Father of lights, with whom there is no variation or shadow of turning.

James 1:17 (my translation)

There is such a thing as glory
And there are hints of it everywhere.

Rich Mullins, "Such a Thing as Glory"

Beauty is an idea whose attractiveness is as immediately apparent as the attractiveness of those things that are called beautiful. The sense of beauty—that is to say, the feeling that some things are beautiful—seems to be universal, and the commitment of each person to the value of beautiful things precedes any argumentation or justification. More than the good or the true or the just or the useful, we exhibit an allegiance to the beautiful that declares that we think its value is self-evident.

It is interesting then that beauty has remained one of the most stubbornly resistant of all the grand concepts that exercise the philosophical and theological mind. It is difficult enough to characterize, much less to define. As a result, many reflections approach the topic somewhat obliquely, turning to concrete instances of beauty (art) to get some purchase on the topic. These reflections are fruitful and, when carried out with specific reference to theological claims, make up that burgeoning field of reflection to which the term "theological aesthetics" refers.

This, however, will not be an entry in that rich conversation. I am not concerned in what follows with art, except peripherally, as offering examples of that central dynamic I am treating. The question this book will consider, in its broadest form, is: What is beauty? But, more narrowly, I am interested in understanding what beauty is in light of the theological realities revealed by God in Christ. So the question is transformed into the following: What theological account can we give of beauty? It is thus not a theological aesthetics but a theology of beauty that will take shape in what follows.

Defining the Question

Three Senses of the Word "Beautiful"

There are, however, various forms of even this more narrow question that could be considered. This appears when we take note that we may mean "beautiful" in multiple senses: broadly, properly, or most properly.

Most properly, when we say "beautiful," we are referring to beauty itself. This may be construed as a transcendental property of being, and thus, in theological terms, as a property of God; or it may be understood as a privileged concept within human thinking (one to which no thing as such corresponds). But insofar as, within a theological landscape, such abstract and non-individual human thoughts find themselves constantly referred to God, beauty in the most proper sense, taken either way, turns out to be largely about the same sort of thing: the doctrine of God. God is beautiful and the source of beauty; God is its source both because God is the cause of God's own beauty and because God is the cause of all beauty that is not divine.

In the second sense, the proper sense, "beautiful" refers to some creature or created state of affairs. Such things have been established in their beauty by God, and their beauty is a participation in original beauty, the ground of beauty, God the beautiful. Thus, it is implicitly the case that creatures are beautiful insofar as they actually image (and not merely are thought to image) God. It is to this sense that theological aesthetics belongs, for the artifacts of human industry are themselves creatures, and the beauty with which we imbue them is still a participation in the divine beauty. This second sense of "beautiful" is therefore concerned with the doctrine of creation.

In the third and broad sense, however, we use the word "beautiful" to refer to the experience of beauty—that is, to a situation in which something strikes me as beautiful. Beauty in the broad sense has to do with how the creature's character as image is subjectively encountered in the common space of the world. Thus it requires an explication of a different category than the other

two senses. The first and second senses of beauty are correlated to fundamental theological loci (the doctrine of God and the doctrine of creation,
respectively), while the third sense has rather to do with the encounter with
a reality described by a theological locus. Put another way, beauty in the first
sense is a doctrinal statement made within the doctrine of God; in the second
sense, it is a doctrinal statement made within the doctrine of creation. But in
the third sense, it is not a doctrinal statement in any theological locus. Rather,
it is an implication of such statements, and specifically of the doctrinal statements that constitute the earlier two senses of beauty.

As such, much of the excellent theological work done in the first[1] and
second areas[2] addresses questions that stand as presuppositional to the third
sense of beauty. An account of the third sense could therefore be considered
to require an antecedent account of the first and second senses, such that a
complete theology of beauty would consist of a full treatment of each of
these three. However, our situation in the history of theological reflection
does not require this. For even though the account I would give of the first
two senses of beauty differs materially from existing accounts, it is not the
case that the particularities of an account of beauty in the first or second
sense predetermine exactly what one can say of beauty in the third sense.
Rather, accounts of beauty in these first two senses are generically related,
and all the accounts within one or two genera can converge upon a common
account of the third sense.

Thus, it will be enough to know the genus to which my understanding of
the first two senses belongs. Briefly, as is perhaps already apparent, I treat
beauty in the first sense in the genus of positions that consider beauty to be
a name or property of God; in the second sense, I hold that creaturely beauty
stands on divine beauty in such a way that divine beauty not only is a necessary
precondition but also is determinative. Creaturely beauty is related to divine
beauty by means of participation, such that the beauty of creatures is never
disconnected from the beauty of God, though it is also not reducible to it, nor
is it any part of it. Individual theologians who share these commitments offer
specific accounts, with differences and nuances that modulate these generic
accounts of beauty in the first two senses. However, I do not think that the
specifics of the answers to the above questions greatly impact the nature of
the answer to the third question I am developing here. If I am right about this,
someone whose account of beauty in either or both of the first two senses

1. E.g., Balthasar, *Glory of the Lord*; D. Hart, *Beauty of the Infinite*.
2. E.g., Wolterstorff, *Art in Action*; Wolterstorff, *Art Rethought*; Begbie, *Theology, Music and Time*; T. Hart, *Between the Image and the Word*; Jeffrey, *In the Beauty of Holiness*.

differs from mine materially (that is, specifically but not generically) ought still to be able to derive fruit from the analysis conducted here by a kind of analogy. That said, there are places where my account avails itself of a greater degree of specificity about an antecedent claim (for example, in the doctrine of analogy), and in such cases I will provide the necessary grounding.

It is not only the case that beauty in this third sense requires a different type of discussion than beauty in the first two senses, but it also seems to be the case that much less work has been devoted to it. Indeed, given the type of description that has been given of the difference between the third and the first two senses, it is not difficult to understand why this would be the case: only once some significant progress has been made in explicating the first two senses could one really turn to the third sense at all. It ought also to be clear that this third question is necessarily synthetic, joining together precisely the discourse on beauty as a transcendental and beauty as represented in creatures.

However, it is not enough to delineate these senses of "beauty" and to indicate that our focus will be on the third, for throughout we will have to make reference constantly not just to the experience of beauty but also to the beautiful creature. A brief word about the nature of the relationship between the second and third senses of beauty will help the reader navigate these interrelated claims.

The experience of beauty may not be reduced to the beautiful creature, even as subjectively experienced, for the sense of beauty may be mistaken: I may find the ugly beautiful. This would really be an experience of beauty, but it would not be an experience of a beautiful creature. Thus, while it would be a real experience, it would not be a true one. True experiences of beauty are the experience of some creature that is truly beautiful as beautiful—that is to say, my experience is true because it corresponds in some significant measure to the reality of the creature that is the occasion of the experience. To anticipate a little, the following general claim may then be made: the experience of beauty is grounded in what I will call "anamnesis" (which means, in this case, "to be reminded"), while the beauty of creatures, relatedly, is grounded in the type of image that may remind us or elicit anamnesis. Such ability to elicit anamnesis is of great relevance to the following analysis, even though it is not the focus of this study.

Our Concern: Beauty Broadly Speaking

If we are to treat beauty as a particular sort of encounter with another something in the world, then we have immediately brought subjectivity into play: for it is undeniable that there is truly an experience occurring, and so some subject is having an experience. But objectivity also enters here, because one is having an experience *of something*. The objectivity in question is complicated, however, because there may or may not be an objective beauty present in the moment of the experience of the beautiful. This is because false experiences are possible: on the one hand, there may be an absence of an extra-mental reality in the moment of experience, removing, perhaps, any possibility of an objective correlative to what is experienced; and, on the other hand, there is truly ugliness, and the ugly can be mistaken for the beautiful (more on that shortly).

Subjectivity and objectivity are thus both involved in such experiences. I call subjective that which is private, and so not subject to any standard outside the individual. The objective, by contrast, is not private, and is subject to a standard that exists outside the individual. Thus, every objective reality has a measure, and so claims about them are able to be disproved (falsifiable). This must not be confused: it is not objective because it is falsifiable, it is falsifiable because it is objective. Hence, even if we do not know the standard (and so no human can actually falsify the claim), it is still objective because the standard exists, and one *could* falsify the claim if only the standard were known.

Thus it should be clear that the standard of objectivity is not to be allied with either physicality or extra-mental existence. For even an idea in one's mind is such that a claim that it is beautiful is falsifiable. Indeed, even when the thinker is the first to have a concept and never shares that concept with anyone, there is an objective dimension because *were* it to be shared, a claim about its beauty *could* be falsified. This conditional falsifiability is sufficient to defeat the claim that the experience is merely subjective.

The subjective is thus the realm of relativity. Here what the individual says may be determinative precisely because there is no external norm governing the situation in question. Only when the experience is in no way bound to anything transcending the perceiver is the subject free to determine the nature of the experience without abuse or blame.

From this it should be clear that almost nothing is purely subjective, precisely because human making happens in the context of divine making. And yet in every encounter with any thing, the subjective element is not able to be eliminated, for what is not falsifiable is the particularity of my encounter with that thing (though it may yet be blameworthy). An experience falsified by reference to objectivity is revealed to be objectively false, even though it is, as experience, subjectively true. And thus the subjective is judged by the objective, and they may be in concord or discord without being reducible to one another.

In the experience of beauty, it seems at first glance that subjectivity is more central than objectivity, for it is necessarily involved, while objectivity seems to be only potentially involved. And yet this only seems to be the case, for in the moment of the experience of beauty, we experience *something* as beautiful. Indeed, I said a moment ago that it is possible that in such moments there might be no objective correlative, but this would be true only if we took "objective" in the strongest possible sense as "really existing outside the mind"—a sense I have just denied. It is impossible that such experiences occur without anything whatsoever filling the role of object. What I am experiencing may not be "real" in the sense of existing outside of my mind, but it is nevertheless a real phantasm or perception that is the object in the experience. And this is the upshot of objectivity in this context: something is encountered as the object of the perception, regardless of the ontological status of that object. So the objective element turns out to be, like the subjective, ineliminable, and neither may be reduced to the other. All such experiences draw on the dynamics of both subject and object.

As such, we have clearly entered the realm of epistemology as the particular set of questions that explicate the dynamics of the subject. But if we have entered only the realm of epistemology, then we run the risk of not respecting the objectivity operative in experiences of the beautiful. This would collapse the objective beauty encountered in such moments into an epiphenomenon of subjectivity, and by extension be equivalent to a claim, at the least, that what is beautiful in that moment is something about me and not something about the object encountered, and at worst, that the object encountered has no meaningful existence apart from the subjective use to which I can put it. If this is to be avoided, and the reality of the ineliminability of the dynamics of the object outlined above indicates that it is, then we must acknowledge that in coming to the third question of beauty, not only do we enter the realm of epistemology but simultaneously and as fundamentally, we also enter the realm of ontology.

However, it is important not to move too quickly beyond the complications of objectivity, because they underscore several important dynamics. For I have allowed that not every experience of beauty need be a response to something beautiful: one may, on the one hand, be responding only to an experience of something subjective, a reality internal to one's own mind; on the other hand, one may be encountering something that is in fact not beautiful but ugly, and one may find it beautiful precisely according to that which makes it ugly (that is to say, it is not that the thing is ugly in one respect *a* and beautiful in another respect *b*, and that one is actually responding to *b*; one may find *a* beautiful). This represents a fundamental breakdown in the faculty responsible for recognizing beauty.

The simplest solution is to take a path of pure subjectivism, to say that such experiences have no non-arbitrary connection to objective realities, and that beauty in this third sense is not the kind of thing that has any point of reference beyond the mind of the one experiencing it. But there are several reasons for resisting this conclusion. First is what has already been said—namely, that in instances where there *is* clearly an extra-mental stimulus for the experience of the beautiful, such subjectivism would reduce the stimulus to something about the observer. For what we are after is an account of the fundamental nature of the experience; thus, if we base that fundamental nature on the particular instances in which an external object is lacking, what we say will also apply to instances in which such an object is not lacking. Rather, the dynamic of subject and object is foundational, and the differences between these different types of experiences are due, as has been said, not to the presence or absence of an object but to the type of object.

A second reason to resist this subjectivist conclusion is to be found in the way in which the third sense of beauty is founded on the first two: if God is beauty itself and creatures are beautiful by participation, then the claim that there is no external standard by which to judge the veracity of particular experiences of beauty is already excluded. There are in fact two related standards: the standard of creaturely participation and the actual thing in which they participate (and these two standards are analogically related to one another).

There is a third and highly important reason to resist the subjectivist move, though it is somewhat subtle. The supposed impetus for the subjectivist move is a certain failure in the objective side of the situation. The fact that the experience may arrive whether or not there is an object outside the mind suggests that perhaps the dynamics at play are entirely internal to the mind. But if error is to be allowed to cause us to doubt the place of the dynamic in which error has occurred, the second instance of failure in correspondence—namely, those instances in which the ugly is judged to be beautiful—counts as a reason for rejecting the subjective component. For the failure in such instances is not on the part of the object, but on the part of the judging subject. So it would seem that on the criterion of failure, we would look neither in subjectivity nor objectivity for an account of the experiences in question. Or (an equally valid conclusion), we would not look to either alone.

Take note: if we anchor ourselves in a commitment to such objective standards (though not exclusively to such standards), then the realm of purely subjectivist talk about beauty and aesthetics is closed to us. Not only are some things objectively beautiful, but it is at least possible that some things are objectively ugly.

This sets a limit to our reflection that must not be trespassed but that is also quite fruitful (as limits generally are): we have to be able to account for the ugly. Ugliness belongs to the second question of beauty—that is, to the doctrine of creation; it could not belong to the first question without Manichaean consequences.[3] And so we must beware of too-facile definitions that do not have the power to address the existence of ugliness, but also, and most importantly for our purposes, the role that the ugly plays in experiences of the beautiful: the misidentification of the beautiful as ugly and the ugly as beautiful, and the failure to see either beauty or ugliness where they in fact exist. Such errors in the judging faculty are of great interest to this account because the power of perceived ugliness is so great that it can erode the confidence we feel in an ontology of beauty. I shall call this the challenge of the ugly, and I intend to meet it head on.

The Challenge of the Ugly

An Ugly World

As we turn to a consideration of the ugly, we must beware of treating ugliness (and also, throughout the account that follows, beauty) as merely external. The ugly is not merely the unattractive, for the unattractive may yet be beautiful, just as the attractive may yet be ugly. Beauty and ugliness in creatures (the second sense of beauty) go deeper, beyond the surface to the very depths of things; likewise, the experience we are talking about is not mere fascination or revulsion but a deeper response. The one who has this experience is convinced of the rightness of it, that it is in some way expressive of the way things really are (and thus such a one is always interested in and pointed toward an objective dimension to this experience).

The ugly in this strong sense strikes us with offensive moral force: we feel greatly that it should not be, that its existence is a challenge to the very rightness of things. This moral force is evidence that the ugly is, at least in our thinking, allied with evil. This allows us to understand the particular nature of the challenge that ugliness sounds: it is, in fact, the problem of evil. The ugly is founded on that which does not resemble God as it should, and so its source cannot be in the divine realm without positing either a second, non-divine eternal principle or positing both good and evil in God. Rather, ugliness is born out of the rebellion of the creaturely will, as evil is. Ugliness is a sort

---

3. This will be clearer in a moment, when the connection between ugliness and evil is discussed.

of vicious nonconformity. The preponderance of the ugly makes us doubt whether there can truly be meaning, whether life could be worth living in the face of such ugliness. At a fundamental level, it is the question of whether, given the great amount of evil that exists in the world, any good could ever be sufficient to even balance it out, much less to conquer evil without itself becoming evil.

Against this, it must be said that the darkness is not absolute: the world is not in fact pure ugliness but is shot through with pockets of beauty, radiant havens that push back the inky blackness and give us strength to press forward, to carry on, to dare to hope that all may yet be well. On these moments of beauty all the hopes of humanity are built: we believe that we can extend them, expand them, and, by so doing, gradually push back the power of darkness until no ugliness remains and we enter the beautiful light of utopian harmony. This (ultimately secular) optimism is grounded in the belief that the collective powers of humanity are always growing; it therefore mistakenly takes such powers to be infinite (and thus more than adequate to any problem).

A theological outlook resists this, maintaining instead that though we have cause for hope, even in the age after Christ's resurrection this hope rests more on faith than on sight. The appearance of beauty within the world is fleeting, elusive, and easily missed. Beauty rarely abides, and it remains vulnerable to exploitation, marginalization, and disfigurement. Faced with the rarity and instability of beauty, we are often satisfied with what we perceive to be merely not ugly. This is in part because the ugly is not simply an element within reality or a statement of the fact that there are many ugly things; rather, the ugly is a dynamic and a principle, a systemic degradation of the good into the useful and thence to the subservient. The world as we know it presents itself as an ugliness machine, churning out greater and greater evil and ugliness.

The ugly is therefore parasitic on and corruptive of the beautiful. Where there is ugliness, there is always profanation (sin). But what is the nature of this profanation? It must be correlated to the senses of beauty laid out above if we are to avoid equivocation. Thus, there will not be one sense of profanation but two: (1) the profanation of beautiful creatures, which is to say, the damaging of the being of the creatures themselves such that their beauty is marred or destroyed, and (2) the profanation of our experience of beauty. Additionally, although beauty in the first sense, as a property or characteristic of God, is not subject to profanation because God is incorruptible, one may nevertheless attempt such profanation, may attack the way that God is understood—and this will be blasphemy.

The first profanation requires a change in the nature of things, and a change in their nature precisely according to the way in which they are in the image of God. That such a profanation may result from human sin is the lesson of the biblical narrative of creation and fall, for along with the fall of humanity, the rest of creation fell, and subsequent biblical reflection on that fall indicates that at least part of what was lost was something of the ability of creation to image the Creator (cf. Rom. 8:20). The witness of creatures is muted since the fall, and this directly touches their beauty.

It is not clear, however, how far to go with this. How extensive is our ability to mute the ability of things to refer to the Creator? To qualify as this type of profanation, a change in the image-character of the creature is required, but one that stops short of destruction. I would not say that a tree destroyed by fire has lost its ability to image God; I would say, rather, that it has simply ceased to be. In order to qualify, it would need to be the case that the tree is still a tree but is now no longer as reflective of divinity as it once was. I suspect that the claim that this kind of profanation has happened is often erroneous, and that in fact it is profanation of the second sort that has occurred.

The second profanation touches not the actual beauty of the thing in question (any more than the failure to experience something as beautiful renders it not beautiful) but rather our ability to experience it as beautiful. This is above all the profanation that is rampant, and this is where we see the dynamic of the ugly at such ceaseless work. For objectification does not render the thing objectified a mere object; rather, it *treats* it as such, even though in fact it is not. But this is not therefore harmless to the objectified creature. The reputation of the thing is harmed, and this has real consequences: in the case of a rational creature, it may cause deep and lasting emotional pain. Part of the evil of the objectification of a person is not the theft of personhood (for this is impossible) but that one says to that person, "I do not accept your personhood." This marks out the limits of dehumanizing forces: they bring massive and terrible power to bear on their victims, but they can never actually touch the humanity and irreplaceability of the victim. This is why such forces must work so hard to convince the victim that they have done more than they have, that they have successfully rendered him or her non-human. Otherwise, the victim would see that his or her identity cannot be coerced and would discover a wellspring of strength from which to mount a dangerous and ineradicable resistance.

But in damaging the reputation of the creature, one has also rendered it less capable of bearing meaning to other rational creatures. The objectified creature has not been made ontologically less, but it has been made to be thought to be less. This grounds loss both on the part of the considering subjects, for they are impeded from seeing the thing well and understanding all it could convey, and also on the part of the objectified creature, which is now hindered from fulfilling part of its role as a bearer of meaning. It should be clear that blasphemy is of this sort; it does not change God, but it does damage God's reputation, and in so doing may make it harder for us to recognize God.

The victims of this latter sort of profanation are twofold: the things or persons objectified as well as those for whom they are objectified. When I lose my ability to experience the beauty of the tree, I suffer a genuine loss. My world is impoverished, and my life will be characterized by many fewer experiences of beauty. It is the beginning of the slide into a world without wonder.

So the challenge of the ugly can be explicated as the assault of evil on the good, of injustice on justice, of falsehood on truth, of meaninglessness on meaning. At stake is the very character of the world we inhabit: Is it a good place, or is it not? Or rather, given that it is not wholly good, is it good enough? Can it be salvaged, and what kind of power would be required to do that?

It is important that we understand the reason for this situation. Much philosophic ink has been spilled trying to determine the origin of the ugliness principle (usually discussed under the name "evil") and in trying to deflect the charge that God could have done and should be doing more. Such talk is, however, always somewhat dishonest, for it is the type of blame shifting to which our race has been prone since God first asked Adam whether he had broken the commandment (Gen. 3:11–13). We are the ugliness in the world: we are broken and twisted, inside and out, fundamentally and beyond any but divine power to correct, and we have broken the world to make it match our brokenness. Not content with the damage we have already done, we continue to break the world more and more every day, introducing hate, pain, suffering, loneliness, exclusion, and every manner of evil, even with our most well-intentioned actions. It is not only in our weak moments when we know we are acting selfishly that we break the world; in our strongest moments, in our best, shining triumphs, we are also always breaking the world.

The relevance of this is difficult to overstate. Even as the objective element in the experience of the beautiful impresses itself on the one having the experience, convicting the one having it that this is a true experience and that the world corresponds meaningfully to how it is being experienced, this objective element is at the same time challenged by the possibility that the object in question has undergone profanation and so may be a false beauty. Likewise the subjective element, which cannot be controlled for or elided, is problematic precisely because the experiencing subject is the prime agent of profanation in the world, and its reductive narcissism may even in the moment of experiencing beauty be engaged in the project of rendering the beautiful merely useful, or actually ugly. A theological account of this experience must be careful to explicate the nature of these failures.

Apart from a theological perspective (and, increasingly, internal to certain theological perspectives), it would seem that God does not care about our experience of beauty, because God is conspicuously absent from the entire dynamic of the profanation of the beautiful that characterizes our daily existence. And yet the allegiance between the ugly and the evil suggests that there may, and perhaps must, be an opposing alliance of the beautiful and the good (and that, in fact, the axis of ugly and evil is only a poor imitation of the original unity of beauty and goodness). And indeed, we can say that God has demonstrated that God is ultimately concerned about the beautiful, for God has dared great things to bring about a beautiful conclusion to the story of the world.

And yet questions remain. On the one hand, can we affirm the beauty of an ultimate state of affairs that includes an eternal Hell, as Jesus seems to have taught? On the other hand, are we to conclude that God only cares about beauty beyond the horizon of this world, in that place where every tear is finally wiped away, but that here and now, in the Vale of Tears, the divine concern for beauty is muted or absent? The answers to these questions are important but can be given only in the wake of a theological explication of the nature of the experience of the beautiful.

Structure of the Work

This work is divided into two parts. Part 1, which comprises chapters 1–3, deals with the explication of the encounter with beauty. At issue is the positing of the ground of the experience of the beautiful in what I will call "theological anamnesis" and the explication of this understanding and its corollaries (chap. 1); the nature of the type of vision that the experience of the beautiful recommends (chap. 2); and the ontological ground of such an experience in the analogical relation of creatures to the Creator (chap. 3).

Part 2 extends this understanding of beauty by considering its implications for major areas of thought that are controlled by the notion of reference—namely, linguistics (chap. 4), metaphor (chap. 5), semiotics (chap. 6), the sacraments (chap. 7), and iconology (chap. 8). This section of the work not only makes clear some of the systematic implications of the account of beauty developed in the first half but also, by giving a consistent account of these other areas, develops tools that themselves allow further specification of the nature of beauty and theologically anamnetic moments.

Every facet of the following account could be deepened with a stringently technical analysis showing how it can stand up to rigorous critique and situating it within the broader conversations of Western culture.[4] However, this will not be my concern in what follows. Instead, I intend to focus attention on the arguments themselves and on an understanding of these fundamental and powerful experiences that I think is theologically true. I will only say as much about sources and contemporary conversations as either materially moves the arguments forward or demonstrates that such grounding in wider discourse *can* be given. This is advantageous, for the argument made here is only partly logical; the other part is aesthetic. And for the force of aesthetic arguments to be felt, the reader must not be distracted from the overall form by a proliferation of details. Accordingly, what follows remains somewhat programmatic and suggestive, though the main contours are sufficiently delineated to convey a whole that is greater than the sum of the parts.

---

4. One might, for example, bring the account into conversation with Hume in chap. 1, Kant in chap. 2, and Barth in chap. 3. To continue the list, an encounter with Saussure, Sapir and Worf, and Derrida would be demanded by chap. 4, and dialogues with the major figures of analytic philosophy would be appropriate throughout. The absence of reference to these figures is partly in keeping with the constructive nature of the account. I am trying to express this view on its own merits without saddling it with an undue anxiety of influence. But it is also partly due to the fact that the perspectives those authors represent on the problem are rejected to such an extent that discussion of them would only distract from rather than advance the argument here. Nevertheless, such discussion would, in a different version of the project than the one I have chosen to write, clarify exactly where there is similarity and difference to these giants.

PART 1

The Encounter with Beauty

1

Eternity in Our Hearts

Memory, Beauty, and Divinity

For there are many who love beauty, but beauty lies not in external things, but in His likeness.

Bonaventure, Hexaemeron, col. 20, no. 24 (my translation)

It is difficult to find words strong enough for the sensation which came over me. . . . It was a sensation, of course, of desire; but desire for what? . . . Before I knew what I desired, the desire itself was gone, the whole glimpse withdrawn, the world turned commonplace again, or only stirred by a longing for the longing that had just ceased.

C. S. Lewis, Surprised by Joy

Beauty is a key to the mystery and a call to transcendence. It is an invitation to savour life and to dream of the future. That is why the beauty of created things can never fully satisfy. It stirs that hidden nostalgia for God which a lover of beauty like Saint Augustine could express in incomparable terms: "Late have I loved you, beauty so old and so new: late have I loved you!"

John Paul II, Letter to Artists

"Beauty is the word that shall be our first. Beauty is the last thing which the thinking intellect dares to approach, since only it dances as an uncontained splendour around the double constellation of the true and the good and their inseparable relation to one another."[1] Consistent with this claim, beauty in all its senses has remained famously resistant to definition, so much so that many who have come to the task have either intentionally or unintentionally taken refuge in merely characterizing it. It is my intention to go beyond that here, but it will be helpful to begin with a characterization of it, both to introduce operative intuitions and to clear the ground of certain things that seem attendant upon the experience of beauty but that do not, strictly speaking, enter into its definition.

Characteristics of Beauty

Pre-argumentative

No arguments or reasons have to be given to enable the experience of beauty. While we may offer such arguments after the fact, these arguments are no part of the moment of recognition. We notice the beauty of the thing apart from any arguments.

Now, it may seem that this is not so, as the following counter-examples show. First, there are what may be called intellectual beauties: concepts or thoughts that are the stimulus for experiences of beauty (for indeed we may find ideas beautiful, and this is often stronger than their logical coherence in determining our acceptance of them). One cannot find a concept beautiful until one has understood it, and often this requires explanation and argumentation. In fact, it could be argued that one often sees the beauty of an idea only when one "sees the truth of it," and that these two moments coincide in such a way as to count as the same thing. But if seeing the beauty of an idea is synonymous or even merely coterminous with seeing the truth of it, then precisely because it is possible that the truth of it only be seen after argumentation, it is also possible that the beauty of it may be seen precisely as the result of such argumentation.

This account flounders on a misunderstanding of the nature of argumentation and the process by which a mind comes to accept something as true. It assumes that to accept a proposition as true is the result of being convinced (one is tempted to say "compelled") by the force of the argument: undeniable premises and a valid syllogism lead one to a certain conclusion by necessity. At the earliest, recognition of the beauty of the conclusion is contemporaneous with the acceptance of its truth and perhaps occurs at some time subsequent

1. Balthasar, *Glory of the Lord*, 1:18.

to that moment. But this just is not the way that belief formation works. Such an account does not help us explain why some minds reject valid syllogisms built on premises they accept and find undeniable, and also why so many accept invalid arguments. To go further, and much more to the point, such an account is weak on explaining why an argument that begins from premises that I do not accept may yet be successful in convincing me to accept not only its conclusion but also its premises. There is another dynamic entirely going on here than the irresistible force of deduction.

What is happening in such moments is that I am seeing the beauty of the idea before I have come to be convinced of its truth and that the beauty of it does work in convincing me. I am willing to allow myself to be persuaded of the conclusion, and even to shift ground on certain premises, because it is worth it to hold an idea of such beauty. Indeed, sometimes I do not have to get to the end of the argument to know that I want to accept the coming conclusion, because its beauty is already apparent. (This may be disturbing from the standpoint of a desire that logic be objective or dispassionate, but it is just the way that fallen human minds work. It is also not clear that such a desire is even to be lauded.) This means that the beauty may be perceived *before* the truth and that it may be seen before the process of argumentation has reached its conclusion.

I take this to mean that the recognition of the beauty of the idea is not tied to the process of argumentation. Argumentation may cause it to appear, but it may also appear apart from that process. One does not see the idea as beautiful because one has been argued into it; rather, one sometimes needs help just to really see the idea. But once it is seen, its beauty does not depend on arguments.

The same is true in a second case, the case of something physical that may not be seen as beautiful at first, but that one later comes to think of as beautiful. Much art may be this way: an observer may not find a ballet, a piece of music, or a painting beautiful until someone has explained it. What is happening in such moments is not that the person is being argued into finding it beautiful but that the person is being helped to really see it. But once seen, if it is not judged to be beautiful, no amount of arguing about its importance or its objective qualities will convince one that it is beautiful. Thus, again, the experience of beauty lies beyond the realm of argumentation.

Imperative

Beauty greets us with an over-mastering force, and there is an immediate recognition of this force on our part, and often as immediate a submission.

Even when we resist, we often find ourselves incapable of eradicating that first powerful moment of encounter. The beautiful is rarely resisted, and even more rarely conquered.

I do not mean that beauty overrides our freedom or agency. We are always free to decide how to respond to beauty—with, for example, reverence or hatred. But *that* we find this thing beautiful does not respect our intentions or agency. We have very little say in what we find beautiful.

But what about the case of changing tastes, and the fact that one can even purposefully override the beautiful? In the first instance, what one once found to be beautiful may cease to seem beautiful with the passage of time; in the second instance, one may intentionally train oneself to stop finding beautiful what one previously found beautiful.

It will be easier to respond to this objection about changing tastes when we have defined beauty, because then it will be clear that what is happening in such cases is that one's idea of the divine is changing. The next chapter will add the ability to assess the degree to which moral culpability is to be assigned to such change. For now it is enough to point out that one is not defeating the imperative character of the beautiful in such moments; one is resisting and redirecting it. For in the examples in question, the one thing that one cannot do is to make it the case that one never found a particular thing beautiful. I may not like that song anymore, but before I convinced myself that the lyrics are deplorable and the music formally bankrupt, I did like it. It got to me, and while I may be ashamed of that or angry about it, it is nevertheless true. Indeed, to truly unlearn seeing such things as beautiful is very difficult, and perhaps more rare than we would admit if we could be truly honest with ourselves.

Subjective

The same things are not found by all to be beautiful, and there are striking instances where some things generally acknowledged to be ugly are considered beautiful by a very few. This is the other challenge of taste: that it is not universal, whether across cultures, within cultures, within subcultures, or within families. No amount of homogeneity produces identical responses to things; different individuals always have non-identical senses of beauty.

Expansive

Generally, we celebrate the ability to see beauty where others cannot. This is why the artistic soul is prized—these are the ones who can see beauty in rare places and who can therefore open the eyes of others to recognize beauty where they do not otherwise see it. In this instance, the old German proverb is true: "The one who sees more is more correct."

However, this must not be allowed to trespass: there is a distinction between calling the ugly beautiful and seeing the beautiful within the ugly. The latter is laudable, but the former is reprehensible. There appears to be such a thing as sinning against the notion of beauty, and this occurs when we call what is ugly beautiful. A visceral reaction ensues, and we instinctively feel this to be a most dangerous error.

If we begin to call the ugly beautiful, we will lose our ability to distinguish between the two. And whenever we find our ability to distinguish things diminished, we tend, because of original sin, to distinguish improperly. Thus, if we lose the ability to recognize the difference between the beautiful and the ugly, we risk converting everything into the ugly. Only the fact that the beautiful does not allow us escape—that it comes pre-argumentatively and imperatively—keeps us from applying the touch of evil (and it seems that the lightest touch would do) to utterly wipe beauty from the face of the earth.

The Theological Definition of Beauty

The central claim of this book is that beauty in the third sense, as the experience of the beautiful, is a moment in which we are being reminded of God. To find something beautiful is for that something to remind you of God. To be reminded is to have a memory activated; thus, the experience of the beautiful is founded on memory, *anamnesis*. And since it is specifically of God that one is reminded in such moments, the nature of this anamnesis is theological. Thus, an experience of beauty is a theologically anamnetic moment.

This definition assumes that we know God, or at least that we have known God. There must be some memory that is activated in such moments if this account is to work. I take it to be revealed in Scripture that there is such a memory in every one of us, in a twofold way.

First, both Psalm 19 and Romans 1 declare a minimal natural theology, a base level of knowledge about God that humanity cannot be excused for not possessing. Romans 1:20 is especially clear: "For his invisible attributes, namely, his eternal power and divine nature, have been clearly perceived, ever since the creation of the world, in the things that have been made. So they are without excuse." This passage teaches not that we *should* know God and so cannot be excused for not knowing God but rather that we *do* in fact know God and that attempts to claim that we do not are a suppression of the truth

(v. 18). Taken seriously, this constitutes a claim that there is an empirical knowledge of God that is basic to every human, however much we may attempt to diminish it or deny it.

Second, Ecclesiastes 3:11 says, "He made the whole beautiful in its time; indeed, he gave the whole to their hearts so that humans will not discover the deeds that God is doing from beginning to end" (my translation). The divine strategy for suspense, to ensure that we will not be able to lift the curtain on the world and see exactly what God is doing, is not to hide the divine work from us but to give the whole to us. We have implanted in our hearts a sense of the whole, and it is on the basis of this that we cannot grab hold of it: it is placed in our hearts as an irreducible knowledge and an unshakeable desire, and as such we are able neither to thematize it sufficiently (for it lies at the root of all our thinking) nor to be truly satisfied with any substitutions. We are driven by what already lies within our hearts to seek what we would not seek if we were not already in possession of it. But it is bigger than we are, and bigger than we could ever be: it is very eternity. As such, we possess such knowledge not comprehensively but apprehensively—that is to say, we do not grasp it but are rather grasped by it. The law of subject/object holds true here: the lesser belongs to the greater. Since we are the lesser, we belong to this eternal whole that lies within us, and so at the center of our being there is an ecstatic knowledge that constantly pushes us beyond the bounds of our systems and methods. It is a *semper maius* (always more) that haunts and drives our being.[2]

Only God is eternity: eternity is not something other than God that contains God, is co-extensive with God, or is co-primal with God; rather, it is a *quality* of God. Thus God's relation to time is analogous to God's relation to space: there is no place where God lives. Heaven is not the place where it is proper for God to live, for Heaven is a creature (that is, a created thing).[3] It is the dwelling place of God because it is the place God created in order to live at one with God's creatures. Likewise, there is no time that God inhabits, nor is eternity a never-ending but successive present. It is no time, but is rather the ground of time, an expression both of the idea that God always was and always will be and of the fact that God is immediately present to every time, and so for God the end is in the beginning and the beginning is in the end. This is not to say that the end is latent in the beginning or that the beginning survives in a transformed way in the end; rather, the end and the

---

2. Cf. Augustine, *Confessions*, book VII, chap. 17, no. 23.

3. Cf. Ps. 113:5–6: "Who is like the LORD our God, / who is seated on high, / who looks far down / on the heavens and the earth?"

beginning are unified in the one who grounds both and is present to both, and so every moment of time lies open to every other moment by a kind of transitivity through their relation to the Lord of time. Eternity is this supratemporal transcendental quality that, while *distinct from* time, is not *outside of* time. This is why our belonging to eternity by the infusion of it into our hearts is effective at keeping us from laying hold of eternity: it ensures that we can only ever interface with eternity discretely—not in pieces, for eternity is in itself indivisible, but as the whole appearing in a part that is able to mediate the whole without containing the whole. To have eternity in our hearts is to possess the whole as whole but in a partial way, as is most suited to our being. We see that there is more to see, and in this seeing we become aware that we cannot see all the way to beginning or end. Were this not the case, we would still not know what God does from beginning to end; but we would also not be able to see any of what God is doing now, *in medias res* (in the middle of things).

This complicated reflection on the nature of eternity is meant to underscore that what is in our hearts according to Ecclesiastes is not other than a knowledge of God. This knowledge is innate to us without being connatural: it is above us in kind, and so not of a similar nature to us. We belong to it in knowledge rather than it belonging to us; but it is irreducibly basic to all human thinking.

Taken together, these two biblical strands outline how the claim that there is a ground for theological anamnesis in a concrete memory of God to some extent transcends the debate about whether our foundational knowledge is innate (rationalist) or empirical. For there is irreducible knowledge of God in every rational creature both according to an innate mode (Eccles. 3:11) and according to an empirical mode (Ps. 19; Rom. 1), and these two sorts of knowledges are not identical, though they are complementary. Of course this does not entirely transcend the debate, because the assertion of any innate knowledge is already to come out on the rationalist side of the question; nevertheless, the scriptural texts also support the assertion of a type of irreducibly basic empirical knowledge that fundamentally grounds thought in addition to thought-grounding innate knowledge.

The result is a compound "memory" of God. It is compound in its origin, for it is partly innate and partly empirical; but it is also compound in its orientation. The empirical knowledge of God looks backward to things we have seen in creation, to prior moments of recognition that, although they may not have been attended to as such, are nevertheless so foundational to our empirical experience that they are already entrenched before we come to self-reflective analysis of our empirical experiences. The innate knowledge of

God looks forward to someone we have not seen yet but whose appearance our being is attuned to desiring. In this way the theological memory with which we are concerned participates in the dynamics of eternity by taking the whole of God's presence in time as its content. Thus, even though both arise in time (one at the very beginning of the creature and the other at the very beginning of the creature's encounter with the world), both are correctly keyed to that within each temporal moment that transcends time—the eternity that God is.

This memory is the operative element in C. S. Lewis's experience of joy, and it is the element of the familiar in every experience of the beautiful. A favorite Beethoven symphony or a favorite novel, or your beloved's face—these all excite longing because they contain an element of inexplicable familiarity. We cannot point to what it is or say exactly what it reminds us of, but it is there nevertheless. This is the fundamental and indelible memory of our Creator that each of us has. We may deny it or attempt to alter it, but we can never forget it. It is the memory that we shall see face to face in Heaven or be tormented by night and day in Hell. Our worldly experience of beauty is keyed to this, and we call beautiful that which excites this memory in us.

Corollaries

The definition of the experience of beauty as a theologically anamnetic moment has rich implications that touch a variety of topics, doctrines, and claims. The second half of this book will consider several specific instances. At this formative stage, however, our task is the examination of several corollaries that follow as immediate consequences of this view. Each one performs a clarifying role with respect to the definition itself. It must be said that some of them are not corollaries in the strictest sense of following immediately from only the terms of the definition. But they are corollaries for me because they do follow immediately upon the definition if only the terms are understood as I in fact do understand them—that is to say, given a God of a certain sort, given a certain understanding of memory, and so on.

COROLLARY 1: It is not only through the physical that we approach beauty.

This is true because something does not need to be physical in order to remind us of God. Indeed, even when what we are to be reminded of is itself physical, the reminder itself need not be. A thought, emotion, or mood may remind one of one's beloved just as strongly as a smell, a touch, or a sight. But especially in this case, when the beloved is not physical, it is possible that perhaps anything, regardless of whether it is physical or not, is capable of reminding us of our beloved.

This will mean that the experience of beauty is not only or primarily about the physical. For even if it should turn out to be the case that the majority of experiences of the beautiful are of physical things, this is merely accidental to the experience of beauty as such: the physical is not more capable of reminding us of God than non-physical things, and no reason can be given why the physical would hold primacy. The numerical advantage the physical may have as the stimuli of such experiences is easily explained as a result of our carnal state: that we are disordered internally due to sin and so inordinately preoccupied with bodily things.

However, it is equally to be affirmed that the physical *is* capable of reminding us of God, because creation is able to refer to God even in its concrete, physical realities. "And the Lord God saw all that he had made and it was very good" (Gen. 1:31). The body is neither a penalty for sin nor a necessary evil: it is essential to who we are as human persons. Thus, the corrective to an inordinate preoccupation with physical things is not to denigrate the physical but to restore the physical to its proper place as only one of the important types of things to which we must attend.

COROLLARY 2: Longing for that which is not present in the desired way is an integral part of the experience of the beautiful.

When we come across that which reminds us of our love, the pain and poignancy of the similarity is fueled by the insufficiency of our possession of our love. This is why those childhood experiences of beauty are so powerful: the intervening time strips out the negative parts of the experience until all we are left with is pure, unsatisfied (but unadulterated) longing. This longing, which is grounded in a recognition that we have lost something or that we stand at some distance from what we desire, is part of the experience of the beautiful.

To put it more clearly: because the beautiful is what reminds us of God and God is not present to us in the way that we desire, every experience of the beautiful has in it something unsatisfying; it has in it the recognition that this thing, the stimulus, is not the thing that we are really after, the thing that means most to us in all the world. I treasure the stimulus because it reminds me so deeply and powerfully of what I really want, but it is not yet that thing. This is the reality of a fallen world where we are distant from God experientially and also ontologically (due to our lack of holiness): even our best moments are undercut by a poignancy of sorrow.

In my experience, this poignancy has been best described by C. S. Lewis in *Surprised by Joy*. There he speaks of

> an unsatisfied desire which is itself more desirable than any other satisfaction. I call it Joy, which is here a technical term and must be sharply distinguished both from Happiness and from Pleasure. Joy (in my sense) has indeed one characteristic, and one only, in common with them; the fact that anyone who has experienced it will want it again. Apart from that, and considered only in its quality, it might almost equally well be called a particular kind of unhappiness or grief. But then it is a kind we want. I doubt whether anyone who has tasted it would ever, if both were in his power, exchange it for all the pleasure in the world.[4]

This last sentence strikes me as quite true. As such, the poignancy of which I speak is not to be assessed in a purely negative manner, and in my mind this is what makes it integral to our experience of beauty. It is not attendant upon such experiences; it is a characteristic quality of them.

Now, it is true that it is not necessary for our beloved to be absent in order that we be reminded of that person. So the fact that anamnesis is integral to the experience of the beautiful cannot be used to prove that God is not present as we want, or that God must remain distant if we are to have space for beauty. We would, in fact, still find beautiful that which reminds us of our true love, even in the company and possession of our true love. In such moments, however, there is a sort of loss in the very mediation of the experience. If I am walking with my wife and I see a necklace at a stall that reminds me of her, I do not encounter her in the same way in the necklace and in turning to her to draw her attention to the necklace. The necklace, by making me think of her without being her (in other words, by mediating an experience of her), presents her to me *as if* she were not present, though in fact she is. I cannot enter at leisure into this experience without turning away from the living reality next to me. In such moments I have sometimes stored up the treasure with the knowledge that there will be a future time when my wife is not present and I desire her to be, and I can then go to the necklace for the mediated experience that it can offer.

This still seems to entail that the work of reminding demands the absence (real or virtual) of what one is to be reminded of. And to some extent this is to be maintained: insofar as anamnesis of this sort is a mediated encounter with its object, there is some such absence of the object, for mediation is generally reflective or productive of distance (though we will have occasion to

4. Lewis, *Surprised by Joy*, 17–18.

consider how in the sacraments mediation becomes the locus not of distance but of the overcoming of distance, precisely in re-presenting the work of the mediator who reconciles all things in himself). But the distance may be only subjective. Thus, God is neither *necessarily* distant nor in fact distant; yet God is *felt* to be distant. This feeling is already a strong indicator that our sense of beauty is greatly damaged, or we would be unable to feel that the one who "plays in ten thousand places, / Lovely in limbs, and lovely in eyes not his"[5] is distant. But it is the undeniable reality of our experience (even the mystics long for more experience of the Lord, whose presence they are more greatly attuned to than the rest of us), and so it is an irreducible element in the worldly experience of beauty.

One could perhaps go further: the insatiability of the appetite of the mystics indicates that no degree of nearness to God suffices to still the desire to be ever closer to God. This may mean that the element of poignancy in the experience of the beautiful is inherent to all creaturely experience of the divine, not just those mediated by other creatures during the time of testing. But, consistent with Lewis's insight that this poignancy, though painful, is not undesirable, in the consummation of all things this poignancy would remain but would not be experienced as pain. It would perhaps be the pang of the heart, the wound of love, by which one simultaneously receives proof that one's love is deep and genuine and also undergoes a deepening of that love.

COROLLARY 3: The experience of the beautiful, properly speaking, is of creatures.

This corollary follows because what reminds us of God is not itself God, and therefore it must be a creature. However, one may object that God is able to be experienced as beautiful. Indeed, would it not be exceedingly strange and a major shortcoming of a view like this one, that claims to be rooted in the idea that God is original beauty, if God could not be experienced as beautiful directly? But if God may be experienced as beautiful, then does this not call into question the entire understanding developed here? It seems unlikely that what is happening in that moment is that God is reminding one of God.

I would not want to be too quick to acquiesce to this objection, because there does seem to be an instance when exactly what the objection rules out— namely, that in seeing God we are reminded of God—is true. This seems to be so specifically when we gaze upon the Son. In the mystery of trinitarian personhood, one may look on God and be reminded of God precisely because there is differentiation in the Godhead of a robust enough sort to allow

5. Hopkins, "As Kingfishers Catch Fire," 51.

this. Nevertheless, in another sense the objection holds, because it is not the case that the beauty of the Son is *only* the Father; rather, the Son is himself beautiful and in many ways is uniquely suited to be the one we are reminded of in such moments.

What the objection actually reveals is not the inadequacy of the definition but the imprecision of the taxonomy with which we began this work. For while there may be three senses of beauty, the third sense of beauty (the one we are concerned with) is itself divided into two: (3a) the experience of God as beautiful and (3b) the experience of creatures as beautiful. This is to divide the question of the experience of the beautiful according to what type of beauty is being experienced. If it is beauty of the first kind—that is, Beauty itself—then we have one type of experience; if it is beauty of the second kind—that is, the creature as participating in God's beauty—then it is a different experience. The fact that the subdivision of the experience of beauty follows the two different ways in which things can be beautiful confirms that this is not a spurious or purely procedural distinction.

It is of course 3b, the experience of creatures as beautiful, with which we are primarily concerned in this present work, and it is of 3b that I have offered a definition. How then do the two types of experience relate to each other? 3a is different from 3b insofar as in 3a we are not being reminded of God, but rather we stand before God. As such, the dynamics of reference are not the controlling dynamics, and the two experiences are fundamentally different, just as being with one's beloved and remembering one's beloved are fundamentally different. And yet, as is also true in the two noted ways of relating to one's beloved, the two modes are not disconnected, but are rather analogously related. 3b is analogous to 3a in that it is a 3a-type experience mediated through another. Thus the two experiences are related in just the same way as the two realities referenced (God and creatures) are related—namely, through analogy. The analogy between the two ways of experiencing beauty is in fact grounded on the very thing that is the analogy between God and creatures. We will have occasion to speak more of this in chapter 3.

To return to the corollary, because the experience of the beautiful is an experience of creatures, it is an experience of creation coming alive in its original, intended role as sign or indicator of the divine presence. This is the sacramental character of creation: its ability to mediate the presence of the Creator (in a sense that brings the mediated reality closer rather than making it more distant). Thus, the experience of the beautiful is grounded in sacramental realities. In this way beauty and holiness run hand in hand, with holiness as the grounding condition for beauty. This is why the experience of the beautiful is often given a sacral character, even by non-theological reflection.

COROLLARY 4: God is the remote yet proper referent in the
experience of the beautiful.

What the experience of the beautiful is pointing to is God, and this referent
is distant. More immediately, the experience points to the beautiful creature.
So there are two different referents: the one that is the closer point of reference and the one that is the further point of reference. The meaning of this
corollary is that the remote referent is the more important of the two; it is,
in fact, the *proper* referent of the experience.

It is important to clarify what I mean by "remote" here: this is not a claim
that God is distant from creation, or from particular creatures. God is not
in fact distant but is closer to us than we are to ourselves, if we understand
things properly. What I mean is a "referential remoteness" whereby God is
not immediately or proximately intended but only mediately or remotely. If
God were not referentially remote in the experience of the beautiful, it would
be a 3a-type experience, not a 3b-type. And it is this referential distance that
allows us to fail to notice that an intimation of the divine is active in our
experiences of beauty.

When two things are related, it is often the case that one of the things related (*relatum*) is controlling, at minimum, the character of the relation and
perhaps even the other *relatum*. For example, in cause-and-effect relationships,
the cause both determines the quality of the relationship (if the cause is fire
and the effect is heat, then we could call the relationship "warming") and
also generally controls the effect (it is making the iron hot). In cases where
two things are related such that one is the goal of the other, the goal is the
controlling factor. For this reason, Aristotle called the goal a final *cause*, even
though it often exhibits no agency. But beyond these standard creaturely relational situations, whenever God is in a relationship with a creature, God is
the controlling factor in that relationship (this follows upon both the qualities
of divinity and the fact that God is the Creator of each creature and as such
both may and does set the boundaries to that creature's being).

This makes God the objective correlative of the experience of beauty: God
is the actual real objective thing to which our subjective experience must be
correlated. So to test an experience of beauty—to know whether one is finding the beautiful within the ugly or just calling the ugly beautiful—one must
consider God. There is a limit to what can be called beautiful and that limit
is nameable with the trinitarian formula.

So, however remote God may be referentially speaking, God can never be
removed from the field of play, and neither does the divine lose its power in
proportion to its remoteness. The former is true because God is neither referentially nor in any other way *absent* from creatures. The second is true because

divine power is infinite, and so does not lessen with distance, even referential distance. This means that however far God may be from the thoughts of the one experiencing beauty, the divine is never powerless to break through that experience and strike the individual with clarity. But it also means that even when the divine is denied and remains unrecognized in the moment of finding something beautiful, such moments still arrest and captivate, not in spite of the divine referent but because of it. The experience of beauty is a moment of theological anamnesis, even where the most stringent barriers have been erected against the slightest suggestion of a divinity.

In some sense, the more remote God is in the consciousness of the one experiencing the beautiful, the more powerful God is felt to be when such moments are finally seen for what they are; for the engine that runs the beautiful is *longing*, and longing is increased rather than decreased by distance. It is not that distance increases the value of the relationship; but it does sometimes increase the awareness of how much one values it. Sometimes it is those who do not have what they long for who best understand it.

> COROLLARY 5: However much the beautiful creature is dear to us for its own sake, it is more importantly dear to us for God's sake.

The beautiful creature, once seen as beautiful, may be loved on the basis of its beauty, but this is not the fullest possible response. One may even take the next step and praise God that such a beauty should exist, and, as a result of this, love God more. But even this is not the most authentic use of this experience. Rather, the recognition of the creature's ability to remind us of God renders that creature more dear to us. Experiences of beauty, when used rightly, cause us to love the creature more than we otherwise would, on the grounds that this creature is capable of reminding us of God. And, on analogy to something that is loved because it reminds us of our beloved, this will always be the most poignant and important dimension of the beautiful creature.

The claim is that we find things beautiful when they remind us of God. Thus, insofar as perceived beauty is a quality that makes something dear to us, such dearness is always grounded in theological anamnesis. This is the sense in which I would take up Augustine's famous distinction between use and enjoyment: not that God alone is to be enjoyed but that God is the only object whose enjoyment does not also bring a deeper, more fundamental enjoyment to the moment of *frui*.[6] Everything else, when enjoyed, is to some extent (just to the extent that we find it beautiful) also an enjoyment of God.

6. Augustine, *On Christian Teaching*, book I, p. 9.

But then "use" is a bad word to describe this dynamic, because the creatures are not pointing us away from themselves; rather, it is in showing us what they truly are that they also open us to the deeper enjoyment of divinity.[7]

> COROLLARY 6: Because what reminds one person may not be the same as what reminds another person (for various reasons), the subjective element in the experience of beauty is irreducible.

The reason experience is subjective is because no two people see God the same way. No matter how alike we are, theologically or culturally, we all see God differently. I take this to be what Revelation means when it records God saying, "To the one who conquers I will give . . . a white stone, with a new name written on the stone that no one knows except the one who receives it" (2:17). Each person may offer a praise to the Lord that no one else in all creation could ever offer. We are created to see God differently because God is so unfathomably large that no one view—or ten thousand views or ten billion views—could ever be adequate to who God is. All the angels and all the humans together would never have an adequate vision of God. But the Father is lavish and goes out of his way to create more and more and more and more, not because by doing so we get an adequate representation of God but because by doing so God gives a representation that is adequate to the purpose of witnessing to God's majesty while remaining inadequate to the purpose of exhausting it. Reality is a symphony composed of the melodic and harmonic lines that we all contribute by virtue of being created as this particular image of God.

As a result, that we find different things beautiful is not primarily a result of the fall; it is part of the way in which we have all been created to teach one another about our common Lord. In paradise we would have been eager to talk with one another and with the angels about the Lord we serve, just as a man who has recently fallen in love is eager to talk to others who know his beloved: to compare notes, yes, but also to hear any new little detail that was previously unknown. And in the kingdom of Heaven we will have not only our perspectival differences to share with one another concerning who God is but also what the trinitarian persons have done for us in our own personal story of redemption.

This is of great importance for the ability of this definition to account for both diversity of taste and errors in judgment (which will be taken up in the next chapter).

---

7. In the next chapter we will speak more of this dynamic of the creature revealing the Creator.

Preliminary Conclusion: Subjective Objectivity

From correlate 4 (that God is the remote yet proper referent in the experience of the beautiful) and correlate 6 (that the subjective element in the experience of beauty is irreducible), there follows the notion of subjective objectivity. This means that in the experience of the beautiful there is a subjective appropriation of an objective reality in which the categories of the subject are irreducibly important and yet the whole encounter is controlled more by the object than by the subject.

The resulting account is therefore not subjectivist, for it is bounded and grounded in the reality and concrete qualities of the object. Neither is it merely objective, however, for it depends on and makes use of a robust understanding of the role that the subjective element plays in the encounter. The object is not simply encountered according to its true being, resulting in a predictable experience that is uniform across all possible subjects. Instead, the object is appropriated in the experience—that is to say, it is taken into the proper space of a subject. And this appropriation is subjective—that is, according to the conditions of the subject (moral, intellectual, volitional, religious, cultural, and more).

The appropriation is free, which is to say that the autonomy and freedom of the subject are respected. However, the subject is neither absolutely autonomous nor free, thus respecting its autonomy and freedom does not entail handing over control of the appropriation to the subject. The subject gets a say, but it is a finite say, a say that is always already a response to a prior address, a say that in this instance is grounded in existence and efficacy by the prior activity of the object that is now being appropriated (God). Subjectivity qualifies the appropriation and makes it a particular and unique appropriation; but the encounter is still objective, and the appropriation itself is still more controlled by the object than by the subject.

In this way the dichotomy between subjectivity and objectivity is overcome not in some Hegelian synthesis that issues in a tertium quid or by the rejection of one or the other of the poles, but rather by the elucidation of a hierarchical relationship grounded in the proper understanding of the ordering of the realities in question.

This holds not just for the divine object that is the proper referent of the experience of beauty but also for every creaturely object. Additionally, because our experiences may be manipulated by willful distortions of the conditions of the subject (choosing to ignore significant facts, habitual submersion in the type of sin that tends to alter one's view of the world), it is possible to disconnect the experience from the objective element to an increasing extent, rendering the resulting experience less objective. To do so is not only to harm the self (by distorting subjectivity) but also to transgress the object. But this can be made clear only after the discussion of objectification, which follows here, and contuition, which will take place in the next chapter. What remains in the current chapter is to see what account of the ugly such a definition of beauty generates.

Beauty in an Ugly World

Understanding Ugliness

On the supposition that ugliness is not original but is a falling away from the good, then ugliness can only be understood in relation to beauty. Beauty, by contrast, is not understood in the first instance in contrast to the ugly; neither are they mutually required for understanding, for that could be true only if the ugly were at least equally original with beauty in some sort of dualistic sense. Thus, the ugly does not enter into the task of defining beauty. And yet, if we have an account of beauty, we are also in a position to give an account of ugliness.

All things were created good by God, and in that original goodness they pointed to the Creator, and as such were necessarily beautiful. This referential dimension is not just proper to each thing as creature but also proper to each thing as this *type* of creature and as *this* creature. This means that a cat does not just refer to God by virtue of being created (though it does); it also does so in a special way by virtue of being a cat (that is to say, different from how dogs do) and by virtue of being the cat Tom (and so different from how other cats do). Every metaphysical universal (every genus of whatever level, be it animal, cat, Siamese, etc.) and particular is a creature and points in its characteristic particularities to God.[8]

Thus, it should be clear that there can be no question of ugliness apart from damage to the created order. And ugliness that would correspond to the sense of beauty that we are talking about must strike at precisely those qualities according to which the creature refers to God. To be ugly is thus to be wrested away from God—not in the sense that God is no longer Lord over the creature or no longer has authority over it, but in the sense that the creature's ability to remind us of God is affected. And it will not be enough for this ability to merely be lessened, for what is not as beautiful as it could be is still not yet

---

8. Whether the particularities be understood as that which distinguishes one species from another (*proprium*), that which distinguishes individuals from one another (haecceity), or whatever else.

ugly. Nor will it be enough for its ability to remind us of God to be silenced, such that it is simply not recognized; for to not be seen as beautiful is not yet to be ugly (though silencing is still an abuse that violates its nature, it is the silencing that is evil; the silenced creature is not thereby made ugly). No, this ability must be not just muted but shattered. It is not just silent or distant in its witness to God; it becomes a challenge to God, a counter-argument in creation to the divine goodness and sovereignty. This reveals the structural similarity between the problem of the ugly and the problem of evil.

This shattering may happen in two ways: either something is forced into this position, or something places itself in this position. I will consider each in turn.

First, creatures forced into this condition may be of two sorts: those without will and those with will. The latter are human persons who have been violently sinned against at the very heart of their personhood: victims of torture, rape, slavery, persecution, and wrongful imprisonment, and also those who have been abused emotionally, bullied, devalued, ignored, and cast aside. The former are the lower things of creation that have done no wrong in themselves (and indeed, have no capacity for such wrongdoing) but that are subject to vanity and objectification. Paul speaks of this dynamic in Romans: "For the creation was subjected to futility, not willingly, but because of him who subjected it, in hope that the creation itself will be set free from its bondage to corruption and obtain the freedom of the glory of the children of God. For we know that the whole creation has been groaning together in the pains of childbirth until now" (8:20–22).

Vanity (futility) in this context is the emptying of the ability to refer to God, and thus it is the obstruction of beauty. This passage speaks of God's act of subjecting the creation to vanity, which is a punishment for human sin; but we also may make creatures (both persons and non-persons) vain by our actions. This is not simply to remove the ability to refer to God (which would merely render the creature not beautiful); it is to obstruct and distort it. To completely efface the anamnetic dimension of creatures lies beyond human and demonic power: we cannot annihilate. But we do have the power to shatter the ground of anamnesis, to break it so thoroughly that we are no longer sure whether even divine power could restore it. This is a great abuse of the creature: the obstacles cast in the way of the mind journeying from the creature to God are what cause us to question whether the creature ever *could* resemble God and thus to question whether the creature is in fact good.

Objectification is the other involuntary evil that creatures suffer, and in this context we are able to make our understanding of objectification much more precise. Normally it is used to refer to the reduction of a person into an object: treating a human as merely a sexual object, treating a person as merely a service that person can provide, and so on. In this sense, to objectify something is to take away its native subjectivity and to treat it as a mere object for one's own subjectivity. It is a refusal to acknowledge that the other person has their own subjectivity (that is to say, *is a person*) and that the proper response to that person is not use but dialogue and interaction: romance, if you will. Understanding objectification in this way and then resisting it protects the authenticity of persons; but there are more creatures that need protection.

In light of the understanding of beauty developed here, objectification may be understood to be treating the creature as *only* an object—that is to say, not also as a sign pointing beyond itself or, better, a site where the glory of God is revealed. To objectify something is to take away its proper and originally created intention of revealing the glory of God. Non-personal creatures are not capable of wrongdoing, and yet they are, like persons, subject to vanity and objectification because the will and power of persons forces these evils upon them. The exploitation of the beautiful notices *that* something is beautiful without caring *how* it is beautiful. But in that "how" lies the creature's whole particularity. In that moment we declare that we do not care who or what this is, only that we can use it.

One sees here how necessary it is that the world fall with us, for in our fall we toss away much of our ability to let things reveal God, and we also become bent in our wills such that we habitually twist things away from this revelatory function. Even if there were no curse to make creation groan, creation would groan because it is screaming out to us the glory of God, and we are deaf to its pleas. The material world cannot be all it was meant to be, cannot fail to groan, as long as those whose job was always to cultivate the garden and name the animals (that is, make known how each animal refers back to God)[9] have abdicated this responsibility and in so doing are also robbing things of their proper recognition, of what they were meant to do.

It must also be said that while persons may be shattered by the agency of another, this shattering is greatly qualified due to a fundamental lack of power of determination of one rational being over another. The self-determining ability of persons is never stolen or erased (though it may be surrendered, as, for example, in the case of demon possession), and as such persons remain beautiful even when subjected to the most ugly-making of abuses. Indeed, persons are not so much shattered as disfigured, and disfigurement does not block beauty (especially after the cross of Christ) but only hides it beneath a veil. Disfigurement is a mask of ugliness drawn across the face of beauty,

---

9. This will be discussed in detail in chap. 4.

but it is never stronger than a veil: the glory of beauty may at any moment shine through the disfigured mask.

The divine response to this type of ugliness takes the form of mercy, for no crime has been committed by the ugly things themselves, and there is no guilt. In the case of persons who have been attacked in this way, this mercy comes in the form of healing or liberation from the disfiguring powers. For non-persons, since it seems to have been partly in themselves and partly for us that things were meant to be beautiful (that is to say, God does not just make a tree so that it can reveal divine glory to humans; God also makes the tree to be in itself a declaration of divine glory), so the divine restorative action addresses both dimensions. The general rubric for the divine restorative action toward those things that have been made ugly by the agency of another is sacrament.

Much more will be said in chapter 7 about the sacraments in connection to this understanding of beauty, but a couple of things may be said here. First, consider infant Baptism: traditionally speaking, Baptism has been held to be a remedy against original sin. That is to say, the guilt inherited from Adam's fall that is not one's own fault is taken away by Baptism. This view of original sin and Baptism would make infant Baptism an instance of something that has been made ugly by the will of another (the infant) being restored through the sacramental remedy.

Perhaps more to the point, the Eucharist is a symbol and a remembrance, representing the God who took on our flesh and died for our salvation; therefore it restores to bread and wine the proper dimension of reminding us of God, of carrying the mind back to that story we all long most of all to hear. It is thus a promise, sealed by the actual presence of the first instance of that which is promised (the new creation in Christ's resurrected body), that creation will, when it has been remade, be restored to its original beauty as the place where God's glory is revealed. So the fact that the Lord's Supper is a symbol representing what Christ did for us in his sacrifice restores to creatures (bread and wine) their proper ability to carry and convey our minds back to God. Thus is the beauty of things that is directed toward us redeemed.

But insofar as the Eucharist is more than this—that is to say, to the extent that it is not just the symbol of the body but the actual presence of the body and blood and divinity of Christ—it declares the divine will to dwell along with creatures and even to be borne by them, and therefore it restores the per se beauty of each thing. For now, in the mystery of the real presence, not only are the creatures of body and blood that have been taken into real personal identity with God affirmed in their eternal glory but also the creatures of bread and wine (or whatever creaturely parts of them remain to form the sacramental elements after consecration) are returned to the original glory of a creation in which God walked and delighted, for the Lord is truly among them.

The second way that shattering may occur is when a creature loses by its own will its ability to remind us of God. Only persons (specifically, angels and humans) are capable of this. In these cases, violence is not done to the will, but rather the will itself rebels and turns from the font of light and the beauty of holiness. It is in this key that ugliness is evil: evil is the ugliness of rational creatures.

Like the prior ugliness, this is a challenge to the divine goodness and sovereignty, but the challenge is deeper and more serious: for when I wrest myself away from God, declaring in doing so that God is not good, I set myself up over and against God as the good. When I rebel against God, I declare to every watching creature that I do not think that God is the good; rather, I am the good. I prefer myself to God. But experience and introspection show that in so doing, I am not a good but an evil; I am *the* evil, the broken falseness that darkens the creation and harms the other good things God has done. This is because precisely in turning away from God to myself, I turn everything around me away from its ability to reference God and turn it instead toward myself. I steal the divine sacraments, reappropriating them to make only myself present, and convert beauty from that which reminds me of God into that which reminds me of me.[10]

Given this, the form that God's response takes must be very different. Victims need to be rescued, and that is what we saw with the previous type of ugliness; but criminals and rebels are not so much in need of rescue as punishment. Or, if you prefer, their rescue cannot be without regard to the need for judgment. And judgment is of absolute and unwavering importance, for judgment is not the punishing of evil for the sake of vengeance; rather, it is the *response* of good to evil, working justice. As such, it is that which takes away evil's power, that which defeats the syllogism of evil by the inerrant demonstration of the power of beauty. For evil reasons thus: "There is no God in Heaven, and only God can ground transcendent ethics: therefore there is no right or wrong. Therefore I can do whatever I like." Justice demonstrates the falsity of the minor premise.

This is the deepest and truest reason why God cannot simply forgive sin and why it is not only not inimical to the final beauty of the universe that there be an eternal Hell but in fact necessary to it: because a world in which there is no justice is a world without beauty. A world where there is no judgment for

---

10. This dynamic of secular sacraments will be explored in chap. 7.

the perpetrator means that there is no justice for the victim, for perpetrator and victim are symmetrically related to the same unjust moment. Were there no judgment, ugliness and evil would remain without a response. The lack of a response of good to evil is a capitulation of good to evil, and capitulation is no response, but rather a *surrender*, and the surrender of the beautiful is the victory of the ugly. In Genesis 4:10 the blood of Abel cries out from the ground: this is a clear sign that God feels an obligation to the innocent victim to respond to the challenge of evil, to defeat evil by good; that resistance to evil is not evil, but rather is centrally characteristic of the good.

This is both easy and hard to understand. It is hard to understand because, fundamentally, we do not treat sin very seriously. It looks to us like the ignorant error of a child, more worthy of indulgence than wrath. This is vilest fantasy; we cannot even begin to conceive how bad sin is, because we are trapped within it and endowed in this prison with a will devoted to excusing ourselves.

It is difficult to overstate our lack of moral objectivity when it comes to understanding our own evil. We are those who have eaten of the Tree of the Knowledge of Good and Evil, and so we have lost the pure knowledge of the good. To us, it seems natural to wonder whether it is really possible to know good without knowing evil: Are they not dialectically entwined and mutually entailing such that without knowledge of the one there can be no knowledge of the other? But that is the question of someone who has eaten of that tree. Someone who has not eaten of the tree knows the good properly in itself and can therefore recognize everything that is not it. It is our legacy as the people of the Tree of the Knowledge of Good and Evil that our knowledge of good and evil has become reciprocal, and we now only know the one by the other. Therefore, for us, to come to know the good is always mixed up in knowing the evil, to such an extent that we begin to suspect that good cannot be known unless evil is also known. But this is not absolutely true; it is only true of us.

Consequently, we will never understand why the Good wears such a severe face until we understand how truly dangerous an enemy the Evil is. Here one thinks of what Lewis has Mr. Beaver say of Aslan: "Who said anything about safe? 'Course he isn't safe. But he's good."[11]

But it is also easy to understand why justice is necessary to beauty, for when we feel righteous anger, we believe in punishment. For each of us, there are news items of such horror and ugliness that we, perhaps even against more general progressive tendencies, quickly agree that in this case, something more extreme must be done. And yet no genocide, no act of terror, no sexual

---

11. Lewis, *Lion, the Witch, and the Wardrobe*, 75–76.

assault comes close to revealing the horror of sin. We cannot even come close to understanding how bad genocide is because we do not even know how bad it is to tell a lie: in reality, the severity of lying is much closer to our conception of the severity of genocide than to our conception of the severity of lying. And so the things that we think of as the deepest and most distressing of evils are much more deep and distressing than we think they are. We are fundamentally incapable of wrapping our minds around how momentous evil is.

Therefore, God's response to evils of this sort must take the form of justice. And yet, what is characteristically divine and so unexpected is that it also takes the form of mercy. God's justice is always merciful, and God's mercy is always just. In fact, the idea of merciless justice or unjust mercy only shows that we do not really understand what either of those concepts are. We do not know what justice is until we understand how it cannot be separated from mercy and vice versa. The demand for God to be merciful but not just is the demand for a round square (all of this follows from divine simplicity).

More importantly, God is not just suppressing the ugly but restoring the beautiful. Thus even the ugly that has come to be ugly through its own rebellion is not simply to be judged, but also, like those things that are ugly through no fault of their own, to be restored to beauty. We may consider divine justice the work of tearing down the ugly, and divine mercy the work of restoring the fallen beauty to its place, but only so long as we do not forget that these are not sufficiently distinct to ever be placed at war with one another.

And what of that place where a creature is so given to ugliness that it cannot be made beautiful again, because it will not relinquish its allegiance to ugliness? Such an eternal decision for ugliness, which is easier to make than we think, can only be met with eternal rejection, for the ugly will never and must never be affirmed for being ugly: it must either submit to having its nature restored or be rejected as unacceptable. Thus, even when the will of the rational creature persists eternally in its rejection (demonic wills and the wills of unrepentant humans), there is a restoration to beauty, but it is under the sign of a justice that offers an eternal "no" to this twisted way of being.

Beauty and the Rejection of God

Our reflections do not just issue in the ability to give a theological account of ugliness and God's response to ugliness; they also provide additional insight into the nature of beauty and our relationship to it. For the predominant project in a secular society is not the rejection of beauty (rather, we are all hardwired for it) but an attempt to seize the beautiful apart from or without reference to God.

Concerning this, it must be said that to possess the beautiful apart from that reality in relation to which alone it is beautiful is not to possess it in truth. This can mean one of two things: (1) to possess the beautiful in this way is not to truly possess it, or (2) to possess the beautiful in this way is to possess it but not in a manner in accordance with the truth. I mean the latter of these two, because general divine grace does not begrudge us good things. The secular heart seizes upon beauty just as truly as the inattentive believing heart, and no less really than the attentive believing heart. But the secular heart does seize upon it less truly than the attentive believing heart. The secular heart possesses in reality but not in accordance with the manner of existence of the thing.[12]

Such beauty consoles, but it also harms, because it exacerbates the feeling that something vital is missing; and so, in its own inability to satisfy in an ultimate sense, it witnesses that as an image of the desired reality it is no replacement for that reality. This is analogous to when one clings to that which reminds one of a lost love: the possession is bitter, a wound in the heart kept open by the presence of that which does the reminding. Beauty used in this way wounds, and eventually the heart sickens and longs to be free. Thus, ironically, the attempt to domesticate the beautiful by severing it from the truly transcendent leads to a deeper rejection of beauty.

And so, despite the pervasive ugliness of the world, the ongoing presence of beauty is a pointer to the tireless divine activity on behalf of the beautiful in the world. The opposite claim, that God is not doing enough to respond to ugliness, is either hopelessly or dangerously naive. It is hopelessly naive if it does not realize that God is radically at work everywhere, tirelessly leaving no stratagem untried to pry our hearts away from our fascination with and allegiance to the ugly, to captivate us once again with true beauty. It is not that God is not doing enough; it is that we are fundamentally ill-disposed to recognize what God is doing. Were we able to see just how much God is doing in this regard, we would be astounded. Learning to see the world sacramentally will help with this.

It is dangerously naive if we forget that there is still to come a mighty working of the divine power with regard to the ugly. God has not yet done all that God will do to respond to the threat of darkness, and for that we should be grateful, because the stay of that Great Day is to give more time for those who have not yet switched their allegiance from the ugly to the beautiful to do so.

In this world, beauty reminds us that we were once more than we are now, that we will only be happy with more than we are now, and that it is possible

---

12. What I mean will be clearer in the next chapter when we consider various forms of explicit and implicit contuition.

that we can be more than we are now again. At the same time, beauty opens our hearts to something else, for it forces us to acknowledge that we are not sufficient of ourselves. By reminding us of what we most love and most desire, it also gives us the sure knowledge that we cannot live without what we love. Through the cracks thus revealed in our armor of self-sufficiency, wondrous worlds pour.

2

The Eyes of Faith

Contuition and Spiritual Vision

For from the greatness and beauty of created things comes a corresponding perception of their Creator.

Wisdom 13:5 NRSV

Indeed the whole world was led before his eyes as if gathered within a single ray of the sun.

Gregory the Great, Dialogues, book 2, chap. 35
(Patrologia latina, cursus completus 66:198B)

> Two worlds are ours: 'tis only Sin
>   Forbids us to descry
> The mystic heaven and earth within,
>   Plain as the sea and sky.
>
> Thou, who hast given me eyes to see
>   And love this sight so fair,
> Give me a heart to find out Thee,
>   And read Thee everywhere.

John Keble, "Septuagesima
Sunday," in The Christian Year

Shall I tell you the secret of the whole world? It is that we have only
known the back of the world. We see everything from behind, and
it looks brutal. That is not a tree, but the back of a tree. That is not
a cloud, but the back of a cloud. Cannot you see that everything is
stooping and hiding a face? If we could only get round in front—

G. K. Chesterton, *The Man Who Was Thursday*

Since the experience of the beautiful is an encounter that reminds us of God,
it is necessary to consider the means of apprehension by which this experience is encountered. This consideration will ultimately map the basic ethical
dimensions of the experience of beauty: what one must do to have it more
often, what accounts for failure to see beauty where one should, and how to
understand what happens when one sees beauty where it is not.

In what follows, the experience of beauty will be considered primarily
from the standpoint of the human sensorium. This is, of course, somewhat infelicitous, because it is simply not the case that the experience of
the beautiful unfolds only in the space of the senses. Thoughts, emotions,
concepts, and intuition are all also places where this experience may unfold.
The scope of the experience of beauty is in fact precisely as broad as the
scope of possible human experience: in whatever way we may experience
anything, we may also experience beauty. Therefore, this focus on the senses
should not be taken as exclusive or even as normative in any way besides
that in which it is representative. Rather, I have chosen to think from the
senses both because it is somewhat easier to find common ground in that
area and because it is somewhat traditional in theology to use the senses
as analogues for other aspects of human experience (notably, the idea of
"spiritual senses").

Furthermore, within the sensorium, vision will be given primacy. Again,
this is not meant to suggest that hearing beautiful sounds, for example, is
somehow a lesser instance of the experience of beauty than seeing a raging
waterfall. No particular primacy is asserted for vision over other senses; it is
chosen to give some degree of specificity to a discussion that would be difficult
to follow if carried on at the abstract level of sense experience in general.
This specificity lends the ability to consider certain intuitions that are well
founded and that would show up in any sense (hearing or taste in addition
to sight, for example) but whose law is hard to adduce. But to discuss at the
level of generality would require clearer vision of that law.

There is a substantial critique to be leveled at the privileging of vision, and
this is related to the particular limitations that visual analogies introduce,

precisely because of the nature of vision. Jeremy Begbie has expressed this concern well:

> Sound is employed largely in a way which opens up a spatiality which does not depend on the discrete location and mutual exclusion of entities. In the world I see, an entity cannot be in two places at the same time, and two things cannot occupy the same place at the same time. Visual experience and discrete location become inseparable—seeing this lamp "here" means I cannot see it "over there." But in aural experience, although a sound may have a discrete material source whose discrete location I can identify ("the trumpet is on the left, not on the right"), the sound I hear is not dependent on attention to that "place." It surrounds me, it fills the whole of my aural "space." I do not hear a sound "there" but "not there"—what I hear occupies the whole of my aural space.
>
> This opens up a space which is not that of discrete location, but, for want of a better word, the space of "omni-presence." And when more than one sound is present, occupying the same space while remaining audibly distinct, we may speak of a space not of mutual exclusion but of "inter-penetration." Sounds do not have to "cut each other off" or obscure each other, in the manner of visually perceived objects. The tones of a chord can be heard sounding through each other.[1]

The point is well taken: vision is of the types of bodies for which it is repugnant to share space. That is, visible bodies compete for locations. As a result, the visual metaphor impresses on us a competitive notion of space occupancy that makes it hard to make sense of things like the two natures in Christ. Sound, by providing a model for non-competitive interpenetration (or coinherence), avoids this problem.

A full answer to this challenge will be given later. For now, I can say that the account of vision that follows differs importantly from the purely competitive account just given. And if vision is not always or necessarily competitive, this objection loses some of its significance.

Indeed, there is a certain propriety in talking about vision when talking about beauty. This propriety is not based in any sense that the experience of the beautiful is proper to vision, and then proceeds analogically to the other senses, and then even more remotely analogically to other, non-sensory experiences. That is to say, it is not a propriety of *proprium*. Rather, it is a propriety of *decorousness*, that it is greatly fitting that we should talk about this experience in terms of vision. Why?

1. Begbie, *Theology, Music and Time*, 24.

Either for the same reason that vision and knowledge have been so closely linked, or, if there is no reason grounding this (which I find unlikely), simply *because* knowledge and vision have historically been so closely linked. Thus, even though recognition is proper to all of the senses (I have smelled this before, I have heard this before), we most readily reach for visual experiences and metaphors when we come to talk of recognition (e.g., déjà vu) because we habitually treat vision as the most intellective of the senses.

What follows, then, is a reflection on the type of vision that would best suit us to be adept at experiencing beauty.

The Need for Eyes of Faith

What has been said so far has many implications, but what is perhaps most glaring is that it means that (1) the longing for beauty, (2) the way to see more beauty, (3) the proper response to beauty, and (4) the purpose of beauty will all converge on a simple and familiar theological concept: the vision of God.

1. We long for beauty because beauty is the connection (sometimes closer, as in the beauty of worship; sometimes more distant, as in physical beauty) to that for which we all long most deeply and truly, that which alone can activate our proper joy. We long to see God, and following upon the Incarnation, we long to see Jesus.

2. The way to progress in beauty is to progress in the vision of God, for the more clearly we have seen God, the more readily will we be reminded of God in all the things that are not God.

3. The proper response to the experience of beauty would be to respond to the beautiful according to the very part of it that makes it beautiful. But this beauty-bestowing property is nothing other than its capacity to remind us of its Creator. Thus, we honor beauty most when we turn it into an occasion for seeing God more deeply.

4. The purpose of beauty is that in seeing the creaturely thing, we might be made capable of seeing the Creator whose creature it is. Beauty, without being self-negating, points us beyond itself to the God of all beauty.

Because we are primarily concerned in this work with the experience of beauty had within the bounds of this world, it is not that ultimate vision of God, the Beatific Vision, that is at issue here. However, the Beatific Vision does lie in the background as a horizon, though not because it is the fulfillment of all the experiences of beauty that we have in this life. Those experiences are fulfilled not in the vision of God but in the vision of glorified creatures using glorified eyes. Because Heaven is still a world in the sense of a context for finite, bodily-spiritual beings to inhabit and interact with, seeing the creature does not pass over into seeing God; it is instead joined by the vision of God. The Beatific Vision is not, therefore, the fulfillment of the type of vision operative in theological anamnesis. Rather, it is the fulfillment of that memory or knowledge of God that is the condition of the possibility of experiences of beauty. The Beatific Vision is what happens when the eternity in our hearts becomes the eternity in our eyes.

In this life, then, what we need are eyes that are primed for the eschatological conversion into the vision of glorified creatures. These will be eyes that are able to look beyond the degradation and objectification of creatures into their truth, which lies hidden in the mystery of the divine Word. But it belongs to faith to pierce the veil of worldly appearance and touch the inner truth of things, and thus to deliver a knowledge that surpasses merely objective or experimental knowledge. What we need then are eyes of faith.

The Importance of Vision

The relationship between the one who sees and that which is seen has long been held to be of immense and mysterious import, especially in Western culture. For example, Medusa and the Greek gods represent a spectrum of extreme ugliness and extreme beauty, but neither is safe for human vision. The sight of Medusa was the destruction of the seer (by petrification), and the sight of the unveiled glory of the gods was no less destructive (Semele, on seeing Jove's unmasked glory, was consumed in flames).

The concern is not merely a Greek one, however. Isaiah expresses the same concern: "Woe is me! For I am lost; for I am a man of unclean lips, and I dwell in the midst of a people of unclean lips; for my eyes have seen the King, the LORD of hosts!" (6:5). God seems to confirm this to Moses when he says, "No one may see me and live" (Exod. 33:20 NIV).

Because of this, there was in both Greek and Jewish cultures an understandable fear of seeing. And yet, in spite of this fear of seeing that which is too great for us, the human race is also condemned for this lack of vision, for having eyes and yet failing to see.[2] This is because what underlay this ancient idea was the sentiment that divinity and humanity were fundamentally ill-suited for each other, that there existed between them a radical

---

2. Ps. 115:5; 135:16; Isa. 6:10; Jer. 5:21; Ezek. 12:2; Matt. 13:15; Mark 8:18; Acts 28:27.

incommensurability and otherness such that they could not come together without the destruction of the lesser.

And yet the ancients could also not shake the idea that somehow it *was* possible to put the two together and to do so at the most fundamental level. The Greeks expressed this idea with the notion of demigods: the half-human, half-divine offspring of a very intimate union. In Israel, this was expressed in the notion that the Lord would dwell among his people[3] and in the hope for a Messiah who would be "God with us," the Lord Almighty dwelling among his people in endless peace.[4]

Thus the Incarnation clarifies that the ancient expectation of destruction is not about any meeting of the divine and human whatsoever but about the encounter of the sinful with the divine; at the same time it affirms a union closer than any ancient people ever dared to hope for, for in it God becomes entirely human but does not cease to be God in order to do so. And so in Christ we see God and we are not destroyed, but rather saved: "We have seen his glory, glory as of the only Son from the Father, full of grace and truth" (John 1:14), and "Whoever has seen me has seen the Father" (14:9).

This transforms vision into a theological duty but also into a most unexpected grace. For, as has been mentioned, we were always bound to see (both in the sense that we were obligated to do so, and that doing so was inevitable). We have been given eyes for this very purpose: that we see and, specifically, that we see God. But this command opens into grace in the Incarnation because now not only is it false that to see God is to die, but it has also become the case that *only* by seeing God can we find life at all. Our deepest longing and our deepest need unite in the divine demand to be seen.

There is also a powerful connection to be made between the one who sees and the one who is seen. Now at last the deep-seated double longing of Western civilization is exposed and may be dealt with: we long to be seen as who we truly are, and we long to see God as God truly is. This comes to a marvelous culmination in the cultural production of central Europe in the nineteenth and twentieth centuries: the idea of the ethical responsibility that comes immediately on seeing[5] and on being seen.[6] No less than the fear of the ancients,

---

3. Exod. 29:45–46; Lev. 26:11; Num. 5:3; 35:34; 1 Kings 6:13; Isa. 57:15.

4. Isa. 7:14; Ezek. 43:7; 48:35b; Zech. 2:10–11.

5. Exemplified in Berthold Brecht's play *The Caucasian Chalk Circle*, in which the characters' seeing or not seeing is directly tied to their culpability and desert, and developed famously in Emmanuel Lévinas's philosophy of the face.

6. Shown marvelously in Rainer Maria Rilke's poem "Archaic Torso of Apollo," in which the poet argues that the power that resided in the divine head of the statue, forever lost to time, remains latent in the torso. The headless statue is transformed into the agent here, and in a reversal of the theme of having eyes but not seeing, the statue, without eyes, sees omnipotently:

these cultural products emphasize the danger of seeing; and no less than their predecessors, they do not really consider seeing to be avoidable. But, since the Incarnation, we have access to an awareness that the apocalypse caused by seeing may be not the end of worlds but the beginning of relationship.[7]

So, vision is complicated. But it is essential to the whole question of beauty, for beauty is all about seeing God. It is therefore important to spend some time considering the nature of vision.

The Nature of Vision

There is not a single way of seeing, for God, angels, and humans are all said to be able to see. While the divine and angelic ways of seeing are fundamentally unlike the human in that, as non-material, angels and divine persons do not have a physical organ that interacts physically with the world to produce an image, we need not conclude that spiritual beings do not in fact see but are said to see only metaphorically. One could just as easily conclude that vision is bigger than merely human vision, and so human bodily vision forms only one type of vision. Since the divine persons and angels are in fact said to see, this second conclusion has the advantage of being able to take such talk seriously.

It will therefore be helpful to consider the full range of vision, precisely because it seems that the experience of the beautiful requires a mode of seeing that in some way goes beyond the normal instance of seeing a physical object as physical object. By examining vision in its broader sense, we will find resources that may be used to help explain what is happening in theologically anamnetic moments.

Divine Vision

God sees everything; to say otherwise is to have already denied omniscience. But *how* does God see? Traditionally, God has been held to have a form of vision that is unique among rational beings. This position is grounded in a problem directly related to the claim that God sees all things: Is such vision successive?

"There is no place in which it does not see you," leading to the abrupt and shocking final line of the poem, an ethical imperative that rests easily on the divine authority that the poet has ascribed to the sculpture: "You must change your life." Rilke, "Archaic Torso of Apollo," in *Selected Poems*, 81–83.

7. That is, to see truly causes an apocalypse, but this is not in the secondary sense of "apocalypse" as the destruction of the world, but in its original sense as a revelation of the future glory.

Surely it cannot be the case that God sees multiple things the way that we do—namely, by first seeing one thing (or group of things), and then seeing another thing (or group of things), and so on until everything has been seen.

One reason for this is because God is thought to see infinitely many things (because God sees not only real things but also possible things), and if this were by successively seeing them one after another, even if in groups, God would never arrive at the vision of all things, for one never finishes progressing through an infinite series. Another reason is that if God were to see things successively, then imagine a time (T1) in which God is seeing the first one thousand things. Then imagine T2, at which God sees the next one thousand things. It will be obvious that at T1 God does not yet see the one thousand things that God will see at T2, and so at no time, up until the end of the series, is it true that God sees all things.

But there is also a deeper problem: because vision is so closely tied to knowledge (God can only have knowledge of things that God can "see," such that seeing becomes a metaphor to describe the fact that God knows something), there must be a deeper dis-analogy between our way of seeing and God's, precisely because there is a deeper dis-analogy between our way of knowing and God's way of knowing.

In our case, our vision of a thing is caused by the existence of that thing. That is to say, if there is no car there, normally we will not see a car there.[8] But if things had to first exist in order for God to see them, then God is not the Creator of those things; for God certainly needs to know a thing before God can create it, but on the present supposition, God can know only those things that already exist. Rather, God's vision cannot be caused by things; instead God's vision causes things, and thus it precedes them.

These two claims about the way God sees—namely, that God does not see things successively and that the divine vision is causative rather than caused—lead to the following account of divine vision: God must see all things simultaneously, and God does so, not by turning the divine gaze upon the things themselves (which do not yet exist at the moment God "first" sees them) but by turning the divine gaze upon Godself.

---

8. Hallucinations are an interesting case. On the one hand, we will often say of a person who hallucinates that this person "thinks" he or she sees something, indicating that we are not entirely comfortable classing hallucinations as a type of vision. On the other hand, we have the expression that such a person is "seeing things." What is interesting about this latter locution is that, although the person is said to see, the intention is to point out a fundamental failure in the visual faculty: she sees, but she should not be seeing. Such "visions" are noteworthy for not being true instances of seeing, and in older lore the power of "true seeing" could dispel them.

What this means is that God knows all things as extensions of the divine power. That is, knowledge of horses for God looks like this: "If I exert divine power in this way, a swift, four-footed, equine animal would be the result." Because the particularities of things rely on divine power, this allows God's knowledge to descend all the way to particulars: American Pharoah as opposed to Secretariat. God is even able in this way to know those things that will be actual from those things that are possible but will never be actualized: God knows me as accomplished, but God knows the person I would have been had I been born to a race of martians as something the divine power could have done but did not.

The result is that God's vision is simple, for God only ever looks at one thing (Godself), and in that one thing all other things are comprehended. It is important not to understand this in a pantheistic way: it is not that all things are God; it is that all things can be understood from God. I suppose it is similar in mathematics: if one knew all the potentialities of the number 1, one would also know all the other numbers that are formed by iterating or dividing 1, but all of which depend on the fundamental unity expressed in the number 1.

The major challenge to such a view is God's vision of evil. On most accounts, evil is not something that God can do, and so it cannot be known by God as an extension of the divine essence. So either God is ignorant of evil, or God does not see in this way, or God does not *only* see in this way.

In response to this it can be said that God can in fact know evil in just this way, because while it is not something that God can do, it is still derived from the divine power because it is a power of a power derived from God. Thus, because God has the power to create beings who would have the power to do good or do evil, God can cause a world in which evil can be done. The evil actions of free-willed beings are not outside the powers and abilities that come from God; they are particular (bad) uses of that power, and so they are able to be understood from the primal power.

Additionally, nothing impedes that God also see things in other ways, and in fact this has often been asserted.[9] But the type of divine vision described here is the primary or most proper form, as far as we can tell, because it depends on nothing but God, and so is able to be eternal and to not depend on creation in any way.

From Uncreated to Created Vision

We should expect that when moving from divine vision to angelic vision we would be crossing a very significant dividing line, for we are moving from

9. E.g., Bonaventure, *Breviloquium*, part 1, chap. 8, no. 1, p. 50.

a power of an uncreated being to a power of a created one. Further, we should look for this disconnect in something that has to do with the infinite ontological distance between the two. Thus, the very fact that divine vision is uncreated should ground a significant difference with created angelic and human vision. This is in fact the case, and the difference lies precisely in the action and passion implied in the verbal description of seeing.

When one considers the dynamics of vision, there are two important things: the seer and the thing seen. Thus, there is naturally in vision a subject and an object. In the case of divine seeing, the subject and the object are the same, because the act of vision is reflexive. As a result, a concern about which takes primacy, subject or object, never arises. This is an expression of the fact that the divine vision is uncreated: it depends on nothing other than itself, and so it cannot take another for its object.

One might wish to object to this view on the grounds that it seems to remove God too far from creatures. Instead, one would desire a more direct contact between God and creatures: that in creating, God is precisely making an object that is other than the divine self, and this is a sort of self-emptying (kenosis) by which God chooses not to be all in all in the most literal sense without thereby sacrificing the divine all-sufficiency. But this is accounted for by the claim that God has varying modes of vision: it is in this way that God sees sin, and it is by some combination of modes that God sees that I fall short of the divine vision of what I should be. But, again, these other modes of vision, precisely because they are grounded in the condescension of divine creation, are not proper to God as essential but as conditional, and therefore not what is meant by vision in the first instance when referring to God.

But once one crosses from divine vision to creaturely vision, the situation changes. Now the subject and the object will differ, for no creaturely essence contains within itself all other essences in an ideal form, and so creatures cannot see things other than themselves by a reflexive act of vision. Thus created vision, as much angelic as human and sub-human, is characterized by a non-identity between subject and object. Since this is the case, it is possible and necessary to ask whether one side is dominant in the visual encounter and, if so, which. The goal of such inquiry is not to denigrate one or the other (as has too often happened); rather, the goal is to ask whether one plays a controlling role in the experience.

It might seem that the subject is controlling, for without the subject, there is no vision, and it is the subject who is said to see. Further, things are not always seen as they really are, which seems to indicate that the subject controls the encounter.

However, there is also no vision without the object. Indeed, in those instances in which the thing is not seen to a significant enough extent according to the way it is, we do not call it a true instance of seeing. Also, "to see" could be understood as to be affected or to receive—as for example if our account of vision is that something outside of ourselves strikes our sense organ and causes a representation of itself to become present in our minds. This would make the object the active and controlling element in the visual encounter.

Both are important, because correspondence is an essential aspect of true vision; but it is, on the ordinary understanding, what is seen that is most important. Upon seeing a breathtaking landscape, one is not astounded that one is *seeing*; rather, it is the qualities of the thing seen that are arresting. The act of seeing is normally fairly unremarked on by the subject. Thus in creaturely seeing, the object plays the determinative role. This is an expression of what it means for this act of vision to be created: it is dependent on another.

This then is the ground of difference we were looking for, and it is founded on just the thing that separates the beings in question—namely, uncreated or created nature. And so, in what follows, we must keep in mind that we have already crossed a determinative threshold when we have moved from God to angels, however much commonality may exist in their modes of vision.

Angelic Vision

Angels hold a very important place in theology, because they are between God and humans and share some characteristics with each. Like God, they are spiritual (which here means mainly non-material); like humans, they are creatures and therefore finite. In what follows, I will assume a more or less classical understanding of the angelic nature.[10]

Unlike humans, angels were not created apart from possession of the Beatific Vision; rather, it seems to be the case that angels were created with the Beatific Vision and that their testing came in the form of a choice to prefer the sight of God or the sight of themselves. Thus, angels were made to always gaze on God from the first moment of their being. It stands to reason then that, unlike humans, they also see primarily by looking on God. However, like humans, angels are not infinite and so are not capable of seeing all things. Therefore, angelic cognition functions in a mode similar to God's (it is simple), but it is less effective (it does not see as much). God sees all things with a simple gaze; angels see whatever they see with a simple gaze.

10. As one might find, for example, in Thomas Aquinas, *Summa Theologica* Ia, qu. 50–64.

Demons and their mode of vision form a challenge to this account: surely it is not the case that demons see whatever they see by looking on the divine essence, since they have chosen to look away from God and toward themselves and have thus lost the Beatific Vision. Either they have a changed mode of vision, or angels never saw in this way.

It seems to be in keeping with the general account of the fall of the angels to affirm that the demonic mode of vision has changed. For their natures are changed and darkened by their fall, and the result is a reduction in their power that nevertheless leaves them quite efficacious (much as humanity has suffered a reduction in our abilities because of sin, and yet we are still capable of much). Indeed, it would be a fitting *contrapasso* if the very faculty in which the offense occurred (averting their gaze from God) is affected. Because they have preferred not to find their good in God, they are now forced to seek it elsewhere. Their mode of vision is perhaps now more like human vision (though still non-bodily). In addition to this, it is possible that they retain something of the knowledge they had as angels. This possession would be imperfect because their memories are probably not what they once were before their fall, and yet they are not entirely effaced, and so in this way they may have access to a type of knowledge that they could not now otherwise come by experientially.

To return to angels, both the angelic way of seeing and the divine way of seeing may be called spiritual, because they are not physical (neither in the faculties employed nor in the object intended), and, at least on classical accounts, they involve the entirety of the substance of the seer (because both angels and God are simple).

Human Vision

Human vision is unlike both divine and angelic vision in that for us vision is a bodily, and therefore a physical, function. Thus the proper object of vision for us, especially in this life, is also something physical, and therefore not God. As a result, our vision is not simple but complex: we see successively and we see things discretely, apart from their formal unity in the divine essence.

Thus the distinctive difference between corporeal (human) seeing and spiritual seeing may also be reduced to a question of the object of vision. In spiritual seeing, such as God and the angels have, there is one object, and through that object all other things are seen. For that reason, all that is seen may be seen simultaneously, and the act of vision is single. In corporeal seeing, no one object contains any of the others (for it is repugnant to bodies to be in the same place at the same time); therefore, what is seen is an object that shows nothing but itself. In this way, to see multiple objects requires multiple acts of vision. This is why vision is successive (because not all that can be seen is able to be seen at once) and compound (several different acts of vision combine to form what we are normally accustomed to call "seeing").

The composite aspect of human vision is characteristic: human vision is *reductive*. It has a tendency to group things in order to present multiple things as a single object of vision. Thus when I see a room, the tendency of my sight is to see the whole as a single uniform thing, not as discrete objects of vision. This is compositional, for I am in fact seeing many different things at once. Vision reduces, but it cannot simplify: the end result remains a composite, never truly becoming one, as the divine and angelic object of vision is. Thus, when I see two things at once, this is not with a single act of vision; rather, what I have is a simultaneity of two distinct acts of vision.

And yet, as already discussed, our longing is to see God. Now, while it may be the case that this longing will only be fulfilled eschatologically, Christ's claim in John 14:9 ("whoever has seen me has seen the Father") indicates that there is also a type of vision of God that is possible in this life—namely, one mediated through the Son. What does it mean to see the Father through the Son?

At the outset, we must avoid interpreting this in any sense that will lead to heresy—namely, as if the Father and the Son are not distinct. So this is not to be understood in the same way as if someone were to say, "If you have seen Tullius you have seen Cicero," because Tullius and Cicero are the same person (Marcus Tullius Cicero). Instead, we see one person, who is his own person and who has characteristics that do not belong to any other divine person (notably, incarnation into a human nature), and seeing this one person somehow also counts as seeing a totally different person, one who is not in himself visible to us in this current life (and who may or may not be visible to us apart from Christ in the next life).

Examples drawn from the world we know are tricky because there will always be an important element of difference between anything in this world and God, but perhaps the following may serve as a plausibility enhancer: Bob and I drive the same model of car. Our cars are the same year and have the same options. Both cars are silver. It seems that I could say, in a non-trivial sense, that if you have seen my car, you have seen Bob's car. However (and this is where the dis-analogy comes in), in the simplest of senses, you simply have not. Bob's car is not my car, and so seeing my car is not actually seeing Bob's car. It is, instead, knowing what Bob's car would look like without actually seeing it.

Now, is this what Christ means? Perhaps, but what if he in fact means something stronger? Not "You know what I am like, so you know what the

Father is like" but rather "In seeing me, you are *also* really seeing him." Such a claim would mean that there is at least one situation in which human vision (which normally sees by means of discrete acts of vision) sees more than one thing in a single act—namely, when seeing the Father through the Son. Bonaventure has a name for this type of vision: contuition. This is going to be a central concept for the notion of beauty I am developing.

The Nature of Contuition

Literally, contuition means "co-seeing." This is not double vision, for that would mean two acts of seeing that are taking place concurrently. Instead, contuition is to see two things with one simple act of seeing. In order for this act not to be compound, however, the mode of vision must be different. The two things are not merely adjacent or juxtaposed; rather, one is seen *through* the other. The version of this that we are concerned with here is the vision of the creature along with the God after whom it is patterned: for example, when one sees a mountain and by means of it also gets a vision of the majesty of God. Note that one does not cease to see the mountain in such moments; rather, it is the vision of the mountain as what it is in itself that opens space for the vision of the mountain to also be a vision of God. This could happen only because the mountain is truly an image of God, even if not so express an image as a human or an angel.

Here is another example: when Christ was revealed to the disciples on the road to Emmaus in the breaking of the bread (Luke 24:30–31), this was not contuition; rather, one whom they did not recognize before suddenly became recognizable. But when Christ is recognized by the faithful in the breaking of the bread in the Eucharist, this *is* contuition; for though many of us hold him to be truly present bodily on the altar, nevertheless what is seen is either bread or the appearance of bread, not the actual body and blood of Christ. Thus, when the body and blood *are* discerned, they are seen together with the bread as distinct realities but in the very same act of vision by which the bread is seen.

Thus contuition is spiritual vision. It is a human mode of vision that is analogous to how God and the angels see. And yet it is different from how the angels see, because we do not cease to see physically when we see spiritually. And so there are three ways of spiritual seeing, just as there are three spiritual natures. Contuition unfolds within the physical, and so contuition is a combination of a spiritual and a physical mode: a single act with multiple aspects. And there are modes analogous to contuition for non-sensory experiential powers, such as intellection.

Contuition is enabled precisely because the second object (God) is seen *within* the first object, as that object's inner meaning and that to which it points. Each creature, when it becomes an occasion for contuition, opens up a space within itself, or better, allows itself to become translucent, so that while one continues to see it, one sees also that which it images. To be an image of God is the original purpose of creatures, and so we use creation most rightly when we enable it to usher us through its inner mystery to its proper meaning, which is hidden in God.

Contuition and Beauty

So it is my claim that the experience of the beautiful is implicitly or explicitly a contuition.

Implicit Contuition

Implicit contuition is the most normal form of the experience of the beautiful in a world characterized by willful God-forgetfulness, where we do not see God because we do not want to. Indeed, even when we want to see God, we also do not want to see God, because our hearts are divided (cf. Rom. 7:15–24). So, in this type of world, implicit contuition is the most frequent experience of the beautiful. It is this that has enabled us to fail to notice that the experience of the beautiful is always about God.

Many are they who worship in the temple of beauty: some explicitly, like the Romantic poets and their successors, the aesthetes; and some implicitly, like Hollywood and we its many hangers-on. The rhetoric of the worshippers of beauty is always concerned with the ineffable: beauty is inexpressible and undeniable; it compels us without revealing its true nature; it summons us we know not whither, and we follow gladly. But this is disingenuous: we in fact are not at all interested in knowing where beauty leads, for this would bring us face to face with the ground of beauty, the one who dwells in the beauty of holiness. Rather, what we want is just the thing we find beautiful. Our desire is to convert the beautiful thing into the final end rather than allowing it to be a sign on the way to the true destination. In thus objectifying the beautiful, we suppress contuition, deny spiritual vision, and ally ourselves with the bodily tendency of human vision to reduce all things down to one.

This is not to say that the body is bad and the spirit is good or that bodily vision is bad and we have to get away from it. There is a right use of bodily vision's reductive power on which I think contuition hangs: we cannot follow things back to God if that reductive power of bodily vision is not at play.

But there is also, as with all things in this sinful world, a bad use of bodily vision: there is a laziness about it that we tend to ally ourselves with. Among the two things on offer—the occasion for the experience of the beautiful and the thing it is about that makes it to be beautiful in the first place—we choose the less noble one, the occasion rather than the reason, the moment of recognition over that which is recognized. The religion of beauty is a chasing after the wind because it treats the penultimate as ultimate; in confusing the means with the end, it sacrifices its ability to arrive anywhere.

Ineffability is challenging, for there are varying ways in which something can be unspeakable. The most proper use of the word "unspeakable" or "ineffable" is for that which, because of its nature, is not able to be spoken. God is not ineffable in this way, for God speaks Godself to us in the Word, revealed in Scripture and incarnate in history; but God also invites our talk about God, summons us to the task of theological reflection by encouraging us to tell of the goodness of the Lord (Ps. 71:15; Isa. 63:7). Nevertheless, the fullness of the divine nature surpasses the power of speech, and so there is a meaningful sense in which God can be said to be ineffable. There are things about God, but also the totality of who God is, that just cannot be spoken.

We also call unspeakable that of which one is not allowed to speak. This does not have to do with the nature of the thing itself, which can certainly be spoken; rather, it has to do with an injunction laid on the speaker by a higher authority. Often this is a religious authority, such that the unspeakable is that which would cause offense to the gods: in this way, the unspeakable is just a way of describing blasphemy.[11]

Finally, there is that which is unspeakable because it causes horror or great revulsion, not to some higher authority but to the partners in the conversation. Societal examples include topics like incest, pedophilia, and so on.

Now, which of these types of ineffability attaches to beauty? Its worshippers would argue that it is the first sort: beauty is in itself ineffable, because it is so high above our realm that our language cannot touch it but can only point to it. This is probably a big part of why beauty in its various senses has remained so long resistant to definition, because of a reverent awe that attaches to it and makes one hesitant to try to name the mystery. The language of worship is recognizable here: this sounds like temple language.

But on the one hand, our incessant desire to speak of it belies this claim: we find it eminently effable. It may, at best, be like God: speakable, but not exhaustible. On the other hand, the ineffability of beauty seems to be grounded on our inability to explain why it comes and goes as it does, why it affects us

---

11. The Latin word *nefas*, "that which is not to be spoken," conveys just this idea.

so strongly, and so on. But this is not hard to explain once we have accepted that beauty is what reminds us of God: now each of these questions of ineffability becomes very answerable. Beauty comes and goes as it does because we have an imperfect vision of God and so we are not very good at recognizing God in the things around us. So the fact that I find one person beautiful and another person not beautiful reveals a failure to understand God, because I cannot see how this other person is as beautiful an expression of the divine nature, as beautiful an image as the first. A residue of ineffability remains, but it is the ineffability of the God of whom it reminds us and of our relationship to him, not of the beautiful as such.

Thus, it does not seem that the first type of ineffability best describes the experience of the beautiful, but rather that which is the horizon of the experience of the beautiful. And surely it is not the second type: no authority, sacred or secular, forbids talk about the beautiful. I would like to suggest that the ineffability that we continually run up against in the experience of the beautiful is of the third type: an ineffability of horror and revulsion.

Is that not strange? What are we afraid of? What horrifies us, if the experience is of being rapt in the joy of the beautiful? Is it not exactly the thing that we do not wish to admit in such an experience? It is, in short, precisely the divine of whom this beauty reminds us that we remain terrified of. Thus, we claim ineffability in order to disconnect beauty from its moorings: it is the fig leaf behind which we attempt to hide from God. As a society, we have agreed that God is not to be talked about, that God must not be named, and so we go on seeking the beauty without the power, and we wonder why it keeps slipping through our fingers, why it never satisfies.

The experience of the beautiful indeed belongs to general revelation, which is the witness that God has left of God's majesty, glory, and faithfulness in every corner of creation. In our world, this revelation is not recognized as such: it is not seen to be a revelation but is thought to be merely facts, which have no meaning behind their ability to point to impersonal laws that we can manipulate for our technical purposes. This is perhaps why the poets have an uneasy relationship with technology—because there is a tendency to cut the meaning out of things in order to manipulate and control. The revelation is not disproved; it is simply denied.

Explicit Contuition

Explicit contuition is the province of the religious and the spiritual, of those who have begun cultivating the eyes to see that there is more to this world than what appears on the physical surface. Precisely because contuition involves a *spiritual* mode of seeing, it demands that we go beyond mere physicalism. And contuition only becomes explicit when one recognizes that God is the other reality that one is seeing in the moment of contuition, and so it is true that "whoever would draw near to God must believe that [God] exists" (Heb. 11:6).

It is important to distinguish what I do not mean here, in two senses. In the first sense, I do not mean that explicit contuition is, in the first instance, a mystical vision, although such visions are interesting in relation to contuition. For as visions of spiritual truths represented in bodily things, they are perhaps the most intense form of contuition: the physical world here achieves such transparency that it finds the complete fulfillment of its role as servant to the spiritual realm. Nevertheless, the physical things are often in danger of becoming so transparent that they are *nothing more* than the other thing that they represent, and at this point we leave the realm of contuition for the realm of allegory. Allegory may be useful pedagogically and delightful in a literary sense, but theologically it is weak on the affirmation of the good of the creaturely and the bodily, and so it tends toward docetic misunderstandings of Christology: allegory as a principle in theology tends toward the idea the Christ just appears to be human, rather than that he is really and enduringly forever human.

Second, explicit contuition is not merely a vague religious feeling that senses behind nature a "higher power," a "deeper meaning," or whatever other impersonal expressions one wants to use. The God to whom beauty is indexed not only is personal but is personal to such a radical extent that he is three persons and may meaningfully take on pronouns, even gendered pronouns. All impersonal understandings of God stop short of touching who God most essentially is.

Such feelings are not necessarily bad: one who senses through nature that there is more is on the right track and is easier to bring along the road to faith than one who denies that nature means anything other than itself or that there is anything more to reality than what we can quantify. Nevertheless, these experiences are not explicit contuitions, because of the very vagueness: nothing is really seen; nothing has been made explicit. Instead, they are implicit contuitions, and as visions of the truth they are only intuitions or, better, intimations. They are the seeds from which explicit contuition may spring, but they are not yet germinated.

And so what I mean by explicit contuition as the province of the religious is other than either of these. And no one religion has a monopoly on explicit contuition precisely because it is offered in general revelation. There is properly religious contuition that is not Christian: it terminates in the vision of God as deity—that is, in the divine oneness, power, holiness, and so on. This is to see God rightly but not yet well, for God is not well conceived apart from the Trinity of persons.

Thus the truest explicit contuition is Christian contuition, which sees not just the Creator God but also the God who is Father, Son, and Holy Spirit in the richness and goodness of created things. The various forms of implicit and explicit contuition that have been mentioned so far may be stages on a journey, but the goal is here, in the vision of God through creatures in accordance with the essence of God. It is clear, both because of human finitude and because of divine infinity, that such contuitions are apprehensions rather than comprehensions, and it is this that grounds their ability to transport, to rapture. For in comprehension the object belongs to the subject, but in apprehension, the subject belongs to the object.

It is the duty of the Christian to cultivate eyes that see in this way. To the eyes of faith, God's glory is declared everywhere and God's power is at work everywhere. Such eyes are the needed response to the functional deism most of us in the West have fallen into. It is also the natural result of sanctification that such eyes develop. The more one sees of God and the more one experiences God, the better one becomes at finding God in other places and the more apt one becomes for receiving more of God. Grace builds on grace: nothing can make a person better prepared to see light other than light.[12] Little bits of light enable a person's vision to strengthen to see more of light, then more and more and more; this is Dante's journey in *Paradiso*.

Let us return to the moment of the beautiful and say that one has overcome the sinful urge to shrink in horror from the God it reveals and so has moved beyond the ineffability of revulsion. Is it not true that there is an ineffable residue that clings to the experience? Again, this is no longer the ineffability of horror; at this point, one has returned to ineffability of the first type (of that which exceeds the power of speech and reason). In this sense, it is not the beautiful itself that is mysterious, it is the God to whom it points who is mysterious. But that is not all: the creature itself is beautiful, and the mystery of its beauty is grounded in its relation to something that very greatly exceeds it. Thus, the beautiful creature's mystery and ineffability are participations in the divine mystery and ineffability: as such, the creaturely and divine mysteries are distinct, for where there is identity, there is no participation; two things must be different for the one to participate in the other, and yet the lesser would not exist apart from the greater.

Thus, the beautiful creature is not ineffable in the first way as if it belonged to the category of immensity that grounds the first way. There is an ineffability

12. Cf. Ps. 36:9: "In your light do we see light."

about the beauty of my wife, but it is not because she is as immense as God; rather it is because she participates in God's beauty, which belongs to the first way of being beautiful. Something of God's immensity is reflected in her smile, and that is why it is so beautiful. Her smile can be properly (but not most properly) said to belong to God's immensity.

In this way both the beauty of the creature and the beautiful God of whom the creature reminds us are ineffable precisely in relation to being beautiful. Both of these ineffabilities contribute to the experience of beauty in which we, in recognizing the beauty of the creature, are also moved to see the beauty of God. And this experience also has a certain ineffability. This last ineffability is not merely a repetition or iteration of that of either the divine beauty or the creature's beauty. Rather, there is something ineffable about the act of being led by the hand by something beautiful to the ground of beauty itself. The very reminding, the anamnesis that this beauty is, maintains a certain mystery that offers itself to discourse, but only incompletely.

I have said that all explicit contuition is religious; now I must say that explicit contuition is not the exclusive province of the religious. This means that religious experience is not confined only to the religious. Explicit contuition of the divine will sometimes seize hold of those who are hard at work cultivating an unassailable God-forgetfulness. This is revealed in moments when those who are not religious, in describing the intense joy and pleasure they take in something, reach for religious language. When pressed, they maintain that they do not believe in God, and yet they are unwilling to modify their statements. In those moments, they nearly believe, in spite of themselves. In fact, it is just possible that everyone has these moments of explicit contuition in their lives as part of God's strategy to conquer each heart.

Subjective Objectivity Explored

In the last chapter we characterized the type of view being described here as subjective objectivity. This dynamism of a subjectively appropriated objectivity has great power for explaining the varieties of contuitions in encounters with the beautiful, so it will be beneficial to expand on it here.

Symphonic Witness: Virtuosity and the Experience of the Beautiful

The subjective element of the experience of the beautiful (that is, the fact that what is objectively encountered is subjectively appropriated) brings the conditions of the experiencing subject into play in all potentially theologically anamnetic moments. This is ultimately what accounts for differences in the experience of beauty (both in what is experienced as beautiful and in how it is so experienced).

Any encounter with a creature is potentially theologically anamnetic. And yet, of the many millions or billions of such encounters that make up my daily progress through the world, it is only in a few cases that this potentiality is actualized. This is because my understanding of God is insufficient. We were made to know God more than we do: in Eden, God would walk through the garden and call to the man and the woman, and they would speak face to face.[13] We are to be restored to this face-to-face encounter in the eschaton, underscoring that this remains the divine desire and plan for humanity (1 Cor. 13:12).

In addition to this knowledge of God we were meant for, we were also able to be reminded of God more clearly by creatures before the fall than after it, for two reasons. First, creatures imaged God more clearly before the fall. As part of the general curse on creation, the natures of all things have been blunted, and so they are all "dark mirrors," as it were. Second, our imagistic reasoning—our intellectual capacity to penetrate to the essence of a creature and there to contuit the Creator—is also damaged and weakened. We are less good at interpreting creatures than we were made to be. And so, as a result both of the fact that the paths of anamnesis have become more difficult and of the fact that the one of whom we are to be reminded is less well known to us, we often fail to be reminded of that one when we should be, and most potentially anamnetic moments remain merely potential.

At one level, every creature offers the potential for theological anamnesis equally to every possible observer. This is because of the objectivity involved: the first ground of theological anamnesis is something objectively true about the creature. But theological anamnesis is also grounded in the ability of the perceiver to contuit. In this way, creatures do not offer the same potential for theological anamnesis to all observers, because, for a variety of reasons that include the particular gifts of the individual, that person's unique experiences and past choices, and how well that person understands God (which has to do to some extent with the degree of sanctification that person has achieved), some things remind some people of God more easily than others.

Thus it is important to distinguish two genres of difference in what is experienced to be beautiful: failure and individuality.

Failure is always culpable, for it rests on subjectivity, and the subject is responsible for the conditions of the subject. These conditions vary widely from individual to individual as a result of the particular moral and habitual

---

13. As he would later with Moses in a modified sense (Exod. 33:11; Num. 12:8; Deut. 34:10), Jacob (Gen. 32:30), and the whole people of Israel (Num. 14:14; Deut. 5:4; Ezek. 20:35).

choices of individuals. Indeed, because experience is influenced by the conditions of the subject and the subject not only is not static but also is able to be influenced from within as well as from without, it is possible to distort one's own subjectivity in order to prevent certain types of experiences or to promote others. This self-shaping may be used to grow in the ability to see beauty, as happens in sanctification, but also in purely secular ways of turning from the self, for any turning from the self makes one more vulnerable to God. But such willful shaping may also be used to block experiences of beauty: this willful shaping of one's perception is often used to refuse to see the beauty in art produced by those whose politics one disagrees with, for example, and even to train oneself to find the ugly beautiful.

Failure may be understood in two ways. In the first way, there is a general failure any time a creature is encountered and contuition does not follow on that encounter. There is culpability in this failure, because we are the cause of our own blindness with regard to God. But it is a sort of generic failure, and it may be due to nothing more than the general conditions of a fallen world.

In the second way, there is a failure when a person does not see as beautiful a beauty for which that person is in fact well suited. This failure is more culpable, because it requires a special failure on the part of the individual. This individual may belong to a group that is especially well suited to seeing this beauty, and as such, though the individual may fail to see it, it may yet still be seen. In such instances, the group or members thereof might be able to rehabilitate the individual, to bring that person back to the place from which the beauty may be truly seen. Thus a rhetoric of the beautiful is grounded. But it may also be the case that the individual is uniquely capable of seeing this beauty; in such cases failure is tragic, for it robs the individual and the world of what we will speak of next: a unique contribution the individual could make.

Another source of difference in experiences of beauty is individuality. Individuality is an expression of the fact that the one object may be seen differently by different people and yet still be seen truly by each of the observers. Every creature is rich enough to be patient of a variety of approaches. Every creature can be considered more in *this* way than in *that* way, but such that both this way and that way of considering it are profoundly true and thus productive of theological anamnesis. These differences are not the result of the fall; they are the ground of the unique praise that each rational creature has to offer to God. In an unfallen world, such differences would enable us to speak of the Lord along the way, for I could teach you how I see God's beauty and in turn be taught by how you do, such that God's people would be always enriching one another with their particular and peculiar understandings.

Such differences are attributable to the conditions of the subject who encounters the object. They make possible a creative virtuosity in the appropriation of the object that is the necessary condition for both the existence of art and its ability to convey meaning: there must be an experience of beauty that is felt to be deeply personal if there is to be the creation of art, and yet there must also be a conviction that this experience can be externalized in such a way that others could come to see the same thing, or something sufficiently similar. Likewise, if it were not a subjective appropriation of something objective, there would be no possibility of communing in meaning or of communicating the meaning. The purely subjective as that which communicates with nothing outside the subject can also not be communicated outside the subject and so is private in the most lonely of senses.

This virtuosity grounds a symphonic witness to the reality in question (that of which we are reminded in experiences of the beautiful) that is the only type of witness that could in any sense be understood to be appropriate to the infinite depth to which we witness in such moments. If God is to be imaged in creatures, it can only be by means of a symphonic witness, for no one creature or any one creaturely expressive witness could give any sense of the infinite variety that exists in the divine exemplar.

This is what is lost if I fail to see a beauty of which I am uniquely capable. Because there is some unique yet true aspect of the way that I could see God imaged in this creature, the total human understanding of divinity is impoverished if I do not make my potential vision available to others. This is also why it is important never to lose the subjective side of subjective objectivity: it grounds not relativism (for that is ruled out by the objectivity) but harmony and complementarity.

Transgressing the Object: Blasphemy and the Ugly

This has all been essentially a reflection on the dynamics that the subjective dimension of subjective objectivity brings to bear. We turn now to the objective dimension. As previously indicated, the subjective is a quality modifying the objective: the objective is the thing itself and provides the proper boundaries of the experience in question.

The very fact that there is an object that is particular means that there will be boundaries. For even in the case of an infinite object (which is what we have here, since the referent of the experience of the beautiful is God), the object is still particular and so not susceptible of every possible quality, and so it is this and not that with respect to various properties. For an infinite being does not possess contrary qualities as contrary: God is omniscient, and therefore

God is not ignorant. Indeed, although many seemingly contrary qualities may be simultaneously and even necessarily possessed by God (e.g., justice and mercy), the fact of their simultaneous possession by God reveals them to be not truly contraries. Thus there is a boundary of sorts to infinite being, but this boundary is no limitation on the being itself (it is not a limitation of divine being to be unable to be at one and the same time and in the same respect the subject of contraries). It does, however, create a limitation on thinking about and encountering that being.

Thus, there is a fact of the matter about even an infinite object, and so there are predications of that object that pass beyond the boundaries of its being. In this way the objective dimension grounds the ability to examine the validity of experiences, interpretations, or reflections that claim to be of that object. For example, if God is not evil, an experience that seems to indicate that God is evil is either not a true experience of God or is not being interpreted correctly. And so however much space virtuosity may open up, the field of possible experiences is not infinitely broad, and its delimitation is not arbitrary: it is grounded in the concrete reality of the particular God.

This allows us to talk about what happens when one transgresses the borders of the object. This is another type of failure in the experience of the beautiful, but it is not the failure to see beauty where one should see it: rather, it is to see beauty where one ought not to see it—that is to say, to call the ugly beautiful.

It is worth saying that these are probably the only two options. It is unlikely that anything can be merely not beautiful, because, as was discussed in the previous chapter, ugliness requires the assault on the image-character of each thing. Only that which in no way resembles God is truly ugly, and only that which has been shattered by sin can even arguably be this way. There is, in fact, perhaps much less ugliness in the world than we have thought, precisely because Plotinus and Augustine have taught us to recognize that even within the damnedest creatures (Satan, fallen and unredeemed humans) there is still a great ability to reference God coded into their very being. Thus beauty may blossom even within the ugly, for the ugly is not *in every way* ugly. And so what we think is not beautiful and also not ugly is in reality an as-yet-unrecognized beauty (or ugliness).

The ugly as such is in no way beautiful. Only sin can render something ugly, for only sin has no positive relation to God, and only sin has the power to interrupt such relation. Thus, if we call the ugly beautiful, we are transgressing the objective boundary of the experience, for we are saying that something that is in no way like God is in some way like God. This amounts to attributing to God what ought not to be attributed to God. If, for example, we say with Nietzsche that pride is beautiful, we say that there is something like pride in God, and thus pride reminds us of God. But to attribute to God what is in no way to be attributed to God is blasphemy.

This explains why we take such great and emotional offense to the misattribution of beauty: our response is religious in nature, because we can tell that a religious transgression is being committed. Were the object not God, the transgression of its objectivity would be more allowable, for it would be mere(!) objectification—that is, the rendering of it into a mere object—for the sign or image-character of the object is centrally and essentially a part of its conception as a creature, and so to dismiss this character is already to treat, say, a tree as less than a tree.

This also underscores how inviolable and fundamental the objective is: there is no appeal away from the object. Subjectivity is incorporated, but it is circumscribed and delimited from the first moment of its incorporation by the already existing claims of the object.

Conclusion: Analogical Expansion to the Rest of Human Experience

The account given above, as indicated at the beginning of this chapter, is meant to apply also to the rest of the senses and to all of human experience. The account can only apply in an analogical fashion, however. This can be because the dynamics of the human faculties compared may not be the same or because of a lack of correspondence between the physical and the spiritual.

In the case of the other senses, the relevant dynamics seem to apply. For we are concerned with the fact that the senses naturally work by means of perceptions that are compound and successive, and this seems as true for smell, taste, hearing, and touch as it is for vision.

To revisit the earlier challenge about the limitations of vision, we can now offer a more robust answer. For while the problems with vision that Begbie points out are legitimate obstacles to using vision as the basis for a broader imaginary, this does not, for me, constitute a reason to decenter vision as a source of an analogical account of the encounter with beauty. Rather, I find that it underscores the necessity of a corrected account of vision. The notion of contuition reveals that vision is not in its fundamental nature competitive in the way that we suppose from our experiences of merely physical vision. Spiritual vision (whether divine, angelic, or human) reveals that just as two musical notes may coexist in a single act of hearing without canceling each other out, so two objects of vision may coexist in a single act of vision.

The question of the correspondence between the physical and the spiritual, however, is a difficult one. The correspondence in question would be the degree to which a common account analogous to the one produced above for vision (which is able to discuss divine, angelic, and human vision under the heading of a single category with different forms) is able to be constructed. Concerning such correspondence, there seems to be an unequal amount among the senses. For while hearing is often and richly ascribed to God in ways that seem barely metaphorical, the tradition, within either the biblical text or the theological tradition, of talking about divine and angelic touch, taste, and smell is much less clear.

Indeed, what passages there are about God smelling the smoke from the sacrifice and such seem to be either more metaphorical or metaphorical in a different way than passages about God's vision or hearing. The divine vision is often quite clearly speaking of God's knowledge (e.g., "your Father, who sees what is done in secret," Matt. 6:4), and divine hearing speaks of God heeding a prayer (e.g., "I knew that you always hear me," John 11:42), while passages about God's sense of smell seem to refer to God accepting or rejecting what is offered (accepting: Gen. 8:21; Eph. 5:2; rejecting: Amos 5:21). Perhaps in neither instance is God to be thought of as literally seeing or smelling, but between the image and the presumed meaning there is much less distance in the one instance than in the other, in part because the presumed meaning in each instance is unequally anthropomorphic. God may or may not have a reaction analogous to our recoiling from a bad smell; there can be no doubt that God has knowledge and heeds prayers.

In the case of non-sensory experiences, it seems that the dynamics are the same as vision. For our concepts are typically compounded from other sensory or intellective experiences; intuitions are often of connections among things; and in any event we do not conceive or intuit all things at once. Nor does there seem to be a lack of correspondence to spiritual things, for it is to be affirmed that God has concepts (famously, in the Augustinian tradition), and the notion of intuition may in fact be a closer fit to divine and angelic ways of knowing than normal human intellection.

Does this mean that the discussion of vision applies univocally to non-sensory experiences of the beautiful? This simply cannot be right, precisely because vision is a sensory experience, and the sensory just does not work the same as the non-sensory. In fact, what we should learn here is that the vision-based account was insufficiently concerned with materiality (the substratum of the senses), and for that reason it was already slipping into a non-sensory account.

On the one hand, this forms another reason for the propriety of the vision-based account: it is able to be situated between the sensory and the non-sensory, and so it is well suited to describe the dynamics in ways that can be applied in both directions. On the other hand, this means that while the account given would need to be further nuanced to articulate the precise nature of the analogical relationship between beauty experienced visually and beauty experienced non-sensorily, the required clarification lies with properly distinguishing vision from the non-sensory modes of experience, not vice versa. I will bypass the required clarifications here in order to get back to the main theme of exposition.

3

Beauty and Analogy

After all, the nature of the world, even in its tiniest particles, seems to bear the stamp of its trinitarian origins.

Hans Urs von Balthasar, Theo-Logic 3:416

The books or the music in which we thought the beauty was located will betray us if we trust to them; it was not in them, it only came through them, and what came through them was longing. These things—the beauty, the memory of our own past—are good images of what we really desire; but if they are mistaken for the thing itself they turn into dumb idols, breaking the hearts of their worshippers. For they are not the thing itself; they are only the scent of a flower we have not found, the echo of a tune we have not heard, news from a country we have never yet visited.

C. S. Lewis, The Weight of Glory

Lord, how can man preach thy eternal word?
He is a brittle crazy glass;
Yet in thy temple thou dost him afford
This glorious and transcendent place,
To be a window, through thy grace.

George Herbert, "The Windows"

Our reflection next turns to consider the nature of the being of creatures in their relation to God. It is the fact that all creatures stand in an analogical relationship to God that grounds the ability of the creature to remind us of God and that is thus the necessary condition for experiences of the beautiful. This is to be expected, for we accepted at the outset that God is the beautiful itself, and other things are beautiful by participation in God. Likewise, the experience of the beautiful, the contuition of the creature in its proper relation to its Creator, is the apprehension of the particular analogy that holds between this creature and God. This experience is a recognition of a concrete instance of the *analogia entis* (analogy of being). Parsing the experience of the beautiful will therefore require attention to how the creature is like and unlike God.

We are concerned with how all creatures in some way image God, how far this likeness can be pressed, and where to situate the gulf that must at some point exist between God and creatures (the gulf that is the very defining distinction between that which is infinite and self-caused and that which is finite and caused by another). Without such attention to the dynamics of likeness and unlikeness between God and creatures, we run the risk of pantheism and idolatry in referring creatures to God. Such a reflection should at once both deepen our appreciation of the ability of the creature to be the site of the revelation of the beautiful God and further dampen enthusiasm for the religion of beauty by showing the fundamental inadequacy of the creature to fulfill the longing that is activated in the experience of the beautiful.

Such reflection is also necessary given the nature of the account I have been developing. For, as explicated here, the beautiful places the *analogia entis* squarely in front of us as the inner motor of the experience of the beautiful, for this analogy *is* the comparison of the creature to the Creator. As was just said, beauty is the experience of the recognition of a concrete instance of the analogy of being. Accordingly, what follows will develop first a general theory of analogy, and then expand that to an account of the *analogia entis*.

The Nature of Analogy in General

A General Definition of Analogy

Analogy is the meaningful coexistence of likeness and unlikeness within a comparison.

What I mean by "meaningful" is that the analogy is productive of some understanding, perception, or something of the sort. This productivity or meaningfulness I will also describe as fruitfulness: a comparison that issues in some knowledge or some other such gain is fruitful, while one that demonstrates nothing at all is sterile. In the latter case, I would argue that we are not dealing with analogy at all, but mere comparison.

Without likeness, there would be no analogy, because the things are simply not similar: we would be left with pure difference. And without unlikeness, there would not be analogy but identity.

Concerning unlikeness, I side with the older metaphysical tradition that considers reflexive relations of similarity to be merely nominal; a thing is not like itself, because likeness is only present when something is similar to something else.[1] But to be similar means not to be in every way the same, and thus self-similarity would say that a being is both itself and not itself at the same time. However, even if we were to grant reflexive relations of similarity, in that instance there would still not be analogy because numerical difference (that they are two different things) is an essential difference in analogies. That is to say, whatever unlikenesses may exist between two analogous things, one such unlikeness must in every case be numerical. This is why "A is analogous to A" is not meaningfully said; rather, one would in such cases say "A is identical to A."

Since analogy requires both likeness and unlikeness, the proper understanding of analogy requires attention to both of these dynamics. As in all cases where there are multiple dynamics at play within a single situation, we may ask which of the dynamics in question is dominant, if either, and to what extent. It is not, however, the case a priori that likeness or unlikeness will dominate a given analogy. Rather, the strength of analogy is susceptible of more and less; that is, the two things compared may be more or less like one another.

But note that two things are more analogous the stronger the likeness is. This reveals that even though analogy forces attention to the unlikeness between two things, it is fundamentally a statement about likenesses. It is a way of saying that two things are alike. Difference therefore serves an apophatic function, limiting the exuberance of the comparison. Difference reminds us that although the two things are alike, they are nevertheless not the same. And this is the reason for disallowing reflexive relations of similarity in analogical situations: analogy intends, in the first instance, to measure the distance between two things. But it is therefore founded on a prior recognition or

1. Contemporary philosophical intuitions differ on this point: if one were to put forth a unique existent and then ask the question, "How many existents are like it?" one could in contemporary philosophy reply "one," because it is like itself. It was taken for granted by most ancient and medieval philosophy that the answer to the question is "zero," because it isn't *like* itself, it *is* itself.

assumption that there *is* a distance between two things. No one is concerned to measure the distance between a wall and itself, both because we know the answer to be zero and because the answer is not particularly relevant to situations in which one requires measurements.

It is the fact that analogy is a way of speaking of similarity that makes it fruitful for conceptual work: it enables us, by correlating two things, to learn more about one or both of the things correlated. This has a variety of permutations for two things *A* and *B*:

1. *A* may be fully known and *B* only partially known.
   This type of analogy uses *A* to clarify the nature of *B*.
2. *A* may be partially known and *B* only partially known.

Here *A* may clarify *B* if, even though we do not fully understand *A*, we understand it enough to ground the relevant similarity to *B*. It is also the case that this type of analogy may be mutually clarifying: by noticing the relevant likenesses and unlikenesses between *A* and *B*, we learn more about each one (whether the same things about each or different things about each). Most human thought is this way, because in spite of our pretentions to knowledge, very little if anything is fully known by us.

This form of analogical thinking, while helpful, must remain provisional, because we cannot tell whether what we do not yet know about *A* will, when known, alter not only our understanding of *A* in general (which it must) but also our understanding of the very property that grounds the analogy to *B*. Were that to happen, several outcomes would be possible:

1. The analogy could be seen to no longer hold. Or, more precisely, we would now come to think that the analogy was falsely imposed in the first place.
2. The analogy could be deepened: by learning more about *A*, we have also learned more about *B*. This affirms the propriety of the original analogy.
3. The analogy could be unaffected. It still holds, but even though the property that grounds it in *A* is now thought to be different, the consequence to *B* is negligible or unobservable.
4. *A* may be fully known and *B* fully known.

It might be argued, consistent with what was just said in the previous point, that 4 never happens for humans in this life. But even if that is true, the case seems sufficiently imaginable to be worth considering. Beyond this, the fact that we seem to be incapable of avoiding the belief that we fully know things means that we often think we are in this sort of situation when really we are not, which also makes it worthy of consideration.

It might seem that in this case any analogy would be sterile, because we already know all there is to know about each term. In fact such an analogy is not sterile, however, for while the knowledge of A and the knowledge of B might be complete, for finite creatures it does not follow that because one knows A one knows all the relations A stands in to other things. Thus, the analogy can teach us not about A or B but about AB, and that is not sterile. In general, analogy of this sort is the analogy that belongs to the situations in which the whole is greater than the sum of the parts.

To go further (and this point applies to all that has been said in this section so far), analogies are not imposed solely for the purpose of gaining or imparting knowledge. They are also imposed for delight, for the demonstration of beauty. Thus poetry is the most analogical discourse. And when analogy is used for this purpose, this last type of comparison is very fruitful indeed.

    x. What may not be the case is that either one be totally unknown, for analogy is based in predication, the ability to say something about the subject. Thus, both terms must be susceptible of at least some known predicates, for analogy is in fact the comparison of predicates. "Predicates" here indicates not merely linguistic or conceptual realities but ontological ones. Thus, two things can be analogous in three ways:

- linguistically (because our ways of talking about them are similar yet distinct)
- conceptually (because our ways of thinking about them are similar yet distinct)
- ontologically (because their properties are similar yet distinct)

And so it is clear why none of the permutations considered above allow either A or B to be unknown in any combination: if either term were unknown, nothing could be predicated of it, and therefore no ground could be given for either likeness or unlikeness.

The ground of analogy is not just that which grounds likeness or that which grounds unlikeness, but only both taken together. These grounds will be specific properties (verbal, conceptual, ontological) of A and B. In some instances, the same property grounds both the likeness and the unlikeness.

Such instances are the purest instances of analogy because they are simple (as opposed to complex) and so more *basic*. What I mean by this is that in cases where one property is the same and another different, composition has been brought into play to create the analogical comparison. If this composition is linguistic or conceptual, there is greater room for error because there are more moving pieces to the analysis; if it is ontological, it is expressive of a more complex web of relations between the two things: perhaps they are not simply analogous but analogous in respect to several factors. I will say more about this shortly.

As a result, the ground of analogy, in both its positive and negative senses, is specifiable. Indeed, one ought to inspect an analogy until one has uncovered precisely these grounds, for any work the analogy does is only as valid as the relevance of the particular likeness and unlikeness to that which the analogy is meant to support. Nevertheless, the degree to which it is specifiable varies greatly from an intuition that resists verbal formulation, on the one hand, to mathematical exactitude, on the other. When very little specification is possible, one says things like "in some way," "in a certain sense," and so on. When working with this type of analogy, humility is paramount. When greater precision is possible, one may reason more confidently on the basis of the analogy.

Analogical Complexes

The preceding is an account of simple instances of analogy, in which two things are compared. I have also said that the purest form of simple instances of analogy is analogy in which the likeness and the unlikeness are founded on the same property in the things compared. This does not, however, exhaust the dynamics of analogy. Analogies may be coordinated between more than one thing, and they may also cascade (analogies may be made between analogies). I call such instances of a group of analogies working together to form a single larger analogy "analogical complexes," and they deserve further comment.

1. One sort of analogical complex is when an analogy is made between two analogies, for example: $A : B :: C : D$.

The dynamics of this type of analogical complex are identical to the analysis of simple analogies given above: the analogies $A : B$ and $C : D$ are simply functioning in the same way that the entities labeled A and B did in the examples above. Accordingly, we learn more about $C : D$ from the analogy to $A : B$ or any of the other ways in which such analogies have been said to be fruitful.

2. Another, richer sort of analogical complex is when multiple analogies work together, but joined in a cascading chain.

The point of such analogies is to use a series of comparisons to several things to reveal varying aspects of a thing, and thereby to come to a fuller knowledge of it than would be possible on the basis of a single comparison.

Bonaventure provides multiple examples of this type of analogy. Here is one that attempts to situate the change that transubstantiation is relative to other types of change:

> But if you ask under what genus of motion or change it is contained, it must be said that this is a singular change that has no complete analogy; nevertheless it is likened to something. For because in this change nothing common remains, it is like creation. But because the beginning principle is not nothing but something, it is unlike creation and like generation. But because the final end is not something new, but something that existed before, it is not like generation and is like increase. But because the body of Christ does not increase in this, but comes to be in many places, therefore it is unlike increase and like local motion. But because it exists in another place and does not leave its proper place, but something changes into it, it is unlike every motion and change, and is instead a singular motion.[2]

In this example, transubstantiation is analogous to (that is, it is both like and unlike) creation, generation, increase, and local motion. Each likeness is also its unlikeness to something else—that is, because the beginning principle is something, it is both unlike creation and like generation, and so on. (One can imagine that this need not be the case: it could be like B in respect to x and unlike B in respect to y, and like C in respect to q and unlike C in respect to z.) In this instance, the reality under consideration is *hapax* (unique), and so a residue of unlikeness remains (we will consider this residue of unlikeness in detail when considering the *analogia entis*). Each of the terms that transubstantiation is being compared to belongs to the same genus: change. Thus the particular specification being carried out is the degree to which transubstantiation agrees with our larger notion of change. The conclusion is that it does but not entirely, and so it winds up not only clarifying our understanding of transubstantiation but also expanding our notion of the genus to which it belongs.

A diagram of this type of analogy might look like a wheel: transubstantiation sits at the center because it is the common term in each of the analogies. At the circumference would be the other terms (creation, generation,

2. Bonaventure, *Bonaventure on the Eucharist*, 229.

etc.). The lines connecting them would indicate the relationship of analogy. Corruption would be on the circumference as a type of change, but no line of likeness would connect it to transubstantiation. To complete this image, there would need to be a line connecting to no point on the circumference at all, representing a positive aspect of transubstantiation that is theoretically like something we do not know (even if no such thing to which it is likened exists) that remains. This line would extend past the circumference rather than stopping short, to indicate that the lack of a second term is a matter of excess and not of deficiency.

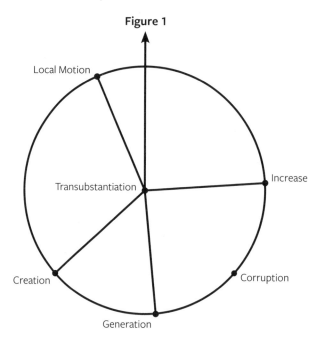

Figure 1

3. Another type of analogical complex would be the sort that proceeds through multiple terms successively: A is analogous to B, and B is analogous to C.

Let us assume for the sake of this example that in each case it is in respect to a property x that both analogies hold. Thus A is like and unlike B with respect to x, and B is like and unlike C also with respect to x. In this case, we know that A's version of x (Ax) is not the same as B's (Bx), but is meaningfully similar. The same relation holds between Bx and Cx. And because it is not the case that $A : B :: B : C$, we also know that Ax and Cx are not the same.

However, the relationship between Ax and Cx is less clear than that between Ax and Bx. It may be more distant, for Ax is not entirely like Bx, and so if

Bx is unlike *Cx* along the same lines, then it will be two steps removed from the quality of *Cx*: still like it, but more distantly so.

Figure 2

It may also be equidistant or closer, for though the property is the same in all cases, the direction in which *Ax* differs from *Bx* may be toward *Cx*, so that the distance between *Ax* and *Cx* is lessened.

Figure 3

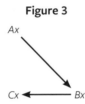

However, in the example given, this rapprochement must stop short of identity, for if *Ax* is the same as *Cx*, then *A* : *B* :: *B* : *C*, which was denied at the outset.

So if the goal is to better understand *Ax*, this type of analogical complex may or may not help—it depends on our ability to specify the nature of the likeness and unlikeness and to then coordinate those between the two instances of comparison. But this type of analogy could be very useful in clarifying the nature of a problem or challenge. It is hard to be very precise about *A*, one might conclude; for although we know *C* well, and we know that *B* is analogous to *C* in the relevant way, and that *A* is analogous to *B* in the relevant way, to the extent that *Bx* is only analogous to *Cx* and therefore lesser known, we are perhaps to be even less confident about *Ax*, which is lesser known still. In other words, because of the non-specifiability of the analogy (or, equally, the lack of confidence we may feel about any given specification), the analogy grounds *quasi*, "in a certain sense." If all we can say is that *A* is somewhat like *B* and *B* is somewhat like *C*, then we have perhaps done a better job of articulating the challenge of understanding

A than we have of actually understanding it. I would still consider this fruitful.

Finally, it must be said that nothing impedes that there be more than three terms involved in such analogies, except perhaps the difficulty of holding too many terms in mind at the same time.

The Nature of the *Analogia Entis*

I take the fact of an analogy between God and creatures to be indicated by the scriptural claim that humans at least are made in the image of God (Gen. 1:27). But it can also be reasoned to, in the following way: I take it as axiomatic that God's aseity means that God is self-determined *and* self-intended. Thus, God is whatever God wishes to be (I mean this in a strong sense), and God acts for God's own ends. However, creatures are dependent on God and were created for God's reasons at God's whim (nothing determinatively explains God's choice to create). The only thing that exists outside of creatures is God, and so God is not only worthily and rightly the object of the creature's intention but also the only object that, when worshiped, does not cause that act of worship to count as idolatry (by establishing a creature as absolute). Therefore, creatures are God-determined and God-intended, when they are rightly ordered.

Thus, we arrive at the Law of Analogy: the creature, like God, has God as its origin and as its goal (likeness); but then necessarily the creature is not its own origin or goal (greater unlikeness). This is a law because it is necessary that the creature be referred to God; even in disobedience, the creature cannot sever this connection or escape this truth. The dynamics of creaturely being will therefore imitate the dynamics of divine being by being God-sourced and God-intended but will differ by virtue of that same fact because, unlike God, for the creature to be directed at God is for the creature to be directed outside of itself. The fact that the origin or goal is not the creature itself but another modulates the being of the creature such that it is qualitatively different from God's being, but the fact that the goal or end is the same for all creatures binds them all to the same logic (precisely to the extent that the logic of the object controls the relation, which is a dynamic we already saw to be the case in creaturely vision).

An example will help to clarify this: if the divine persons are constituted by relations, then it has seemed good to some to say that human persons are also constituted by relations. This could be interpreted to mean that we do not come to the world as fully formed and inviolate persons but that we only become persons through the complex web of our social interactions. But this interpretation transgresses because it is a univocal application of the divine dynamic to the creaturely realm. It is not by any relations whatever that the trinitarian persons are constituted, but rather by their relations to other divine persons. The analogical move would be to say that humans are also constituted by their relations to divine persons. But relations to divine persons, while horizontal for God, are vertical for creatures. Thus, while the divine persons are constituted by their relations to peers, human and angelic persons are constituted not by horizontal relations to other like creatures (society or family) but by vertical relationship to God. So however much such horizontal relations may influence creatures, they are not determinative or constitutive of personhood.

As a consequence of this view, it will be not only human nature that stands in an analogous relation to God but every creaturely nature. I take this, with Bonaventure, to be true in a cascading way: the angels are the most like God, then humans, and so on. However, the degree of likeness is not specifiable. It is not possible to say how much more like God an angel is than a human, or to rank non-rational creation. And even though there is a hierarchical ranking (not all vessels are created for the most noble uses), the point is not the hierarchical dimension but the originary one: the vast panoply of creatures is meant to image varying things about God, and it is from this, and not from their place in the hierarchy, that they draw their worth. The question "Is it better to be a human or an angel?" has no answer; rather, it is better to be what one is meant to be, even if that is not the best type of thing that there is. For "in his will is our peace."[3]

But there is also unlikeness between God and creatures, and this likewise cannot be specified. However, because the unlikeness is founded in the ontological gap between God and creatures, it infinitely exceeds the likeness. Thus, a human and an angel are far more like each other (as are an angel and a cockroach) than they are like God.

Nevertheless, and this is critical, the infinite unlikeness between God and creatures never cancels out likeness. The likeness is, in fact, ineradicable, but this is not the reason it is not eclipsed. It is not eclipsed because it is non-competitive with the unlikeness. The infinity and aseity of God, which are perhaps the attributes that most succinctly name the difference between God and creatures, do not make divinity inimical to representation in non-infinite, derived beings. Rather, they enable a more radical imaging than would otherwise be possible. For the greatness of the difference is what guarantees that

3. Dante, *Paradiso* III.85.

there will be no competition, and so God is free to pour Godself richly into creatures without fear that they will be in danger of no longer being creatures or of being seen as more than creatures. The divine aseity and infinity guarantee a boundless canvas on which the divine can paint.

In the analogy between the divine and the creaturely, it is thus always the unlikeness that dominates the analogy. Theologically, this has been classically expressed as *maior dissimilitudo* (greater unlikeness): the unlikeness between God and creatures is always greater than any likeness. Indeed, we can even allow a *semper maior dissimilitudo* (ever greater unlikeness), but only if this does not transgress the demand that likeness not be swallowed up. The unlikeness is marked as ever greater not because it is constantly growing to keep pace, for that would define a relationship that is ultimately competitive, because the likeness is on the tail of the unlikeness, chasing it. Rather, the unlikeness is always already greater, is fundamentally greater as the ground of the likeness. Thus, it is a priori, even if it is not recognized as such. To state it more clearly: the likeness is founded on the unlikeness; image is founded on the divine self-sufficiency. Whether or not we say with Bonaventure that the divine self-sufficiency, expressed as Trinity, is a necessary condition of the possibility of creaturely being,[4] it is certainly de facto the condition of the possibility of such existence.

The unlikeness of the *analogia entis* is transcendence, and the likeness is immanence. Thus, ontologically speaking, God's being is near to ours in the exemplary relationship that is biblically expressed as the *imago Dei*: the image of God that we are as creatures is not a dead copy; it is a living image of the exemplar precisely because it is enduringly bound to the exemplar as its ongoing measure. The exemplar is not just the measure of our being at the moment of its creation; it is the constant standard to which our being is compared, that to which we are ultimately intended to conform and in fact the truest version of what we can be. In this way God expresses the creature more clearly than the creature expresses itself and is nearer to us than our own hearts.

God is ontologically unlike us in the magnificence of the divine mode of being. Transcendence is not distance but otherness, and so it does not threaten the proximity of immanence. Indeed, transcendence is more meaningful because the magnificent one is near, illuminating and shaping us and everything around us.

In both of these ways, I have just spoken of transcendence and immanence as having to do with something like natures or essences: what God and

---

4. Bonaventure, *Collations on the Hexaemeron*, col. 11, no. 9, p. 218.

creatures are *like*. But God is also personally immanent, residing alongside us in providential and personal care. Our personhood is like the divine personhood, and so we commune in the (unequal) commonality of personhood. And God is personally transcendent because God's way of being persons has a fundamentally different relationship to nature and to numerical constitution than ours does. According to this transcendence, the Trinity is not imitated by us, and the dynamics of divine personhood can only be predicated of us analogically, as previously indicated.

This is the analogical relation between God and creatures indicated at the beginning of the chapter, and this is the necessary condition that grounds experiences of the beautiful. But the way in which the creature is like and unlike the Creator may and must be further investigated. For the likeness and unlikeness of being just noted (ontological immanence and transcendence, whether at the level of nature or person) is general; in the second way, every person can be experienced to be beautiful, and in the first way, every creature can be experienced to be beautiful. This is where the Plotinian notion of the convertibility of the good and existence—that every thing is good insofar as it exists—has its place. But this is rarely the aspect according to which the thing is experienced as beautiful, and the reason for that is plain: to experience a creature as beautiful qua creature is to experience it as beautiful only in a very general sense, a sense that it shares with every other creature. This is a true beauty and is to be appreciated, but it is rarely what arrests us. What arrests us is typically not the generic beauty that all creatures partake in but the particular beauty of this creature in front of us. Its unrepeatable, unique witness to the glory of God is what is most commonly the ground of our experience.

Thus, the task is to identify not the generic likeness and unlikeness to God expressed in its nature as creature but the specific likeness and unlikeness proper to it as *this* creature. This is as much true on the level of particular genera as on the level of individuals: one must descend all the way to the most singular. One must experience beauty not just in creatures but also in trees as distinct from rocks; and not just in trees but also in the manifold species of trees; and not just in this species of tree but also in this particular tree that one is standing before. Because every creature partakes of the image of God and does this in its own unique way even within its genus and species, beauty explodes commonly from within every thing according precisely to its particulars.

PART 2

The Meaning of Beauty

This study of beauty has sketched a set of dynamics and commitments that mark out the contours of a theological account of the experience of the beautiful. What has been said is sufficient to indicate the shape of the account and the direction in which responses to major challenges would lie.

Accordingly, I will now turn to the implications of this understanding of theological anamnesis for signification in general. For both the urgency of our universal allegiance to what we find beautiful and the theological grounding I have given to that allegiance argue that the type of referentiality to be found in that experience is primordial enough to ground other instances of referentiality. The ability of creatures to remind us of God is the first truth of the creature insofar as the creature was created for just this work of imaging and reminding; thus, the entire vast economy of reference, both in its sacred and secular domains, stands on this first creaturely dynamic of reference or signification.

The moment of signification is not fixed: it is not identical with the moment of imposition (when a signifier is first instituted to signify something) or with the first encounter of another with that signification (when you first read a metaphor I have made up) or even with each individual's moment of first encounter. Rather, it travels through time and culture with the signifier itself, such that each encounter with the signified, whether the first or the fiftieth, is the moment of signification.

It is like our inhabitation of the present: the present is always shifting. We flow forward within a moment that is concrete yet undeterminable because it is constantly becoming something it was not without ever ceasing to be what it was. This moment is not ten seconds ago, and yet it is still the present, and so there is a continuity across this continual change. Further, the present as we experience it always has a past and is conditioned by this past without being fully determined by it (for something new may always be injected into the present by those with the necessary causal power). It is pointed at a future in such a way that it seems always to have a future, for we cannot know when it will come up against a decisive break that it cannot cross (such as the transformation of time at the last judgment, which is fittingly called the "Last Day" not because after it there is no longer any time but because after it time is fundamentally and irrevocably altered). In much the same way the moment of signification always flows forward, is always the current instance of the encounter with signification. It has a past that conditions but does not determine it, and it is directed toward a future that cannot be denied to it a priori. We may come to forget our temporal past: this does not rob it of its power, but rather renders us less capable of understanding the present. Likewise, when we forget the past of the signifier, this past is not effaced, but the signifier becomes more inscrutable. We puzzle at a word, for example, wondering how it ever came to be used to mean what it means, unable to answer the question of etymology and filling the gap with guesses that may have nothing at all to do with the history that brings it to us. And this history may yet have left connotations on the word that we are powerless to account for, even though none now know that history. Thus the moment of signification is both fluid and irreducible.

In questions of reference it is important to know *what* is being referenced, and there are essentially two general possibilities: we may be referencing a *res* (or reality)[1] or a concept. These two possible referents will split all categories of reference into two groups.

The first approach to the question of reference must be linguistic, for it is in language that we think and reason, and it is by means of language that

1. I will use *res* to refer to an entity in the world that is independent of a creaturely mind. In this conversation I primarily mean physical things; the extension to non-physical things may be made and is important but requires a more convoluted discussion due to the high level of abstraction involved.

these thoughts will be expressed (chap. 4). In language our concern is with the way words refer: the words themselves (which are distinct from their verbal utterance or written representation) are not *res*, nor do they refer to *res*; rather, they refer to concepts. The relation of those concepts to the *res* they are meant to express is a complicated issue that sits at the center of the battle between realist and relativist linguistics.

The second moment in the consideration of reference comes when we move from the way words reference concepts to the way concepts reference concepts. This is to turn from language to metaphor (chap. 5). The web of interactions established (or, better, highlighted) by metaphorical imposition and interaction further illuminates the nature of referentiality as such.

After this, we turn to the consideration of how *res* refer to concepts, which is the purview of the field of semiotics (chap. 6). This introduces important questions of concretivity and the objective boundaries of the signifier. Beyond this, there is also a striving within semiotics to arrive at something beyond concepts, and in this way it anticipates but is unable to attain to the dynamics of divine reference that are still to come (first part of chap. 7).

These three may all be fruitful; but the first two are not efficacious, meaning that they do not effect what they signify. Semiotics is quasi-effective: in one sense, whatever else things may signify, they also signify a culture. And in this sense, semiotics is productive of the culture that it signifies. This is another way in which semiotics anticipates the dynamics of divine reference. But things never signify culture in the first instance, for culture is a second-order intention of things or a compound or indirect referent. And in this sense the semiotic sign also fails to be efficacious, for it cannot cause the presence of the reality signified in the first instance. The quasi-sacraments of semiotics never quite attain *res*, for the "sense" remains ever at the level of thought (*sententia*) and does not arrive at *sensus* as "something perceived by the senses."

However, the sacraments of the Church open a new category of reference in which things refer to things, to *res*. This is explicitly true: that which is the referent of the sacrament is called the *res sacramenti* (reality of the sacrament). This referentiality of things to things has two directions: one in which the *res* is brought down to us and conferred upon us, and this is the work of the sacraments (second part of chap. 7), and one in which we are ecstatically transported to the *res*, and this is the work of the icon (chap. 8).

These relationships are all summarized by figure 4 (p. 88). The solid lines represent relationships of signification, with an arrow pointing from the signifier to the signified. It will be noted that there is also a line of signification from the concepts that are signified by words, concepts, and *res* to the *res* that these concepts themselves signify (thus "tree" is a word that signifies a concept of a certain type of plant, which concept itself references the things we encounter in the world to which we apply the word "tree"). This relationship between the signifieds of the two fundamental categories of reference establishes a deeper relationship between words, metaphors, and signs on the one hand and sacraments and icons on the other.

Lines composed of dashes appear on the right-hand side of the figure and represent an efficacy that makes something present. The arrow points in the direction of this presencing. Thus, the Eucharist makes the signified to be really present with the sign for the one observing the moment of signification, while icons use the sign to make the one observing be really present to the signified. This is unique to sacred things, for creaturely power cannot institute such effective relationships.

However, the dotted line between semiotics and concepts indicates a dynamic that is analogous to the dynamics of divine reference. For the semiotic sign, insofar as it represents culture, both makes culture present to the observer and initiates or incorporates the observer into that culture. This is, as was mentioned above, a qualified movement, and so remains only analogous to the sacramental and iconic efficacy. But it is a point of contact; it is where human striving reaches after divine things and finds them in an attenuated sense, according to its own proper mode (finite and sinful in the present state of humanity).

All this will become clearer as we progress through the exposition of the various modes of reference. At each step, I will also gather up the fruit of the reflections for the question of beauty in a section devoted to this purpose at the end of each chapter.

Figure 4

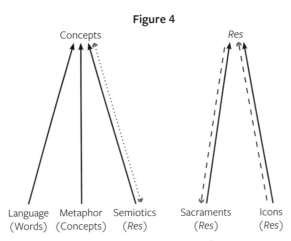

4

Word and Concept

The Nature of Language

There is no cheating in nature and the simple unsought feelings of the soul. There must be a truth involved in it, though we may but in part lay hold of the meaning.

George MacDonald, *Phantastes*

> Yet trees are not "trees", until so named and seen
> and never were so named, till those had been
> who speech's involuted breath unfurled,
> faint echo and dim picture of the world,
> but neither record nor a photograph,
> being divination, judgement, and a laugh
> response of those that felt astir within
> by deep monition movements that were kin
> to life and death of trees, of beasts, of stars:
> free captives undermining shadowy bars,
> digging the foreknown from experience
> and panning the vein of spirit out of sense.
>
> J. R. R. Tolkien, "Mythopoeia"

Realist and Relativist Linguistics

Signifier and Signified

There are essentially two poles to consider in the question of signification as classically understood: the signifier and the signified. Some wish to expand this to three: signifier, signified, and the sign, which turns out to be the instance of signification.[1] This is not what we mean here, however, for this is meant to be an analysis of the instance of signification, and nothing should enter into its own definition.[2] This instance or moment of signification may be controlled by one or both of these poles. One could express this in terms of causality: Does the signifier cause the signified, or is it caused by it?

To anticipate, the first instance is sacramental in this world, to the extent that a sacrament is a sign that effects what it signifies. Note that this is not causality simply speaking but a particular type of causality: It does not cause the *res* signified to *exist*, but it causes it to *be present*. The second instance is an instance of recognition, in which the *res* is foremost.

Linguistic Relativism

Linguistic relativism attempts to treat human language as being of the first kind—that is, that the signifier causes the signified. It does this by emphasizing the separation of the concept from the *res* it is a concept of—that is, it makes much of the fact that the signified is the concept, not the *res*. My concept "tree," for example, is not the same thing as a tree, for no one would claim that the fact that I speak English causes something called a tree to exist, and that no such thing exists to an ancient Roman, Decimus, to whom there are instead *arbores*. Rather, there are these things (*res*) out there, but I come to know them by the concept denoted by "tree" while Decimus comes to know them by the concept denoted by *arbor*. This means that the word "tree" in the first instance means not that thing growing outside but only my concept of it. That concept is then itself referenced, in a secondary moment of signification, to the *res*.

Once the concept and the reality are separated in this way, it is possible to say that language causes the concept. The concept and the reality do not perfectly correspond to one another, as readily appears by comparing concepts from different linguistic systems: If I were to take a walk with Decimus and we pointed out everything we thought was a tree along the way, he would point to some things that I would not. But it is meaningless to ask which is more right,

---

1. E.g., Barthes, *L'aventure sémiologique*, 36.

2. I will reserve the word "sign" for signifiers that are also *res*. As such, the sign or *semeion* (and therefore the subject of semiotics) will occupy the discussion in chap. 6.

because both are arbitrary. It is mere social convention (which may have more or less utility, more or less aesthetic pleasure, and other factors) that has led to the classification of this plant as an *arbor* by Decimus and a bush, rather than a tree, by me. Indeed, I learn my concepts by learning a language. There is a rigorous and continual process by which, as a child, I learn labels, and then I point to things to test out those labels, to be corrected or affirmed by the other members of my culture. In this way, the concepts are cultural products that are delivered to me linguistically. I do not have Decimus's concept *arbor* because I was not inculcated into his culture. I have learned something of it after the fact by learning his language and culture but only imperfectly: I will always be mystified by some of his choices in labeling.

Thus the language I learn as a child controls how I see the world. By learning to speak a language I am by the same act learning a particular and arbitrary way of seeing the world that forever controls my basic intuitions and gives me the concepts from which I must work. As a result, all my thoughts develop from concepts given to me by my language, and thus language is prior to concepts. Thinking is just an internal use of language, and it can only work with concepts delivered to it by my culture. All thoughts are, as a result, thought to be linguistic. Concepts are therefore either only imperfectly translatable or not translatable at all, and we cannot find out which, for we can never know if the foreign other is thinking what we are thinking, even when we have decided that we mean the same thing by "tree" and *arbor*. Thus, when you have learned what "tree" means, you have really learned something about the culture, society, and linguistic system of the people that use that word "tree" to describe certain types of things they see in the world. Language learning inculcates one into the language game, the ability to identify and create references internal to a closed system where every element is at play with every other element.

Language and our mental concepts are thus another instance of the insurmountable barrier of the unverifiability of subjective correspondence. We both see a color and call it red, but we can never know whether we are seeing the same thing. How do I know that it is not the case that what you see when you say "red" is not actually more like what I see when I say "blue"? If your color perception has always been fundamentally different from everyone else's, you would have just learned to call things by the wrong name, and you would therefore think that what most of us see as blue is actually what red is.

Linguistic Realism

Linguistic realism, by contrast, argues that human language is an instance of the second kind—that is to say, that it is caused by the *res* by way of recognition of some prior existing reality. In some sense, we find concepts ready-made in the world, and it falls to us to unwrap them and begin using them. Linguistic realism denies, to varying extents, the claim that language is arbitrary. Language is based on real properties or distinctions of *res* in the world, and thus it is determined by the nature of the *res* we are talking about.

Perhaps the commonsense, unreflective view is that the referent of the word "tree" is the *res*; if so, this would certainly set one up for a realist semiotic. This seems unlikely, however, because "tree" does not pick out any particular tree; but every *res* is particular. To hold that the referent of "tree" is the thing itself, one would seem to need to be a Platonist and thus be able to say that the referent of "tree" is the Idea of tree. Treeness would then be the *res* to which the word "tree" corresponds. If one were to take this strong view, the idea that the signifier causes the signified is simply absurd: *res* do not depend on created utterances for their existence.

The more reasonable realist claim is that the signified is a concept that is best explained as my concept *of a tree* than as *my concept* of a tree. That is to say, the important thing for explaining why the concept looks the way it does is *what* it is a concept of, not the person or culture whose concept it is. Because "tree" references my concept *of a tree* and *arbor* references Decimus's concept *of a tree*, the possibility of meaningful overlap that could extend all the way to exact correspondence between the two concepts is opened. Thus, language "cuts reality at the joints," which is to say that in dividing up reality linguistically we are dividing reality according to the way it really is, and not merely according to what seems right to us (whether it seems right because of utility, aesthetic pleasure, or whatever). When you have learned what a tree is, you have learned something about the world outside of human society and discourse, whatever else you may have learned about discourse.

Of course there must be some level of non-necessity in the imposition of language because not all humans call the same things by the same names. If they did, we would have one language: for we would use the same word to describe trees, the act of seeing, the subject of seeing, and so on. So the words used are different (that is to say, we have different languages), but this does not mean that the words used to refer to *res* are arbitrary. It is not only English but every human language that cuts reality at the joints. That different languages are able to cut reality so differently and yet all be able to be said to be dividing it up accurately is a testament to the variegated nature of *res*, that they may be rightly divided any number of ways. But this also means that the divisions have a non-trivial relation to each other. They are unified precisely in being divisions of the same *res* or ways of looking at the same *res*. Thus, paths are able to be found between them, even though they may be quite circuitous and non-intuitive. So translation is possible, though it may still require great skill and involve great difficulty.

Thus, concepts are pre-linguistic because they arise from the natures of things. This is indeed why this position is aptly called "realist," because the *res* define the concepts ("real" comes from *realis*, which means "*res*-like"). Even though I only learn these concepts linguistically, I am thereby inculcated into a tradition that has read these concepts off of the world, and the concepts point me back to the world (rather than to language). Language learning can thus be a training for reading the world, and it preserves rather than eliminates space for thinking that lies beyond the limits of language.

Adjudicating the Positions

In a sense, the question these two positions attempts to address is primarily about not language but concepts. In a nutshell, we are concerned to know where we get our concepts from and how good they are as representations of the real world.

The relativist would say that we get our concepts arbitrarily: they are simply what seemed best to an older society, which has passed them on to us. It is impossible to know how good they are as representations of the world, though we may speak of how good they are as representations of the linguistic community that gave rise to them and perpetuates them, or of how good they are for the ends of building a society, from one-on-one interactions up through complex structures of government, business, entertainment, and more. The concepts we inherit are modified by our experience of the world and of other cultures; however, they are not inviolable precisely because they are contingent and arbitrary human artifacts, and so they are subject to revision and corruption.

The realist would say that our concepts come from the world of *res* and that they are variously good but pretty good at representing that world. Decimus's *arbor* may be better at describing the world than my "tree," by which I mean that Decimus may be getting the world more right than I am. Nevertheless, "tree" does successfully deliver true knowledge of the world to me because it remains an adequate representation of the *res* in question. However, these concepts are also subject to revision and corruption. We find concepts ready-to-hand in the world, but in unpacking them (which is to say, in appropriating them), we are also changing them. This is indeed what enables the differentiation into various languages: we concentrate our attention on different aspects of the reality in question, and that is what leads to our particular concept. And so *arbor* and "tree" are not the same concept, but they are both concepts of the same *res*, and this creates at worst an analogical relationship between them.

Thus, for the relativist, concepts are arbitrary, contingent, and adventitious, and they arise internal to a linguistic system, whence they are imposed to signify *res* in the world. To the realist, concepts are neither completely arbitrary nor completely contingent; they are natural, and they arise from *res* that are outside the linguistic system.

In a sense, this may be seen to be a version of the problem of universals. For concepts are universals of a certain sort (my concept "tree" is of no particular tree and applies to many particulars). In this light, the relativist is something like a conceptualist: universals are primarily indexed to a creaturely mind, whence they get applied to the world, to which they fit to greater and lesser degrees. The linguistic realist is like a metaphysical realist in that the concepts are not primarily indexed to some created mind, but they have a sort of mind-independent validity and application to the external world. This is a very imperfect correspondence, of course, for one cannot claim that our concepts are what we mean by universals in the strong metaphysical sense without thereby becoming a conceptualist and thus predetermining the question. But it is illustrative: if the dominant intellectual intuition about universals is conceptualist (that is to say, if we have a tendency to side with Aristotle over Plato on the metaphysical status we apply to "chairness"), then there will already be a prejudicial preference for linguistic relativism.

Because the question is about concepts, we are in the realm of epistemology, and the question of the rightness of the concept as a correspondence to the nature that it is a concept of is one with which both positions have to contend. But the question is more urgent for the realist. For if concepts do not map well onto the world, this constitutes a fundamental challenge to the claim that the concepts arise from *res* and in some way remain bound to the *res* even when corrupted by ongoing linguistic use. For the relativist, it is most consistent to claim that whatever correspondence there may be is not verifiable; nevertheless, it does not as a result become simply uninteresting whether there is correspondence or not. The vast majority of the uses of language are concerned with the successful communication of opinions concerning the states of affairs of the world around us. A stringent relativism that would completely disconnect our language from the world would undercut all meaning and be a serious challenge to the correctness of such a view for very many—not all are prepared to take Derrida's path.

It was stated at the outset that the question could also be expressed in terms of cause: Does the signifier cause the signified, or does the signified cause the signifier? Perhaps it will be fruitful to return to this version of the question.

This version of the question, however, assumes that what is signified by language is generally the concept. But this is not simply the case: I do not always use my language to refer to concepts or universals; I also use it to refer to particulars. In fact, I use the same words: "Tree" may refer to my concept, and when I am trying to present to Decimus what I say when he says *arbor*, it is certainly the concept I intend to signify by the word. But when we two are walking and I say, "Decimus, look at this tree!," the signified is not the concept but the magnificent *res* that is before us. Now there can be no doubt that in this type of instance there is no question of the signifier causing the signified. In such instances, the relevant question is not "Where have I got my concept from?" but rather "How well does my concept apply to what I am predicating it of?" This question is not itself answered by realism or relativism, but the type of answer one gives to it is certainly controlled by the position to which one is antecedently committed.

So it turns out that adjudicating these positions is not easy because it does not seem to be obviously the case that one or the other is correct. Language does not seem to be as relativistic as the first position would claim, short of a rigorous subjectivism of the sort already ruled out in the introduction. But likewise, our concepts are not just the realities themselves; they intervene between us and those realities. Thus, all sorts of errors, as much of judgment as of recognition, are possible. Language seems to involve aspects of both realism and relativism.

But then how are they to be related to each other? Is one to be put over the other as the dominant dynamic, such that we have either relative realism or realist relativism? Or are they to be equally related to each other as realism-relativism? I do not consider this last to be a real possibility because the claims of the two positions are not all able to be held at the same time. Parts of each are compatible with the other, but all of each is not compatible with all of the other. And so we must affirm either relative realism or realist relativism. But to determine which one, we will have to introduce theological considerations.

Theological Considerations

In this section we will consider four foundational theological cases: God's speech in the act of creation, Adam's naming of the animals, the Tower of Babel, and Pentecost. Each of these events is formative or transformative, and each lies prior to all our questions concerning the nature of language.

Each therefore contributes something to the makeup of the current linguistic situation.

God's Creative Speech: Calling Things That Are Not

Before even considering the divine speech in the act of creation, an objection arises that it should not be included in this discussion for two reasons. First, it is not human language, and it is only concerning human language that we can develop theories. (Whatever language the angels may have, we do not have access to it, and so we cannot build a single theory that encompasses all language.) Second, surely God can only be said to speak in a sense that is at best analogical to human language. And since we do not know the divine language well enough to be able to say in what ways it is like and unlike human language, we could never assess whether it is sufficiently like human language to ground any specific conclusions.

And yet the very first actions of God recorded in Scripture are carried out by means of speech, and God inaugurates the entire history of God's dealings with us by speaking to us. We are called into being by God and enter the world as addressed by God among a people addressed by God. The Gospel of John deepens this commitment: the identification of Christ as the Word places language in the very Godhead. The fact that the same Gospel continually asserts that Christ pre-exists with the Father before the world began argues that this is true not just economically but also immanently: God is, in one of the divine persons, eternally Word.

Thus, although we cannot construct a unified theory of language that we know covers the divine, the angelic, and the human, we will nevertheless understand language rightly only when we see it as an image and participation in something so true of God that it is appropriated as the name of the second person of the Trinity. This grounds the fact that there must be an analogical relation between the two (for there is not no relation, and no terms applied to both God and creatures can be applied univocally). And there is also good reason to avoid an apophatic move whereby we affirm the analogy but deny our ability to say anything specific or precise about it: God has spoken Godself to us, has told us of Godself but has also given us determinative and powerful instances of divine speaking. Divine speech is an integral part of the divine revelation: indeed, it appears at the beginning and end of God's scriptural revelation.

Further, Jesus Christ is the revelation of God: his whole being is speech about the Father and he is himself the concrete language of God. Our problem with the divine language is thus not that it is too hidden for our inspection, for it lies open for all to see. Rather, it is the transcendent character of it, that it exceeds all that we can say or know of it. But this does not undercut speech about it: it lies within our understanding, but not entirely; when we have reached the limits of what we can know, it keeps going. But that does not mean that we do not truly know.

To turn to the case at hand, then: the first chapter of Genesis shows the primal divine semiotic moment, in which God calls things into being out of nothing, using speech. This seems to be the purest instance of the signifier causing the signified: before God speaks and in the moment that God speaks, there is no *res* that corresponds to the signifier, for all that exists is God, and creatures are not God or parts of God.

We could interpret this as meaning that, insofar as speech requires that the signifier have a referent if it is to be language and not gibberish, God's action is only speech because there is a response, because the being addressed by God indeed comes into being and as such fulfills the potency (both as power and as potentiality) of the divine speech. But this is not quite in line with the account: God does not address the being in question in creating it. God does not say, "Come forth, light" but rather "Let there be light." This is not address but command; and yet the one commanded is not the one who is to exist but rather the nature of reality as such. This locution is best explained not as "I command you, light, to exist" but rather as "The world is now to be configured in such a way that light exist." This is not a potentially failed speech act, then; there is no potentiality but only potency in the divine speech, which "calls things that are not in the same way as those things that are" (Rom. 4:17, my translation). The existence or non-existence of the *res* is not a barrier to God's ability to call to it, for God may, by speaking, cause it, and so God may address whatever God will.

This does not fully answer the question, however. For what I just said about the Romans passage, that God may address a being regardless of its existence because God may cause it by addressing it, still sits squarely in the camp of signifier causing the signified if the being in question is the signified of the divine word. And yet if the *res* is the signified, we are back at the beginning of this argument: God's speech act will fail to count as language if the being does not come into existence.

The *res* does not yet exist when God speaks, but this does not mean that there is no signified. For something specific must be signified if the right *res* is to come into existence and if it is to come into existence according to the way that God intends it. The signified of "Let there be light" is not the light that will come into existence but the divine concept of light. The divine act is not speaking to a *res* to bring it to existence but is rather an externalization of an idea that is already in God. The utterance is equivalent to "Let what exists in my mind also exist in the world outside my mind."

This is definitional to speech. As a representation or expression of what is thought, it is an externalization of what previously existed only in the mind of the speaker. For a human, this causes something to exist in the world that did not before—namely, an utterance—which will from that moment forward have a life that is not under the control of the speaker ("You can't take it back"). For God, speech also causes an utterance to exist, which seems to pass beyond the control of the speaker—for it may be purposefully misunderstood—but which really does not, for it always convicts the one so doing of having refused to listen: The word of the Lord stands forever (1 Pet. 1:25).

But the divine utterance in this primal moment also causes something else to exist in the world—namely, a *res*. And so we must acknowledge that not all instances of divine speaking are the same, for some new *res* is not produced every time God speaks but only when God speaks creatively (which often coincides with the use of the jussive mood). Accordingly, this primal moment of speech is to be compared not to every human moment of speaking whatsoever but only to perlocutionary speaking, in which we attempt to bring about something new by our words.

This is, it turns out, an important clarification: linguistic relativism is not the claim that in every instance in which a linguistic signifier is used, it causes what it signifies. If that were the case, it would be hard to see how signifiers could be reused: each time, they would create a slightly different concept. Rather, it is the claim that in the privileged moments—that is to say, in the primal impositions of words—the signifier caused the signified. Thus linguistic relativism treats human creation of language as very analogous to divine creation of the world through language.

But is the way in which the divine speech causes the signified the same as the dynamic foregrounded by linguistic relativism? It is not, precisely because the signified is not the *res* that is being created but the divine concept. The divine concept pre-exists the divine speech act and is not caused by it.

In a deeper sense, however, the question breaks down because the relativist concern is with the origin of language, not with its use. But in God the language and the concept are so tightly suited to each other that the usual questions of priority fail. One may here assume that the moment the concept exists, the proper linguistic correlate to express that idea also exists in God. And yet logical priority remains with the concept precisely because the linguistic signifier is a signifier *of the concept* and so presupposes the concept in its own definition. Thus, in the relevant sense, the signifier (the divine word) is subsequent to and dependent on the signified (the divine concept).

Naming the Animals: An Irrevocable Choice

The primal instance of human language is Adam's naming of the animals in Genesis 2:19–20: "Now out of the ground the LORD God had formed every beast of the field and every bird of the heavens and brought them to the man to see what he would call them. And whatever the man called every living creature, that was its name. The man gave names to all livestock and to the birds of the heavens and to every beast of the field." This passage is in the context of God's desire that Adam not be alone. Part of the reason the animals are brought to Adam is so that Adam may recognize that none of them were sufficiently like him to be a true companion. The theology of this passage is that whatever similarities may exist between humanity and other animals, there remains a great difference that is evaluatively decisive. This is also the moment in human language that is properly analogous to the divine creative use of language. God's primal speaking creates *res*; human primal speaking names those *res*.

Several aspects of this passage are noteworthy. First, God brings the animals before Adam. That is to say, it is in a face-to-face encounter that Adam names the animals. As a result, Adam's names for each thing are not based on nothing. Because the animals are led before him by God and are seen by him, and only then does he impose a name, his imposition of a name is in response to his inspection of each animal. And this seems to be a real inspection in the etymological sense of that word: Adam looks into each thing and draws forth a name based on what he sees. Thus Adam's naming seems to be based on a recognition of what things are. His naming seems to be a vision of how each animal images God.

However, one could make this objection: the text says, "Whatever the man called every living creature, that was its name." Could this not be read as saying that insofar as the name is connected to the essence of the animal in question, the animal is deriving some character or definition from Adam's naming? But Adam's naming is not creative of the animal. The animals do not await Adam's naming in order for their being to be complete, for God has already accomplished the work of their creation. At this point they already have their kinds according to which they will reproduce; for they come to him according to their kinds, and this was built into the moment of their creation. Therefore this moment of Adam's naming is not ontologically determinative for them. It must then be epistemically determinative. We will return to this in a moment.

Second, God does this "to see what he would call them." There is a kind of indeterminacy here: this is not a test in which Adam has to correctly guess the name of each animal. Adam is truly free to call each what he will. This is thus a creative moment in which names are imposed on things as seems right to Adam. As such, it is an image of the divine creative act because there is an authority to Adam's action that is determinative over other creatures. It is not, in this instance, determinative that they exist or of how they exist but of how they will be called and to a real extent how they will be thought of. For, as was said a moment ago, this naming is epistemically determinative. What is happening is that there are many ways in which the creation could be rightly categorized by humans, and God is allowing Adam to decide. His naming therefore creates the ground rules for human reasoning, the basis even for our logic, the fact that certain things will get categorized a certain variety of ways but no wider. There may be wildly different ways of rightly dividing up the world, but we have already rejected them in Adam and no longer have access to them.

This first moment of naming is also the creation of human language, the first time words will get imposed on things. As such, it may rightly be considered archetypal. This moment then is privileged in relation to human language and may offer clues for resolving our dilemma. How then are we to understand this moment in relation to the dynamics of relativism and realism?

Insofar as this moment is one in which Adam is free to name as he wills (because God has not predetermined the name but has left room for Adam to truly name the animals), this seems to follow the dynamics of relativism, for there is an arbitrary imposition of names that is determinative of concepts and of pathways of thinking and perhaps even of the rules of thinking. The first use of names is therefore one that is creative of concepts and so is an instance of the signifier causing the signified.

But insofar as this is a moment grounded in recognition, it is the dynamics of realism that are in play. For Adam is responding to something about each animal, naming it on the basis of what he sees there. The signifier arises in response to perceived truths about the signified. And while there are many possible right names Adam could give to each animal, there are not infinitely many. There are also wrong names, ones that would not follow on the inspection of the animal God has brought before him. Thus, while there may have been, say, ten different names each animal could be called, with each different name grounding different, correct, fundamental intuitions about the world (such that each choice cuts off nine branches of thinking, each of which could have been productive of as many languages as our history has produced), there is still a finite field of choices, still a right and a wrong way to name.

Given this, the claim that Adam's choice is arbitrary must therefore be clarified. The term "arbitrary" brings to mind the negative connotation of randomness. This is surely a relic of the fact that we believe that things ought to have explanations in the antecedent causal chain, such that if one knew the conditions perfectly, one would also know why the current state of affairs holds. This subtle determinism is the enemy of an account of a will that is free, for the choices of a free will are never fully explicable in terms of the antecedent causal chain. The fact is that the will could always have chosen differently than x, no matter how much the environmental factors persuade toward and recommend x. Free choices always have a residue that cannot be reduced to antecedent causes, and this *ex nihilo* element is the power of self-determination through which the rational creature expresses the highest image of the divine aseity.

Adam's choice is not arbitrary in the sense that Adam could have just said anything he wanted: the real being of the creature in front of him places a constraint on the range of options possible for its naming. A name that went beyond those boundaries would not be based in recognition and so would be an instance of failure. Rather, the naming can be called arbitrary because it could have been different, and there is no ground outside of Adam's will for explaining why this name rather than that name was chosen. That is to say, it is arbitrary not because it is willful but because its ultimate ground is the will.

Still, the word remains infelicitous in the present context and does not well describe what Adam is doing. I will speak instead not of arbitrary decisions but of *ad placitum* decisions—that is to say, decisions that are made according to the good pleasure of the one deciding.[3] This preserves the sense of "arbitrary" according to which there is no ground for the choice other than the will of the one making the choice; but it also avoids the suggestion that the choice is merely random. There are reasons (typically aesthetic rather than logical but not exclusive of logical, precisely because logic may also be pleasing) that contribute to the choice. Additionally, there is nothing that impedes that *ad placitum* choices also be constrained by a sense of what is allowable—that is to say, the right may also be pleasing. And as Adam is as yet sinless and no negative judgment is placed on his acts of naming, we have no reason to think that he was not in fact pleased to name each thing in accord with the truth of its being.

Thus, we have both dynamics at play, but we also have a way of ordering them. There is contingency in the *ad placitum* character of Adam's naming, but it is a naming that derives from an inspection that delivers true knowledge of the thing to be named. The concept precedes the word, and the signified causes the signifier, and so realism is the dominant dynamic.

3. This turn of phrase I borrow from Ockham's logic. It will be discussed in greater detail in chap. 5.

God's act is creative, but Adam's is based in recognition, and so we will call Adam's "aesthetic" (for what he recognizes is precisely how things image God). Thoughts are pre-linguistic for Adam because he looks upon a thing, conceives a concept, and names it out of that concept. Thus, it is proper to human language to function in the aesthetic mode—that is, to be descriptive. For all humans following Adam, thoughts are pre-linguistic because all our words develop from previous concepts that were the referents of words in our language's parent language.

And yet, because we are ourselves in the image of the Creator, and in such a way that we have the power of limited determination of both our own selves and our environment, we may also engage in creative semiotic activity, which is the shaping of culture. Relativism thus remains as the element of freedom in the subjective appropriation of the objectively encountered reality. It is this freedom, iterated across particular language users and language communities, that leads to dialects and idiolects, and ultimately to cultures and sub-cultures. The aesthetic (*ad placitum*) element of language allows for virtuosity at the level of both cultural language use and individual language use.

Babel: The Shattering of Language

The theological material for the analysis of semiotics is incomplete if we stop at the creation account, for that was not the last seminal moment in human semiotics. The Tower of Babel and the shattering of language it represents stand between us and Adam's original act of naming. This event describes a fundamental change in the linguistic situation: language is no longer pure, no longer innocent, no longer unifying. This must affect our account of subjective objectivity.

> Now the whole earth had one language and the same words. And as people migrated from the east, they found a plain in the land of Shinar and settled there. And they said to one another, "Come, let us make bricks, and burn them thoroughly." And they had brick for stone, and bitumen for mortar. Then they said, "Come, let us build ourselves a city and a tower with its top in the heavens, and let us make a name for ourselves, lest we be dispersed over the face of the whole earth." And the LORD came down to see the city and the tower, which the children of man had built. And the LORD said, "Behold, they are one people, and they have all one language, and this is only the beginning of what they will do. And nothing that they propose to do will now be impossible for them. Come, let us go down and there confuse their language, so that they may not understand one another's speech." So the LORD dispersed them from there over the face of all the earth, and they left off building the city. Therefore

its name was called Babel, because there the LORD confused the language of all the earth. And from there the LORD dispersed them over the face of all the earth. (Gen. 11:1–9)

There are a few noteworthy features of this account:

First, it is the human desire to avoid being scattered that drives the building of the tower. But they also wish to make a name for themselves, so they are also seeking their own glory. Even so, it is not the tower itself that is problematic for God; it is the fact that the tower is just the first step in their grand plan. God sets himself against the human plan of establishing a lasting civilization for all humanity because it competes with God's work in a couple of important ways. First, it competes with God's original purpose for humanity: we were commanded to spread over the whole earth, but the desire here is to all gather in one place. Second, it competes with the planned salvific work: in the next chapter of Genesis, God will call Abram and begin establishing the divine kingdom—first in Israel and then in the Church. If humans make a name for themselves in this way at Babel, they will not become a people who bear God's name. God's idea is that striking language will be an effective way to block their ability to establish this name and lasting civilization.

Second, the construction of the tower is an act of creative making, of *poiesis*. It was a technological wonder (for the account focuses on the advances in building technology with baked bricks and mortar), but it was also an architectural wonder ("a tower with its top in the heavens") and thus a work of art as well as of technology. The people would thus establish a name for themselves by the impressive skill required to make the tower and the beauty of the tower's design. It would become an emblem that would be a focal point for the identity of the people: its presence would have an anchoring effect, keeping the people from wandering and being dispersed all over the earth.[4] In short, the construction of the tower as expressive of a desire for an abiding reputation and geographic stability is an act of cultural making, both in the sense that it is a making that derives from a culture and in the sense that it is building a culture. The goal is a single, unified human culture.

According to the narrative, this impulse can only be acted on because there is one common language; no, further, because everyone uses the same words. Everyone calls everything by the same names. Perhaps these are the names first imposed by Adam; even if not, because Adam's original names both control all future possibilities for the naming of things and enshrine a

---

4. One is reminded of Hrothgar's great hall Heorot in *Beowulf*, which also led to disastrous consequences.

certain set of emphases about the natures of things, through their language the humans in this passage have access to a commonly grounded way of looking at the world. It is the realism of language that enables the construction of this monovalent culture.

Interestingly, then, the relativist element has dropped out here. As a dynamism within the truly grounded correspondence between signifier and signified, the relativist dimension opens space for individuality: it is the ground of virtuosity. But the Babel culture lacked individuality or even variety. It was reductive because it shut out one dimension of language in its attempt to focus on the true connection of language to the world. This reduction is not directionless: it is aimed at technology. Language is being reduced in order to allow for technological mastery.[5] If we mine the truths about the world contained in the realist nature of language, they reasoned, we can manipulate the world to our own ends.

Thus linguistic reductionism led to the objectification of the world, the reduction of creation to merely building material. There is then a willful setting aside of the way that creatures refer to God and therefore of the experience of beauty as such. The worship of technology (not technology considered in itself or the sober use of it) is always at odds with the vision of beauty. But this problem is only a species of a larger genus: all idolatry is at odds with the vision of beauty because it turns our gaze away from the one who grounds the experience of beauty.

All this may be seen as a transgression of the divine purposes for language. The divine delight in seeing what Adam would call each thing is not being honored here. A God who is best imaged through a symphony of cultures is not honored where one univocal culture is desired. This symphony of languages would not have been divisive; it is the curse of Babel that introduces that element. Rather, the multitude of cultures would have been mutually intelligible: it would have been no harder to understand how someone from another culture sees the world than it was to understand someone from our own culture. We would be marked as distinct by our cultures, but we would be able to completely enter the world of other cultures without having to *become* them.

And yet, since the fall has already happened, this picture must not become too utopian. For sin has already introduced a wall of separation between

---

5. Jargon, which is a reduction to the same specific words in order to facilitate the transfer of knowledge, is one example of a reduction of language for the purposes of technology. Hence it has come in for stringent criticism by poets, who above all feel what is lost. The critique must not be pressed too far, however, for jargon has its uses (and neither is technology to be shunned). But the reduction of all language to jargon would be as disastrous as the reduction of all human life to technology.

humans and God and between human and human (as the murders that have taken place before this point in the Genesis narrative show). Interpersonal intelligibility is not absolute, but rather is already greatly hampered. And God's response to this human disobedience will deepen that greatly.

The divine response is thus shown to be fitting and obvious: the culture of Babel has suppressed the relativist dynamic in language in an effort to leverage the realism of language for control of the environment and their own destiny. God's response is to restore and strengthen the relativist character of language. The confusion of language is a brilliant stroke: Now that we will no longer use the same words, we are forced to use different concepts as the various signifieds of language. The consequences of this are momentous and relevant to our analysis of the relative strengths of the relativist and realist dynamics in language.

First, however, there is the question of the severity of the curse. Has language been so broken that the realist element is simply destroyed? It is possible that this is a total linguistic break, that any connection to reality that language had before is severed here, and so we as a race lose access to any insight that lay in Adam's original naming, and our language loses the ability to refer in any realist way to concepts derived from *res*. Perhaps what twentieth-century semiotic theory uncovered was the wasteland of language that remains after the Babel event.

It cannot be shown conclusively that this is not the case. However, the dynamics of beauty as described here indicate a situation of genuine connection. The experience of the beautiful is one semiotic moment in which the signified is really attained, and our experience of beauty is the effect of this connection. Additionally, the language of the Genesis passage suggests otherwise. God comes down not to undo or unmake our language but to confuse it. This suggests that this is a shattering of language, not a complete annihilation. The mirror is shot through with cracks and pieces are missing, but it still retains its function as a mirror. And so the confusing of language does affect the nature of the concepts language refers to. Although the connection between these concepts and the *res* is not severed, it is either weakened or made more convoluted.

If the connection is weakened, that would mean that the concepts that are the referents of language are less directly related to the *res* than they were before. If it is made more convoluted, these concepts remain as connected to *res* as they always were, but now the paths from the concepts to the *res* are harder to discover and follow. In either situation, one could be excused for mistaking the situation as non-realist.

To me, this second explanation, that linguistic reference has become labyrinthine, is a better explication of "confused." Our language and the concepts contained therein are now peregrinary: they wander the wilderness as we do, but they are on the journey to a concrete destination, and so there is not eternal deference. We must expect the journey from language to reality to be long and arduous, but we must not despair of reaching our goal. Thus those moments of lucidity when truth indeed shines forth from language via etymology are not fictive or illusory; they are in fact anomalous only because language stands under the sign of Babel.

There is thus a proliferation of non-synonymous and imperfectly synonymous linguistic concepts. Two ancient members of the culture of Babel, call them Nimrod and Semiramis, would have used the same word for a tree, and it would have referenced the same concept. But Decimus and I neither use the same word nor express the same concept. But further, my community does not use the same linguistic concepts as other English-speaking communities. Under the sign of Babel, even the communication of concepts within a single linguistic system is imperfect, and this results in dialectical differences. Again, though my wife and I are of one culture and of similar age, we do not have the same concepts as the referents for our words, and this results in idiolectical differences. The proliferation of linguistic concepts, both between languages and within languages, is generative of a multiplicity of cultures and sub-cultures and also of certain aspects of individuality. This is because cultures form around common linguistic intuitions and uses.[6]

Thus, God's action at Babel restores virtuosity, which realigns language to accord with aspects of the original divine intention. However, it is still a curse. The fact that it has this positive, realigning effect is evidence that God's judgment is concerned not with vengeance but with justice. It is also evidence that all of God's judgments are also mercies. But judgment is no less judgment for all of that. The sign of Babel separates person from person and culture from culture. It was meant to do just this: the purpose of the curse was to make us *not* one people, to keep us from being able to establish a lasting name for ourselves, and to ensure that we disperse throughout the earth.

But cursed language does not just separate us in a neutral fashion: it imparts an entropic principle to language that is analogous to the law of death at work in the rest of creation. The universal downward trend of languages (from complex to less complex and therefore more ambiguous) is an expression of the curse that language lies under. Thus the relativist dynamic within language is stronger than would appear from the examination of Adam's

---

6. Of course, we must not take this too far, as if language were the only building block of culture. Indeed, as only the archetypal semiotic instance and not the full extent of semiotics, it is manifestly not the only building block of semiotics which itself is but one of the building blocks of culture.

naming of the animals, but it does not abrogate the realist element. There is still subjective objectivity, but the emphasis falls more heavily on "subjective" than it did before.

Pentecost: Proleptic Restoration

The theological material for the understanding of language does not rest with Babel, however, for the coming of the Holy Spirit at the post-resurrection Pentecost is the beginning of the undoing of the curse of Babel.

> When the day of Pentecost arrived, they were all together in one place. And suddenly there came from heaven a sound like a mighty rushing wind, and it filled the entire house where they were sitting. And divided tongues as of fire appeared to them and rested on each one of them. And they were all filled with the Holy Spirit and began to speak in other tongues as the Spirit gave them utterance. Now there were dwelling in Jerusalem Jews, devout men from every nation under heaven. And at this sound the multitude came together, and they were bewildered, because each one was hearing them speak in his own language. And they were amazed and astonished, saying, "Are not all these who are speaking Galileans? And how is it that we hear, each of us in his own native language? Parthians and Medes and Elamites and residents of Mesopotamia, Judea and Cappadocia, Pontus and Asia, Phrygia and Pamphylia, Egypt and the parts of Libya belonging to Cyrene, and visitors from Rome, both Jews and proselytes, Cretans and Arabians—we hear them telling in our own tongues the mighty works of God." And all were amazed and perplexed, saying to one another, "What does this mean?" (Acts 2:1–12)

The apostles are enabled by the Spirit to speak in other languages, but this is somewhat ambiguous. For the second reference to language in the passage seems to say not that the apostles were speaking in different languages but that they were being *heard* in different languages (and on the surface level, more cultures are mentioned than there are apostles, if we take this to refer to the Twelve). Whatever the case, it was out of the ordinary. The crowd's response is not to think that the apostles have been busy learning languages but to be shocked that their language is being spoken/heard.

This represents an overcoming of the curse of Babel in that the multitude of languages is no longer a barrier to communication: the message of the gospel has an objectivity to it that commandeers every subjectivity. This does not occur, indeed, by denying or destroying subjectivity: this would be the case if the hearers were suddenly able to understand the apostles' own language. Rather, by making use of each subjectivity, the Spirit shows that

these subjectivities always had the potential to bear the gospel message and
to express it in the contours unique to each particular subjectivity.

In this way salvation from Babel is not the destruction of the cultures created by Babel but rather their redemption. For though disparate cultures are
the result of a curse, the curse was, in this respect, restoring humanity to one
of its original mandates. Our particular cultures are the result of a curse, but
culture is not. So each culture stands in need of redemption, but each culture
is redeemable. The crowd's question ("What does this mean?") is important.
The proleptic presence of the redeemed dynamic calls into question all that we
think that we know about the world. It is a glimpse into a frame of reference
that has the power to recontextualize our every experience and therefore the
power to rewrite our metaphysics, our logic, our intuitions, and everything
else. Just to glimpse this reality is enough to know that such comprehensive
revision is on the table; but it is not enough to know *how* to carry out the
revision, and so we are left befuddled: We do not know how to resolve what
we have experienced. We only know that we cannot explain it away or ignore
it. It will come forward with us and will work on us and our thinking for the
remaining days of our lives.

Language and Beauty

Subjective Objectivity: Naming and Beauty

Insofar as linguistic realism grounds language on a principle of recognition, the realist claim parallels the anamnetic character of the experience of
beauty. Yet the virtuosity introduced by the relativist dynamic within language
parallels the subjective appropriation of that correlate in every particular
experience of beauty.

We have learned from our analysis of the beautiful that the experience
of the beautiful is controlled by what is so objective that it is the object par
excellence, the divinity. Thus, realism and objectivism take the first place
in the ordering of conceptual priorities. And yet, this is the *experience* of
the beautiful, and so we are dealing with a subjective appropriation.[7] Thus,
we arrived at the need to understand the experience of the beautiful as a
subjective objectivity—that is, as a subjective encounter and appropriation
that is controlled more by the object than by the categories of receptivity
in the subject.

7. It could also be argued that because the object par excellence is the highest subjectivity,
our understanding of reality is not in accord with that highest object if it does not enshrine
subjectivity within the very moment of the beautiful.

Analogously, the linguistic moment, when it is most pure, is a subjective appropriation of (understood here as "making use of") an objectivity that controls the manner of the appropriation. There is relativity, and therefore virtuosity and individuality, in the use that is made of language; but this virtuosity and individuality is bound by something other than itself, something objective. In the case of the experience of the beautiful, this is something that, as the objective par excellence, exceeds the subjectivity and relativity of every merely creaturely subject. But even in the case of linguistic imposition, all such actions are based on a prior moment of aesthetic semiotics—specifically, Adam's, which, although hidden behind the fall, Babel, and centuries of cultural drift, nevertheless stands as the primal ground of all human language. Even the creative uses we make of language stand under the sign of recognition and so are controlled more by the signified than the signifier.

The Subjective Concern: Babel and Beauty

Babel strengthens the subjective component in language, restoring the desired virtuosity but also turning language into a dividing wall that separates culture from culture and person from person. Understanding of the linguistic other is greatly hampered, and a limit is set to the extent of understanding that is possible (though a limit neither specifiable by us a priori nor able to be definitively fixed by us a posteriori). And thus in language, as in the encounter with the creature, it is easy to miss the anamnesis. Just as beauty is elusive because our senses are poorly attuned to the God whose recognition is requisite for the experience of beauty, so truth and meaning in language are elusive because our entire semiotic economy lies under the curse of Babel.

And we can go further: the shattering of language widens the space between our concepts and the *res* they are imposed to signify, and this allows us to doubt the degree of correspondence, or whether there is correspondence at all, and even whether there ever could be correspondence. As this doubt deepens, we feel the rift between ourselves and the world widen. In response to this growing rift, a despair concerning our ability to correctly or even adequately conceive of the world can arise (the course of postmodernist philosophical reflection on various matters, but particularly language, reflects just such a despair). In light of this despair, one response that seems reasonable to the one despairing is to abandon questions of meaning, preferring instead questions of utility (pragmatism), domination (exploitation), or facticity (reductionism). Each of these paths leads to an increase in our inability to recognize beauty, for in their own way each objectifies creatures and so strips them of the anamnetic dimension.

The Objective Ground: Pentecost and Beauty

Humanity lies under a cultural mandate. It is a mandate to create cultures as the natural expression of ordering the creation (it is in this sense that I understand the command to subdue the earth in Gen. 1:28 and Ps. 8:6). Pentecost reveals how this cultural mandate remains in force, even though it is currently driven by and subject to the dynamics of Babel. This means, as I said, that every culture stands in need of redemption, but also that every culture is redeemable: the gospel is able to resound in every culture in the unique tonalities of that culture without losing its own unicity.

Similarly, each creature is capable of brokering the experience of the beautiful, but the curse brought about by the first sin must be overcome to some extent before it can do this. Experiences of beauty are a proleptic (and therefore partial and temporary) restoration of the creature to its original and most proper purpose.

In Pentecost moments, God commandeers the subjectivity that each culture represents in order to make straight again the paths of language so that it may arrive by a shorter route at its objective goal. The things of God are made plain by underscoring how they all point to "Jesus of Nazareth, a man attested to you by God with mighty works and wonders and signs" (Acts 2:22): the signs are the creatures Christ miraculously commandeers, calling on their obedience to provide witness that he in fact has the authority to do such things. Pentecost is the coming of the Spirit in order to witness to and make clear the remote referent of each created thing: God. Therefore Pentecost is primarily to do with beauty because it unlocks theological anamnesis.

The potential that Pentecost unlocks is encoded in the analogical relation between different linguistic concepts. Because Decimus and I have different concepts that are both concepts *of a tree* and because each of those concepts is grounded in the objective correlate, the concepts are necessarily relatable to each other to the same extent to which each concept truly corresponds to something of the *res*; for every true correspondence will be grounded in some property of the *res*, and the unity of the *res* grounds a relation among all those properties.

Likewise, in the case of beauty, there will be an analogous relation among various experiences of beauty. This is true of many observers being moved by the beauty of one thing, but it is also true of any two different experiences of beauty, whether they are the same or differ in either subject or object. For they all have this in common, that what renders them experiences of beauty is that they remind us of God, and the divine objective correlate is thus the same in every experience of beauty. Therefore the journey from implicit to explicit contuition includes attempts to unify disparate experiences of beauty in order to better conceptualize the objective correlate that, when better seen, grounds the ability to see beauty more fully and more successfully.

5

Concept Squared

The Nature of Metaphor

The essence of metaphor is understanding and experiencing one kind of thing in terms of another.

George Lakoff and Mark Johnson, *Metaphors We Live By*

In theology both things and words have meaning.

Bonaventure, *Collations on the Seven Gifts of the Holy Spirit*, IV.15

The metaphor is perhaps one of man's most fruitful potentialities. Its efficacy verges on magic, and it seems a tool for creation which God forgot inside one of His creatures when He made him.

José Ortega y Gasset, "The Dehumanization of Art"

Defining Metaphor

Metaphor and Analogy

Bonaventure states that "in metaphors it is not necessary that total likeness be understood, but it is sufficient to find some likeness."[1] In context,

1. Bonaventure, *Bonaventure on the Eucharist*, 117.

Bonaventure is referring to a situation of analogy, in which there is both likeness and unlikeness. A metaphor, he says, requires not total likeness but only sufficient likeness.[2] Is metaphor then just another name for analogy? Like analogy, there must be likeness; but also like analogy, if there is not difference, metaphor is not possible, for nothing is a metaphor for itself.

And yet metaphor and analogy are distinct; for, as we argued earlier,[3] analogy requires attention to both likeness and unlikeness. But in metaphors, although there must be some unlikeness, one is not required to identify the unlikeness. When I say that my beloved is like the sun, I intend to underscore a likeness between my beloved and the sun; but I do not intend to draw attention to the difference, even though without this difference the metaphor would be impossible, and if one were to deny the difference, it would render the metaphor absurd.

Likewise, just as there is a distinction to be made between the original analogy that holds between things and God, and therefore also among things (the analogy of being), and the linguistic imposition of analogy, so here there is a distinction between the metaphor and that on which it is grounded (some property of the two things in question). But unlike the case of analogy, this does not distinguish two types of metaphor. Rather, only the linguistic or conceptual imposition is metaphor, not the similarity of the properties.[4] The similarity of the properties is an instance of the analogy of being.

Metaphor is not, therefore, the same as analogy but is founded on it and may be considered to be a species of *analogia conceptionis* (analogy of concept). This may be made clearer by considering whether metaphor is coextensive with the imposition of concepts—that is to say, is every instance of imposing a concept the creation of a metaphor? But if every imposition of a concept is the creation of a metaphor, since all concepts have a beginning, every concept is a metaphor. But this seems wrong: the concept "tree" does not appear to be a metaphor. The necessary element of reference beyond the *res* in each concept is not metaphorical but analogical: all concepts are analogical, and metaphors are relations between concepts.

Metaphor therefore places a likeness between two or more things in view in order to communicate some truth about one or more of the realities compared.

2. In this chapter I will treat simile as a species of metaphor, so examples will be drawn from both similes and metaphors.
3. Chapter 3, p. 73.
4. Because thought is pre-linguistic, a reduction of metaphor to linguistic dynamics is to be resisted. Metaphors, properly speaking, are not comparisons of language but comparisons, made in language, of concepts. Nothing impedes that there be a metaphor that we grasp but cannot linguistically express.

Thus, what is signified by metaphor is not a concept in the linguistic sense or a *res* but a particular *relationship* between the various things the metaphor makes use of. The metaphor "my beloved is like the sun" is not about either my beloved or the sun, strictly speaking, but about the relationship between them (this in spite of the rhetorical fact that I am using the metaphor to tell you more about my beloved). This relationship is conceptual, but it is grounded on a real relationship precisely because the properties that make the one like the other are real and belong to the same world and therefore have a relationship or relationships to each other.

Metaphor and Contuition

The fact that metaphor places in view the likeness between the things compared is what renders metaphor similar to contuition, in which two or more things are viewed simultaneously. Like contuition, both realities must remain in view if the moment is to be fruitful; neither can vanish into the other without also collapsing the metaphorical moment.

In order for contuition not to be mere juxtaposition (which is in fact merely a compound way of seeing) and because of the repugnance of bodies to one another with respect to space, it is normally the case that one of the two realities in question needs to not be physical: for example, a tree and God, of which one is physical and the other spiritual. Instances of contuition of two creatures are typically of a physical creature and a concept (e.g., a tree and the notion of life) or of two concepts.

Metaphors obey this rule, for they only set forth physical realities conceptually. When I say that my beloved is like the sun, although both are physical, I juxtapose not the physical realities referenced (which would result in the immolation of my beloved) but the concepts of them. Thus, metaphor is a relation between concepts, not *res*.

Ad Placitum *Institution and Human Invention*

No metaphors are natural: every metaphor is constructed by someone. Things in the world are not metaphorical of one another—they are analogous to one another. Thus with metaphors, unlike with the analogy of being or the contuition of God, but like conceptual analogy and the contuition of concepts, human institution is an important dynamic.

Normally such institution is said to be "conventional"—that is, everyone has agreed to use the proposed sign in a certain way. However, this language makes the institution seem arbitrary in the negative sense mentioned earlier.

According to this view, the answer to the question "Why is it this way?" is that there is no answer—it just *is* because that is how people have agreed to treat it. As previously indicated, I find this answer to be lacking and insufficiently attentive to the realist/objectivist element in language, experience, and so on.

Instead, I would substitute Ockham's language of *ad placitum* institution.[5] Such things are "instituted according to pleasure" or "pleasingly instituted." The answer to all "why" questions would therefore be "because it was pleasing to certain people." This pleasure may rest on a variety of factors:

1. Aesthetic: The imposition may be pleasing because of its fit with already existing impositions or because of a certain inherent beauty or because of its fit within a larger intellectual context.
2. Logical: The imposition may seem especially perspicuous according to one or another part of our system of logic.
3. Moral: The imposition may be seen to be in line with or expressive of goodness or justice.

The foregoing examples follow the transcendentals (beauty, truth, and goodness), and each is grounded in some kind of correspondence. But these examples are not exhaustive. Other respects in which something may be pleasurable include but are not limited to novelty, the degree to which it helps one to avoid an undesired conclusion, pragmatism (the accomplishing of some goal or the attaining of some power), the degree to which it will help or harm a certain group or individuals, and difficulty (either because it is easy or because it is hard).

What we are looking for when we are assessing the strength of an imposition or when we seek to impose something anew is a certain pleasure derived from one of the above factors or any combination of them. Generally speaking, the more factors that can be brought to bear, the more pleasurable the imposition, and the more firmly it will establish itself within a culture.

It seems to us that we assign meaning to things, and thus it seems that we create that meaning. I can, for instance, find meaning in a ritual that was not intended by those who crafted it but that is nevertheless consonant with the purpose of the ritual. Such an interpretation will gain force and catch on precisely because of the consonance between the intended purpose and

---

5. Ockham, *Summa Totius Logicae*, part 1, chaps. 11–13 (1:72–77). Interestingly, the translator follows convention in rendering this as "conventional." But on this side of the linguistic philosophies of the twentieth century, such a translation has connotations that are likely not ones Ockham would accept.

my new interpretation. But have I not just assigned this, precisely because it has no relationship to the reason why the ritual is the way it is? But it is this last claim that is dubious, for on what is the consonance grounded if there is truly no relationship at all? Are not those things that are not in relationship dissonant? Or, indeed, they are not even dissonant, for even this requires some sort of relationship; rather, they simply cannot be compared.

Instead, the fact that there is a consonance possible between the interpretation and what it is the interpretation of indicates that I am not creating but discerning the relationship. Indeed, our deepest imaginings have not come close to sounding the types and number of relations that hold between things that inhabit the same world: our world is crisscrossed with a thick weave of relationships and relationships among relationships such that we could never exhaust them all. Are not most cases of metaphorical imposition more likely to be discoveries than inventions? Does not the very etymology of "invention" suggest that we once thought this?

But surely there are also false impositions, the discernment of a relation that just is not there. What are we to say about these? Perhaps this: that all such misattributions are founded on a correct realization that is then incorrectly interpreted or extended; that, in fact, human creativity is never *ex nihilo*, and so even our false creations stand on something true (and true not insofar as it *exists* but insofar as it is related in some way to something). In a better world, even our mistakes ought to lead to deeper truths.

Contuitio ad Placitum Instituta

It is at the intersection of contuition and *ad placitum* institution that I would situate metaphor. Metaphors are, in fact, pleasingly instituted contuitions among concepts (*contuitiones ad placitum institutae inter conceptiones*).

Metaphor therefore works according to a simplifying logic in the sense that it works to create a single whole from two or more things that are normally seen disparately but without denying the specificities of the things in question or attempting to reduce them in themselves. It unifies things in a movement that is akin to concentration: the more unified they become, the more powerful they become.

Thus in English the phonetic consonance of the sun and God's Son indicates the opportunity for a contuition: as the sun gives light to the whole world, similarly the Son gives light to the whole world. But the more similarity one sees between these two (the more unified they become), the more robust the metaphor becomes: the sun is the condition of the possibility of life on this planet, as the Son is the condition of the possibility of existence;

the heat that radiates from the sun is the engine that drives most processes on earth, as the love of the Son is the engine that drives human history; and so on.

Metaphor and language are therefore both grounded in the notion of pleasure. While this pleasure may be of many different sorts, the fact that linguistic and metaphorical imposition are *ad placitum* indicates that at the heart of these enterprises is something fundamentally aesthetic. The imposition of words and concepts (language) and the highlighting of relationships between those concepts (metaphor) may therefore be seen to be a sort of search for beauty where beauty is understood as that which will please. But because this search is grounded in recognition of and respect for the objective qualities of both *res* and concepts, it is the search for beauty understood not primarily as the attempt to create beauty but rather as the attempt to uncover it, to discover it. It is, then, a search for anamnesis. The desired end of linguistic and metaphorical imposition is beauty in the very sense that we are discussing here—that is, beauty as the theologically anamnetic.

This means that linguistic and metaphorical imposition are in fact species of the search for God. Adam first looks on things and recognizes a way in which they image God. Even after Babel and especially after Pentecost, we are trying to recapture that original project: we want to understand things as they truly are, and some part of us knows that this will lead necessarily to theological anamnesis.

But language only takes us so far. The curse of Babel and the tightness of correspondence (that it is hard for words to mean broadly enough to be really synthetic of complex relationships without losing their specificity and precision) leads us to turn to metaphor as a means of expanding the boundaries of human thought beyond the merely linguistic. And here the notion that our thoughts are pre-linguistic comes to the fore: we have thoughts too big for our language, and our use of metaphor is an indicator that we have such thoughts and that we are driven to try to express them.

Every artist who has said something of what he or she means is also aware of what has remained unsaid in that very act of saying. The artistic gaze settles on a truth that our language is incapable of, and the creative act attempts to overcome this limitation by using language in new ways: by combining existing words in surprising ways, and by making new words that nevertheless must have a discernible connection to existing linguistic usage if they are to be at all understandable by anyone but the poet. The kenning of Anglo-Saxon poetry is an excellent example of the former; calling the sea a "whale road" pushes toward an idea that is not totally or well expressed with the phrase "whales ride along the sea the way a cart rides along a road."

Metaphor therefore comes to the aid of language by extending (but not completing) the work of language. Language is locked into an economy of correspondence due to the correspondences between words and concepts and concepts and *res*. It is not rigidly locked: polysemy or multiplicity of meaning, which grounds ambiguity in such a way as to allow for wordplays of various sorts, is a way in which language preserves a virtuosic space even within itself. Language can never be reduced to *mere* correspondence. But metaphor, by virtue of its second-order nature (it intends relations among concepts, which relations may themselves become quasi-concepts as a result of being referred to in the metaphorical moment), frees itself from this economy of correspondence without becoming entirely disconnected from correspondence (which would be to evacuate metaphor of all meaning).

Metaphor therefore aims at a clearer instance of anamnesis than is the norm in language. And because metaphor is less bound to correspondence, it is already more aware of itself as caught up in the attempt to express something ineffable (at least under the current conditions of human language), and so it is more open to the idea that the anamnesis in question is referenced to something transcendent. The artist joins the saint as one exceptionally well suited for contuition because the artist is, as artist, already concerned with something transcendent. But whereas the saint is well disposed for explicit contuition, it is implicit contuition that the artist, as artist, is well suited for.

The root dynamic of metaphor, grounded as it is in recognition and contuition, is both founded on and imitative of the dynamics of beauty. This makes metaphors suitable for brokering the beautiful and indeed makes them one of the privileged sites for human creation of beauty. For although the relations among things already obtain, there is something creative and virtuosic about grabbing just a few such relations and highlighting them in relation to each other.

The Dynamics of Metaphor

Accretion of Meaning

The power of metaphor is in its ability to be polyvalent, which exceeds that of non-metaphorical language; as a result, it is well suited to saying several things at once. Rich metaphors have not one but several meanings, and metaphorical literacy consists in the ability to properly order and relate these meanings to one another.

Whether considered from the complexity of meaning or from the complexity of interpretation, metaphors grow. They do this by the accretion (with no negative connotation intended) of meaning as the metaphors enter new cultural, personal, historical, artistic, philosophical, and theological contexts. This is because the metaphor intends in the first instance a relationship between real things. An excursus on the nature of relations is relevant here, though a full account is beyond the scope of the current project.

Relations are grounded in properties of the things related (*relata*). These properties may be real or conceptual—that is to say, they may be ontological properties of the *relata*, or they may be conceptual categories applied to the *relata* that exist only in the mind of the ones thinking and that may or may not correspond to the way the *relata* actually are.

If the properties are ontological (such as purpleness), then the relation will be real—that is, to assert that *A* is like *B* is to express something real in the world. *A* is not just thought to be like *B*; it really is like it, and so there exists a relationship between them. This relationship is a property of both *A* and *B*, but it is not of the same ontological order as the purpleness on which it is grounded. Relations of this kind are not just ways some subjects have of grouping the world; they are expressive of the very nature of the world and are themselves a part of it (even though it is difficult to fix what the exact nature of their ontological status is).

This seems easy to affirm in the case of the relationship of similarity, but what about other relations? To take a particularly challenging case, what about dissimilarity? Surely there is no ontological property by which *A* differs from *B*. If you say that there is, and that it is the same property by which *A* was potentially similar to *B*—namely, purpleness—then either this proves that these relations are not real but just ways of thinking about the same thing (for the same property is now said to ground contrary relations) or you would have to say that multiple distinct and even opposite relations are able to be grounded by one and the same property.

This last is indeed to be said: by virtue of having some quality (say, purple), *A* lacks other incompatible qualities, such as being black in the same part of the surface that is purple. Every particular property makes *A* both be some ways and not be other ways, and so each one grounds relations of both similarity and dissimilarity. And when we consider that these are only two among very many possible relations, it becomes clear just how complex the web of relations among things is.

If the properties that ground the relation are merely conceptual, then the relations will themselves be merely conceptual—that is to say, there is no real relation between *A* and *B*. To say that they are related is not to say anything about them but rather to say something about the mind that considers them to be related.

Again, it might seem to some that the sort of relational convolution just ascribed to things in virtue of real relations is not in things but in the language or concepts we bring to things. It should be clear by this point that such a conclusion is incompatible with the objective nature of the account given here of *res*, concepts, and language. There is a fact of the matter about the world, and our concepts and language can successfully (though imperfectly, incompletely, and to varying degrees) attain to that fact of the matter, and so there is truly correspondence. But because our language and concepts can also fail to attain to the fact of the matter, it is possible that supposed relations are merely putative and not actually real.

Relations may also be more or less specific. They are made more specific by the specification of the property to which they are indexed. Thus, "A is like B" is less specific than "A is like B with respect to purpleness." It might seem that general relations are of the conceptual type: since they do not reference a particular property, one is not referencing any ontological likeness, but rather one is offering a judgment that the two are alike. Underlying this is the idea that ontological likeness must of necessity be specific. On this view, even though generic likeness (likeness according to its genus) is possible, it is specifiable by the specific difference creating that genus: thus, to say that a human and a cat are alike because they are both animals is to reference a specific likeness, that which separates animals from other things (being animate, for instance).

This belief that only specific relations are real is false, however. On the one hand, declining to specify how A and B are similar is not the same as denying that A and B are similar. And so a general relation may be seen to be a placeholder for a more specific real relation. A general relation correctly asserts a real relation between A and B, but it is not really but only conceptually distinct from one or more specific real relations between them. On the other hand, the notion of a whole—that is, the unity of a particular substance—is in general a mysterious one that we have made little progress in understanding. There always remains a residue that exceeds what we can explain by attending to the parts, some ineffable "more" that is the referent of our notion of wholeness or unity when applied to particulars. But since we have such a notion and it seems not to be vacuous (for things do seem to really be wholes or unities), and since this wholeness does not seem to have to be in every way the same for different types of things (there are different types of unity), we may consider two things to be related (like or unlike, etc.), with respect to such wholeness. It must be admitted that this is another way of referencing a particular property. But it is an unspecifiable property. The notion of unity that I have is not sufficiently well formed to be explicable.

As a result, when I see unity, I do not comprehend it but only apprehend it. And yet that apprehension may be strong enough to assert relations to other apprehended unities.

All general relations then lead either to one or more specific relations or to a notion that, though not specifiable, is nevertheless able to be conceived and probed and thus is a notion in which we are able to make progress.

There is then in real relations a wide range of explorable connections that has no a priori boundary. It does have a boundary, for the number of connections is finite; but one cannot fix how many or what sort they will be ahead of time, and the number of them may be so great that they exceed the human capacity to conceptualize them all.

Now to return to the fact that metaphors grow, both on account of the complexity of meaning and on account of the complexity of interpretation.

COMPLEXITY OF MEANING

The metaphor takes on additional meanings, and this occurs in a variety of ways. First, when the metaphor comes into a situation that recontextualizes the elements of the metaphor in such a way that their comparison is also recontextualized. This is similar to what we said about the way that an analogy between *A* and *B* that elucidates *B* may yield new insights over time as our knowledge of *A* increases.[6]

Second, just as the original metaphor is an *ad placitum* institution, a later institution may add on to the original metaphor. The contingency of the imposition of the metaphor means that the metaphor does not become inviolate once imposed: it always remains vulnerable to modification and expansion.

Beyond these two, there is a yet more mysterious way in which metaphors accrete additional meanings. This mystery stems partly from the fact that it is unforeseeable: no prior calculation or inspection could reveal the direction this dynamic will go. It also stems from the fact that there is often no clear agent in such cases, so that we speak of the metaphor as having a life of its own: it is not being added to; it is adding on new meanings. This mysterious dynamic is the way in which metaphors have a tendency to attract meaning to themselves that was not part of their original imposition and that cannot be easily reduced to an addition of the first two types.

This last form of accretion is grounded in the fact that metaphors are a discovery of and subsequent emphasis on certain relations that obtain among concepts that themselves have referents that share a common world, and so are themselves related in more ways than human research could discover.

---

6. Chapter 3, p. 74.

When we focus attention on one such relationship between concepts and codify it in a metaphor, the light thus thrown on it tends to illuminate nearby relations as well. These may go unnoticed in the excitement of the moment of discovery, but eventually they will be noticed. They will then be thought not to be additions to the metaphor but to be implications or extensions of the metaphor. Unlike logical implications, however, they do not remain in a properly subordinate relationship because they are not properly subordinate. The original relation *AB* is not the cause of the adjacent relation *BC*, and neither is it the ground of it. *AB* is only original because it was contingently chosen to be the object of attention. *BC* presents itself first as an adjacent relation and then as a relation that could just as easily have been the original relation, and at last the mind is led to the conclusion that *AB* and *BC* are aspects of the same thing, such that *BC* comes to be compassed in the original metaphor.

For example, in the metaphor of my beloved and the sun, perhaps I originally meant to convey only that she is a bright, shining wonder, as the sun is. This is the first relation and the original meaning of the metaphor (*AB*, if you will). But as I think on it longer, I realize that the sun gives forth not only light but heat and that this heat is the necessary condition for life on earth. This seems also applicable to my love, especially if I am particularly idolatrous about it: it not only gives light to my life but is such that I cannot live without it. This is the second meaning of the metaphor (*BC*). But this second meaning is not derived from the first; it is derived from other properties of the *relata*. Scientifically it might be argued that the light and heat of the sun are the same energy, or that one is derivative of the other, or whatever. But I have not been thinking scientifically, and so this does not explain the relation of the meanings in this metaphor. Further, I might just as well have meant the metaphor in relation to heat first, and only then realized that the light connection also was valid; but in actual fact, I did not. The process will not stop there. As I continue to reflect on the sun, and perhaps as I learn more about it scientifically, I keep finding new meanings that enrich it as a metaphor for my beloved. Even after I have lost interest in the metaphor (perhaps my love has grown cold or died), another may return to it and continue the task of discovering new connections within the one original contuition.

The result of all this is that metaphors grow by dynamics of which some are analogous to organic dynamics (the first and the third) and some are analogous to artificial growth (the second). All this accretion is grounded in the expansive nature of the complex web of relations that really do obtain among things that inhabit the same world. And in whatever way metaphor grows, the result is an increasingly complex metaphor.

COMPLEXITY OF INTERPRETATION

Metaphorical discourse is not explicit. It does not say directly what it is trying to show; rather, it offers something to view by means of a contuition that must then be interpreted if it is to be expressed in direct, non-metaphorical discourse. When we encounter a metaphor, there are two distinct moments of response: the first is when we glimpse or apprehend what the metaphor is about, and it is attention to this dimension that grounds accretion of meaning in the ways we have just described. The second is when we attempt to articulate what that thing is in non-metaphorical or less metaphorical language. It is to this latter that we now turn.

Strictly speaking, the interpretation of metaphor is no part of the metaphor itself, and this follows the normal rules of hermeneutics. But the very dynamics of metaphor ground a distinction between the interpretation of metaphor and the interpretation of other language. For language is normally grounded in a correspondence that has two levels (first to the concept, then to the *res*), but that exerts a strong controlling influence on language. Thus, interpretation has to do with making these connections clear, with "getting it right." Metaphor by contrast is grounded in the demonstration of a relationship that may be of many different kinds. It is not a correspondence of the signifier (the metaphor) to the signified that is introduced but rather a correspondence among two distinct signifieds (the two things compared in the metaphor). The interpretation of metaphor is not therefore the clarification of the correspondence between the signifier and the signified but rather the exploration of the relationship to which the metaphor points—that is, the meaningful comparison of these two signifieds. And precisely because of the dynamics of relationality that we have been talking about, no boundaries can be set to this comparison a priori. Each point of comparison is generative of many contrasting points of comparison (because each property grounds many relations), and relations among even just the properties of one of the *relata* may themselves be generative of further relations.

For example, say that A and B are similar with regard to property x and dissimilar with regard to property y. Then, not only is Ax similar to Bx and Ay dissimilar to By, but also Ax is related to Ay differently than Bx is related to By, and Axy (the relation of Ax to Ay) is dissimilar to Bxy, but in a way that differs from but is grounded on the difference between Ay and By. And this does not exhaust the implications of just these few relations.

This exploration unveils new depths and aspects of that relation that is the proper signified of the metaphor. As such, it is hard to draw a sharp line between the interpretation of metaphor and the metaphor itself. The interpretive enterprise becomes one of the ways in which the scope of metaphor is expanded and by which new meanings are added to the original metaphor. Interpretations also interact with one another in ways analogous to how relations interact with one another, producing new meanings that exceed the original or any particular interpretation. As the interpretive enterprise progresses, the complexity of the metaphor is increased.

All this means that the destiny of a metaphor cannot be delimited, controlled, or predicted by the one who imposes the metaphor. The metaphor, as it progresses into culture and usage, has a life of its own that is the result of a combination of dynamics that are each too complex to be fully transparent to any human or to be controlled by any human. This growth is sometimes the expansion of the original meaning, but more often than not it is accomplished by taking on additional meanings.

These additional meanings may be closely related to the original meaning A though not any part of it and so be something like corollaries to that meaning. Thus one might see the additions of meaning $Ax, Ay,$ and Az, all of which are grounded in the same thing that grounds A without being identical with, analytic of, or reducible to A. These meanings may also be more loosely connected to A, such that they not only are not internal to it but do not even follow on it, though they still have some meaningful relationship to A. Such meanings might be designated $(A)x, (A)y,$ and $(A)z$. Finally, they may be in no clear way directly related to A. Metaphors sometimes take on meanings that are entirely different from their original meaning. These meanings could be designated $B, C,$ and D. These meanings are related to A by being meanings derivable from the relationship expressed in the original metaphor—that is, because my beloved is like the sun, the properties of the sun and my beloved ground $A, B, C,$ and D, and so each of these is related to the others through the realities described, but not directly through each other. Each of these meanings is also capable of producing derivative meanings of the sort described above, such that one may have $Bx, By, (B)x, (B)y, Cx, Cy, (C)x, (C)y,$ and so on.

Metaphorical Complexes

What has just been described are the processes by which metaphors grow. The result of this process of growth is a metaphorical complex made up of all of the accreted meanings. This is not mere plurality, however, for the new meanings of a metaphor do not create a separate unity from the metaphor itself. Were that to happen, they would be not new meanings of this metaphor but a new metaphor. The fact that these are new meanings for this metaphor underscores the unity binding them all together. This is why I have chosen to speak of complexification rather than plurification: these are the dynamics not of the multiplication of metaphors (such also exist) but of how a metaphor grows into a complex network of meanings all unified under the originally imposed contuition.

At this point it may be said as an aside that the process of accretion is analogous to the Incarnation. As the Son assumed flesh, metaphors likewise assume (take to themselves) additional meanings that are external to them as originally imposed but not incompatible with them (however much it might seem to be the case a priori). These meanings are taken into a unity not at the level of meaning (which would threaten to confuse meaning A and B) but at the level of reference. And so just as in Christ the union is not natural but personal (hypostatic), so in this case the union is not in meaning but in the metaphor itself. And the metaphor, in taking on these additional meanings, does not cease to be what it was before.

There is then a multiplicity of meanings unified under the referential sign. These meanings are all true, but they are not all equally primordial. They are not equally primordial in the sense of being equidistant from the moment of imposition of the metaphor, whether this distance be conceived of temporally or logically; and they are not equally primordial in the degree of their fit as meanings of the metaphor: some are more essential while others more accidental—that is to say, some follow more essential features of the two realities compared than others. They are also not all equally fruitful, whether as generative of further meanings or as productive of understanding concerning any particular purpose to which the metaphor is applied.

There is then a proliferation of true, irreducible, hierarchizable meanings within the normal dynamics of metaphor. But the various meanings may be organized according to different hierarchical principles, yielding different hierarchies. For example, meaning A will be closer to the purpose for which the metaphor was imposed (some particular poetic end) than B, but B may better express the general relationship between the two realities contuited in the metaphor; C, however, may better express some particular but salient aspect of the realities in question. One could go on with no clearly cognizable end in sight.

However, because of the fundamental unity of the metaphor, the proliferation of meaning is not a path to meaninglessness, nor does it dishonor the originally intended meaning; rather, it is the deeper understanding of the context of that original meaning: in digging deeper into the web of relations that grounds the original meaning, we affirm and deepen the original meaning. A metaphorical complex is more meaningful than a simple metaphor, both in the literal sense that it contains more meanings, but also in the sense that the original meaning of the metaphor is greater because of the accreted additional meanings. This is all the more likely to be the case in those things that have been divinely instituted for symbolism; for they carry a second layer of relationships (not just as co-worldly creatures but also as sacrament, for example), and this second layer is no less dense than the first. This will appear more clearly in chapter 7.

Subtle analysis of metaphorical language will therefore have to take into account the larger metaphorical complex and will be especially attentive to what appears in the interactions among various meanings. For the unity of the metaphor is the common space in which the meanings meet and play. It is what is conditioned not just by the individual meanings but by their interaction (and it is only here that space is to be made for something like Derrida's sense of play). Thus it is the metaphor itself—that is to say, an instance of referentiality imposed under the mode of contuition—that is affected and changed by this interplay, and the analysis of the metaphor (not of any one meaning of it) must be attentive to this above all.

This does not forbid the analysis of one or more meanings of the metaphor; it only marks out a different, equally valid, and much more difficult project. What emerges from such an analysis is not the author's intention, which does not extend to the metaphorical complex as such, but the author's achievement, which, in imposing a metaphor of such richness, has allowed the creation of the metaphorical complex.

Metaphor and Beauty

In the experience of the beautiful, two things are contuited: the creature and God. Likewise, metaphor imposes the contuition of two things, which are generally two creatures.[7] The result of the contuition in the case of metaphor is meaning and then an ever-increasing complex of meaning. The result in the experience of beauty is varied:

1. Desire: We long to cling to what we find beautiful.
2. Delight: We take pleasure in it.
3. Rest: There is an experience of satisfaction or satiety in the experience of the beautiful that we long to make permanent.
4. Inspiration: The beautiful strengthens one's mettle and grants the courage to take on great things.

---

7. God may of course also be used in metaphors. This differs crucially from the way in which God is contuited in the experience of the beautiful, however. In the experience of the beautiful, God is the remote referent in such a way that one could miss that God is being referred to at all; in a metaphor, God is directly compared to a creature. It is the difference between examining something (metaphor) and being reminded of it (beauty).

5. Sympathy: Beauty draws us out of ourselves and thus often grounds a greater compassion or kindness toward others.

6. Rectitude: Beauty often inspires us to want to become worthy of it.

7. Confidence: Here we have found something we can trust, something we are willing to stake much or all for.

8. Softening: Beauty makes our hearts vulnerable and opens us to new influences.

9. Restraint: The fortitude and inspiration imparted by beauty may combine with the desire to be worthy of it to produce a true ability to alter one's way of life.

10. Insight: Every experience of beauty is to some degree a true seeing. If this is at all capitalized on intellectually, some insight is produced, and one sees the world slightly more truly than one saw it before.

11. Wonder: We are struck by our own relative smallness in the face of what we have experienced.

Each of these may go wrong in various ways, usually when we direct our attention to the creature in abstraction from the Creator—that is, when we work directly against the beautiful. Whatever our motivations when we do this, we are trying to unsee what we have seen; and while we may not be successful at doing that, we are successful at sterilizing the experience. We also go wrong when we treat the beautiful as primarily or exclusively for us and thus seek to dominate or master it. This is another way of wrenching the creature away from the Creator. The result of these ways of abusing beauty is that we wind up with corrupted desire, corrupted delight, and so on. We want it for the wrong reasons, or we want the wrong thing, or we want it in ways that are not good for it or for us. We delight in the wrong parts of it, or we delight in what we can do with it; on it goes.

But the first nine results listed above are also correlated with the fruit of the Spirit mentioned in Galatians 5:22–23 (love, joy, peace, long-suffering, uprightness, goodness, assurance, gentleness, and self-control), which indicates the direction in which the right use of beauty lies: in a gifted response that is produced in us by the Spirit. I will speak more of this in the postscript.

Metaphorical meaning is grounded in the true relation of the realities contuited, which is an expression of their being co-worldly. The fruit of beauty is grounded in the true relation of the creature to God, which is the creature's way of imaging God. Thus it is not that the creature and God are co-worldly but that God is the ground of the creature, the antecedent condition of its being in a world at all. And so while metaphor considers the horizontal relations in which creatures stand to other creatures, beauty considers the vertical relation of a creature to its exemplar.[8]

In metaphor, the complexity of the relations between the *relata* grounds the proliferation of meaning. In beauty, though the relation is singular, an analogous proliferation of fruit is grounded. This is because the relation of the creature to its Creator, although singular, is comprehensive. In it is contained every possible good thing for the creature and the limits of the evil that the creature can undergo. These are each productive of fruit: The possible goods of the creature ground the recognition in the one experiencing the beauty of how gracious the Lord is, which contributes to the fruit listed above in various ways. The limit to the evil to which the creature may be subjected (which may be expressed as the idea that however far the creature may be objectified, it never loses its capacity to be a reminder of God) teaches the one experiencing beauty about the nature of God, that God remains committed to what God has done ("the gifts and the calling of God are irrevocable," Rom. 11:29) and that divine power is not able to be thwarted by creaturely power. In other words, because the totality of the creature's predestination (purpose) and the possibilities for it with regard to that purpose (whether fulfilling it or failing in it) are all contained in the original relation of the creature to God, the experience of the beautiful, like metaphor, has no a priori assignable limit to the amount or kinds of delight, desire, and so on that it is able to elicit.

Even in implicit contuition these dynamics obtain. For although in such moments it is not clear to me what I am contuiting or, in some cases, *that* I am contuiting; nevertheless I am contuiting, and so fruit is possible. This is analogous to the way metaphorical language continues to bear and be productive of meaning as metaphor, even when the interlocutors have lost sight of the fact that the language being used is metaphorical.

In metaphor, the relations among the meanings produced are themselves productive of meaning, and one has not really understood the metaphor to the fullest extent possible without an analysis of this larger complex of meanings. Likewise, in the experience of the beautiful, the understanding of the experience requires attention to the many different fruits it produces (as much intellectual as affective). The task of examining the experience requires making the contuition explicit and reflecting on the manifold gifts given in the moment of experiencing beauty.

---

8. Metaphors between God and a creature (e.g., "God is like a loving father") are actually expressions of an original analogical relation: they are truncated analogies. This is confirmed by the fact that failure to attend to the unlikeness in such cases has disastrous consequences.

6

Res and Concept

Things as Signs

When first I knew Thee, Thou didst lift me up so that I might see that there was something to see, but that I was not yet the man to see it. And thou didst beat back the weakness of my gaze, blazing upon me too strongly, and I was shaken with love and dread.

Augustine, *Confessions*

For these disguises did not disguise, but reveal.

G. K. Chesterton, *The Man Who Was Thursday*

The philosopher may sometimes love the infinite; the poet always loves the finite.

G. K. Chesterton, *The Man Who Was Thursday*

The Sign Character of Things

Semiotics is, according to Roland Barthes,[1] the study of signs, of how humanity gives meaning (sense) to things. This points to a final dimension of creaturely referentiality, one that moves beyond the question of how words refer

1. Barthes, *L'aventure sémiologique*, 249. Barthes, at the head of the contemporary science of semiotics, occupies a privileged place. And while not every semioticist practices the discipline

to concepts (language) and the question of how concepts refer to concepts (metaphor) and into the realm of how *res*, as the bearers of meaning, refer to concepts. It is to this dimension that we must now give attention.

The study of this phenomenon is semiotics, but what we are concerned with is not the discipline of semiotics (any more than we were concerned in chapter 4 with the discipline of linguistics) but rather with what semiotics is about. We may call such things as are the object both of semiotics and our discussion here "signs." However, insofar as we have spoken of both words and concepts as signifiers of concepts, we could rightly call linguistic entities (*legomena*) and metaphors also signs, and language and metaphor would seem to be species of semiotics.

We should not move too quickly here, however, for this implies that the relation between words and the concepts they signify and a concept and its correlated concept in metaphors is the same sort of relation. But it is not: the relation of signifier to signified (words to concepts) is not the same as the comparison of two concepts, as happens in metaphor. Language is a species of semiotics, but it is not clear that metaphor is, or if it is, it is not divided from the genus by a similar difference.

It remains however that language at least seems to be a species of semiotics. This is to be granted, as long as it is remembered that the species modulates the genus by a specific difference (here, the application of grammar as syntax and morphology) that creates a set of dynamics that are merely potential in the genus and not realizable in the genus as such, but only in the genus as it has become some species ("animal" may be patient of "rational," but "animal" is not rational apart from being the rational animal "human"). This means that the dynamics between the two will be at best analogical and that a univocal reduction of the one to the other is not warranted and is to be resisted.

We will therefore use "signs" as the term for the thing under discussion here, not in spite of the ambiguity with linguistic signifiers but precisely because of it. One *should* hear echoes of words as signs in this discussion, but one should also keep in mind that they are signs of a certain sort and so have a unique set of dynamics.

Res *as Signs*

Turning our attention to *res* as signs has some immediate consequences deriving from foundational truths about the *res* that are not a result of human institution.

---

in the way that Barthes did, his work remains seminal and is marked by a kind of transparency that is helpful in understanding the semiotic task.

1. The first of these truths is that the signifier is now no longer a product of human invention.

No human words are divine: the primal moment of human language is Adam's naming, not God's speech. Thus, though our words, after Adam, do not come from nowhere (they come from earlier words), nevertheless they are products of human ingenuity. Likewise the concepts used in metaphor are not of divine provenance. For even given that there is surely some divine concept to which the human concept corresponds (that is, surely God's concept of purple is that after which my concept "purple" strives and that by which it is judged), it is not the case that we are thinking those divine concepts. We have our own human versions of them, which are incomplete and erroneous in ways that in this life we cannot correct for. Indeed, as I have argued, Adam's primal naming is also a primal conceiving, and so the primordial history of our concepts is hidden in the same place as the primordial history of language. Thus the source of our concepts is ultimately also humanity.

But in the first instance, *res* are not the product of human ingenuity or invention; they are creatures created by God. As such, the relationship we have to them when we press them into semiotic service is different in important ways from the imposition of words and concepts of which we are the authors.[2]

2. The second foundational truth about the *res* is that created things are not created in order to refer to human concepts, because they are not, in the first instance, created *for us*. All things are created for God and the divine glory, and it is part of God's largesse that they are also able to be useful to us without thereby retreating from their original function. It is crucial to note that the original function of creatures is in fact *to be signs*. It is in fact coded into each thing to such an extent that creaturely kinds are predicated on it: to be a frog is to image God in a certain way, which is further differentiated by the nearly five thousand species we know of. Thus our imposition of *res* to be signs is a repurposing of another's sign for our own uses.

Since this is so, it follows that there are good and bad ways of making use of *res* as signs. Because the *res* are not there primarily for us to make use of, the danger of abuse haunts our every use. There are several ways of transgressing the *res* when we press it into the service of our signification:

a. If we deny the already existing sign character of creatures, we objectify them (as was mentioned in chap. 1).

---

2. Our concern in the present chapter is with natural signs, though much of what is said here will transfer even to the works of our hands, *res artificialis et manu facta* (manufactured things). These will be considered in the next chapter.

b. If we deny the objective character of creatures as existing apart from and before our uses of them, reducing them to mere signs, we spiritualize them. Spirit is not bad, but reducing what is both non-spiritual and spiritual or what is only non-spiritual to the spiritual is a transgression of the proper mode of being of the thing in question. This is always a violation and unwarranted, because nothing needs to be other than what it is in order to represent God faithfully and so to have value and meaning (even though in this fallen world all things need to be made more fully what they are to do this as well as possible for each thing).

c. If we use the creature in ways that are incompatible with the way it images God, we profane it by trying to make it say of God something it is fundamentally opposed to saying. This is an attempt to enlist the creature in our own blasphemy, to make it also blaspheme.

There are also ways of failing or falling short that do not go so far as transgression. Perhaps the most common of these is simply to ask a creature to signify in a way that has no relation to its native signification but nevertheless is not incompatible with it. Such signification becomes arbitrary in the vicious sense. If a slug is imposed to signify, say, the unfailing strength of the human spirit, even though it has no natural suitability for expressing any such thing (in this instance, the signification is not meant to be ironic), then why has a slug been chosen rather than, say, a butterfly or a roach? If a rock had been chosen, one could easily answer the question; but of course, the question would not have arisen, because the ground of the imposition in the natural properties of the rock would be clear.

An extreme skeptic may wonder whether all our impositions of meanings on things are not in fact arbitrary to a radical degree. To such a one, we only think the rock is a good sign for strength because of contingent cultural factors and not because of any true connection between the rock and the concept of strength. But such skepticism is in fact unwarranted and proceeds from despair in the face of the subjective elements involved. If we do not allow subjectivity to cloud our vision of objectivity, but only to qualify it, there is no reason to doubt our ability to attain to true correspondences grounded in the beings of things.

What is lost in such a failing is the beauty of the suitability that appears in an aptly chosen signification. The reference becomes purely external to the *res* to which it is attached, and the *res* itself appears dispensable and replaceable. But when the imposition is based on a suitability inherent to the nature of the thing itself, the *res* becomes irreplaceable in the sense that were a different *res* to be substituted for it, even one that expressed a different but equally apt suitability, meaningful content would be lost. Such an imposition, one that is according to the true qualities or properties or characteristics of a thing, affirms the *res* in its being and thus in its way of imaging God.

3. The third foundational truth is that, just as these *res* are already signs, so they are also already full with meaning. A tree has meaning besides, before, and apart from any meaning that we assign to it. In fact, it is perhaps this that attracts us to it as a sign at all: we see that it is already meaningful, and by the same impulse that drives us to expand metaphorical complexes (which is a desire to attain a greater vision of the unity of the world) we desire to add our own meanings to its extant meaning. And this does not require us to recognize what that meaning is, only that some meaning is present. That is to say, we do not need to know what a tree means to be affected by it; we only need to know that it is meaningful.

Thus, the imposition of a *res* to be a sign is going to be even less under the control of the one imposing than in the case of language and metaphor. This is, in part, because the assigned meaning is going to interact with the primal meaning of the *res* in ways that cannot be predicted and cannot be effaced. If the primal meaning were of human origin, it would be theoretically possible to efface it, just as words and metaphors may lose meaning over time when subjected to cultural forgetfulness (which requires either the loss or the neglect of important texts or traditions). But since this primal meaning is of divine origin and is analytic to the *res*, it cannot be effaced any more than the ability of a *res* to remind us of God can be effaced. Creaturely power is just insufficient to wrest things so thoroughly away from their Creator, even within our own thinking (we cannot even succeed at entirely effacing our own ability to be struck by the primal meaning).

The primal meaning and the imposed meaning may interact in different ways. One may be dominant over the other, or both may be suspended equally in view. The use of *res* as signs is therefore fraught with peril, for one always runs the risk of being caught up and co-opted into the primal meaning of the *res*. Whatever I am imposing it to mean may wind up subjected to and even swallowed up in its primal meaning. We see this dynamic even with artificial signs, when a particular meaning becomes so powerful that it cannot easily be effaced. Who knows whether a swastika will ever be able to be used without the negative connotations that have become attached to it; but if such a thing is possible, it can only be after a great deal of forgetting of its use in Nazi Germany.

Every *res* as *signum* is therefore a thicker reality than words or concepts, because they bring a rich and non-negotiable history with them to the moment of signification. Or rather, one may negotiate the history in the sense in which one negotiates a dangerous crossing, but one is not able to barter or bribe away the history. This makes these types of signs especially rich for analysis, because they will ground a kind of relational complexity analogous to what we saw in metaphorical complexes. But unlike metaphor, the signifier is not a concept, which must be to some significant degree abstract. It is instead a concrete reality. Here we must face the question of particularity versus universality in the *res* as *signum*.

The *res* that is imposed to be a sign must always be particular. This is definitionally true: for since universals are not independent of created minds, they are not *res*.[3] Thus, if I impose the abstract notion of a tree to refer to the organic unity of the world, I have made a metaphor. If I use Yggdrasil to refer to that notion, I have created a sign. The concretivity of *res* as signs is therefore foundational to the way in which they signify.

The Opacity and Transparency of Res

One of the most important dynamics that the concretivity of *res* brings to the way in which they signify is the degree to which the *res* is opaque or transparent in the moment of signification. And as the moment of signification changes, so does the opacity or transparency of the sign. There is no fixed value with regard to this dynamic.

It is also not the case that opacity and transparency are to be conceived as two different ends of a scale, with the sign tending more toward one or the other at any given moment. For though this is in some sense true, it will be greatly misleading: The reality is much more complex. There are in fact multiple scales of opacity and transparency, and the sign may at one and the same time be more opaque with regard to x and more transparent with regard to y. The intricacies of these possibilities would take us too far afield. I will limit myself instead to the general dynamics of opacity and transparency, leaving this further complexification as an implication of this general dynamic.

OPACITY

Opacity may be described as the way that the sign intrudes on our awareness in the moment of signification. It is an expression of the extent to which the sign arrests our gaze, slowing down our move to the signified.

---

3. There remain, of course, the divine ideas, which are independent of creaturely minds. But these are not our universals: our universal concepts are not God's concepts but creaturely and human versions of them (the angels presumably have yet a different set of concepts that match God's better than ours do and yet are not God's). Thus no concept independent of a creaturely mind is imposed by creatures to signify, precisely because no creature knows any such concept.

But it is not just the fact of noticing the sign and its characteristics, for we are speaking of opacity not in a general epistemological sense but as a feature of the moment of signification. Therefore it is a description of the way that the features of the sign not only arrest our view but subsequently affect the way that we understand the signified.

For example, suppose an antique analog watch is imposed to signify my soul. At an average level of opacity, one notices the type of thing that it is and draws comparisons: it is a way of keeping time, as my soul, with its repository of memory, keeps the time to which I have been subject. And as it indicates where exactly in time one is, so does my soul in its present state indicate where on my journey through life I am. But because the sign must be particular, one must go beyond the general description of things that are true of any watch to the things true of this particular watch. And the more the watch becomes opaque, the more avenues for reference will be opened up: it has an inscription on the back showing it to be the gift of a loved one; even so is my soul signed by the hand of my loving Creator. If the mind's eye stays on the watch long enough to notice the damage it has received through the years, then the scratch on its face will indicate the scars on my soul from the violence that has been done to me; the wearing of the gears will indicate the way in which my soul has ground against itself in futile rebellion, causing damage to its inner workings that threaten to overturn the entire enterprise. In this way, greater opacity may open up deeper connections and a deeper vision of the suitability of the *res* for the particular signification it has been imposed for.

Both conscious and non-conscious factors affect how opaque a sign is. I can choose to focus more on the details of the sign and so render the sign more opaque to myself. This is what happens when we are, for example, sitting in a cathedral and experiencing great power, and we turn our attention to the details of the place in order to understand what it is doing to us. By turning our attention more consciously to the cathedral, we gain greater understanding of the work it has already been doing; but we also begin a new work, as the previously unremarked-on details will connect to the original experience and deepen it further.

But any number of other factors outside of our conscious control affect how opaque a sign is at particular moments of signification. A symbol such as a statue may start out largely transparent to an individual, but subsequent experiences may render it very opaque as the emblem of something to which one now feels special devotion or loathing. Piety or controversy tend to render signs more opaque.

It might seem that what is happening instead is that the signified is more or less capable of exciting strong feeling and that it is not the statue but what it signifies that has become more opaque. But this is not true: we clamor for the statue to be removed, or we organize a rally to save it. It is true that it is only because it is a statue *of* such and such that there is an issue at all, but that is precisely the point: it is its opacity *as a sign* that is at issue here, not its opacity *as a res*.

Opacity is therefore a positive feature of the sign insofar as it allows the sign to carry more meaning. This is especially true when the sign is well suited to what it signifies: the greater the suitability, the more fruit is to be expected from a greater degree of opacity.

But opacity may also be a negative feature, and this just to the extent that it begins to occlude the intended reference. When I use a clever analogy in arguing, the desire is for a certain amount of opacity: I want you to notice the cleverness of the analogy and the suitability of it. But if the analogy becomes contentious and all discussion turns to the suitability or unsuitability of the analogy, or the rightness or wrongness of the situation described in it, it has become too opaque. It is now blocking discussion of what it was meant to facilitate. It is in such moments that I feel compelled to remind my interlocutor that the clever example was only intended to be an analogy and that I really wanted to be talking about whatever it was an analogy *for*.

Transparency

Transparency describes the degree to which the sign steps aside to allow the gaze more easy access to the signified. The greater the transparency, the clearer the signification. To the degree that a sign is transparent, it helps the signified to appear. Relatedly, transparency is also the way that the sign avoids blocking the view. It must retreat somewhat in order that space be made for the signified to be seen.

In the case of opacity, greater opacity allowed the sign to more greatly affect the moment of the signification. In the case of transparency, greater transparency allows the signified to more greatly affect the moment of signification. A swastika graffitied on a wall is a good example: the sign has become highly transparent, and what it signifies (a certain set of social and political commitments) is forefront. In this instance the moment of signification has much more to do with the events surrounding Nazi Germany than with the complicated (and not exclusively evil) history of the symbol as such: moments of signification involving this sign very rarely contain anything of its eastern or Christian religious meaning; philosophical reflection on the way it is formed of angles and intersections (which would be the fruit of greater opacity) hardly ever arises.

TRANSLUCENCE

The sign may slide entirely into pure opacity or pure transparency, but this is to be described as a semiotic failure, for in that moment the sign ceases to be a sign. If the sign becomes entirely opaque, nothing else is seen and reference is eclipsed. One retains the signifier but loses the signified, and in so doing the signifier has ceased to be a sign and is seen only as the *res* that it is. If the sign becomes entirely transparent, one does not see it at all but only sees what it references. Here the sign has sacrificed itself entirely in the moment of reference, has become entirely dispensable. Such a sign is less than arbitrary because it lacks the requisite existence to be arbitrary. The moment of signification would also be the destruction of the sign. This is unfitting because no *res* exists only to be a sign in our semiotic usage. The epistemological annihilation of the sign transgresses the objective character of the *res* in the sense of spiritualization mentioned above. The ontological annihilation of it in the moment of signification is hard to find examples of, but perhaps this is what happens in the immolation of a sacrifice: at the moment the victim becomes entirely given over to the god, the victim is by the very instance of giving over destroyed.[4]

Thus signification is only possible where there is both opacity and transparency. In other words, signification requires translucence. The connotations of that word—that light is shining through something—are felicitous. In signification, because there is both opacity and transparency, the moment of signification is affected by both the sign and the signified. Thus light beams into the moment of signification from the signified. But light also beams in from the sign. It is the interaction of these two lights that creates the luminosity of the moment of signification.

This is why signification is so powerful and so vital: it is *illuminating*. It does not just or primarily illuminate the sign or the signified, because these are each sources of light in the moment of signification. Rather, it illuminates *the world*. It does this by causing light to shine on the one experiencing the moment of signification, revealing in this light new relations among things in the world.

Signs and Beauty

Herrlichkeit *and the Objective* Res

Hans Urs von Balthasar has placed the German word *Herrlichkeit* in the middle of the theological discussion of beauty as a transcendental property

4. One thinks of the sacrificial victim in Stravinsky's *Rite of Spring*.

of being, and this is felicitous for our present purposes. For the term's dual sense of both lordliness and sovereignty (*Herr-lichkeit*) and as glory rightly unifies the independence and translucence of the *res* as sign.

INDEPENDENCE: *HERRLICHKEIT* AS SOVEREIGNTY

The fact that *res* are not dependent on human activity for existence may be expressed with the concept of independence, understood here not as absolute independence—for they depend on God (and this dependence is irreducible and essential)—but as an expression of the fact that we come upon them already existing in the world. This concept of independence is the ground of the objectivity that anchors the experience of beauty.

The independence of *res* confers freedom upon those *res*. This is not the sort of freedom that rational beings have: that is to say, it is not free *will*, for a tree has no will except in a metaphorical sense. Rather, the freedom they have is a freedom of availability or disponibility. This disponibility is directed at God in the first instance. It is an obediential potency—that is, a potentiality of the creature that can be activated only by God.

Why bother calling this a potency of the creature at all? Why not just consider this potentiality to be an aspect of the divine omnipotence rather than something of the creature? For example, one could say that bread has the obediential potency to become the body of Christ, but why not say instead that divine omnipotence has the power to make bread into the body of Christ, and that this has nothing at all to do with bread's natural powers?

The reason is that when the ability to become the body of Christ is predicated of the bread, then the bread (a) does not suffer violence in being so changed and (b) does not need to become something else or cease to be what it is in order to become the body of Christ. This would mean that as one seeks to understand the mystery, one is not led away from the true essence of bread but deeper into it, to that point at which its created image always carried within it the possibility of this marvelous transformation.

No creaturely active power corresponds to this potentiality—no creature, not even the most exalted seraph, could actualize this potency. It is bound to God, and thus, though it belongs to nature, it cannot come to be apart from grace. This obediential potency is a creature's deepest secret (*mysterium rei*), for it is tied to the particular type of image that the creature is. It is the place where freedom (to be what it is) and obedience (to image God with maximal translucence) meet: and such a place is the freest place a creature can inhabit.

The creature is therefore free with respect to all possible human uses (that is, it inhabits a place from which we can place no claims upon it) because the uses to which we put creatures are not the primary expressions of their essences. They are free with respect to our uses, not free *for* our uses. No potential human use of *res* has any prior claim on these *res*. As a result, no matter how much *res* may submit to our uses, they are never defined by them. An excess remains; it is that *mysterium* that is bound to God and that therefore need not be (and never in fact is) submitted to humanity. We may destroy a creature, but we cannot change its quiddity (whatness); nor, indeed, since the divine intentions for things extend all the way to individuals, can we change its haecceity (thisness).

Transparency, Opacity, and Incarnational Logic: *Herrlichkeit* as Glory

It is out of the freedom that coincides with obediential potency that the experience of the beautiful erupts. The *mysterium rei* is the objective condition of the possibility of theological anamnesis and is what is glimpsed in such moments. For this reason, although my experience of a beautiful *res* reminds me of God, it is the *res* in question that I am finding beautiful. Theological anamnesis cannot be reduced to simply "*I* am being reminded of God," where the passive verb occludes the *res* that brokers the experience (pure transparency). It is always "This *res* reminds me of God." The one who experiences is the object of the action of reminding, not the subject. And yet the subject performs this action not by acting but merely by being, by lying open to inspection by an observer of the right sort. And so the grammar of the experience and the grammar of the words used to describe it are chiastic. More importantly, the *res* must be opaque to some degree if there is to be an experience of beauty at all.

And yet when one has come to the place where the *res* is free, one has simultaneously come to its deepest and most unqualified obedience. This is ineluctable: if you deny the relation of the *res* to God, the very being of the *res* (understood at its most essential and therefore most free) still declares its dependence. For every *res* is part of a world and cannot exist apart from that world. One can think of a tree in the abstract existing in a metaphysical vacuum only because this is a pure fiction enabled by the bracketing of all other attendant things. But one cannot think of a tree with all that is essential to that notion (as living, and therefore as in a certain relationship to sunlight, water, air, and earth) and believe that it could be all that exists. Its essence, as a worldly reality, is therefore epically relational; for everything that is worldly is enmeshed in a wild tangle of things that are co-worldly with it.

But the tree goes further, for its essence declares it not only to be worldly but also to be creaturely, and so it indicates that its being depends on the activity of another who is not co-worldly with it. If it merely declared itself to be caused, one could imagine that its cause is co-worldly to it (at this late point in history, one would perhaps assume it; but such an assumption is in no way warranted on the basis of the nature of causality). But if it is not merely caused but created, then the Creator is not co-worldly with it; for everything in its world also shares this quality of creatureliness. The Creator must be transcendent to them all. Indeed, even if this particular tree is merely caused (which it is not clear we should grant), it is a member of a kind that is created, and by expressing its kind it also expresses that transcendent causality.

Thus the *res* must also be transparent, otherwise the *mysterium rei* does not appear; or, if it does appear, it does not appear *as mystery*, and so it is not seen in its proper dimensions.

Therefore the sign must submit and point away from itself in an abnegation that nevertheless cannot erase itself, and so it must also abide. What is required is a kenosis (emptying) whose result is not nothing (this would be annihilation) but emptiness; and this is not an emptiness of meaninglessness, hopelessness, or despair, but the emptiness of a container that can therefore be filled with glory.

7

Res Sacramenti

The Nature of Sacraments

I am the food of grown men: grow and you shall eat Me. And you shall not change Me into yourself as bodily food, but into Me you shall be changed.

Augustine, *Confessions*

The spring leaps up even more plenteously. To be sure, it flows out of a wound and is like the blossom and fruit of a wound; like a tree it sprouts up from this wound. But the wound no longer causes pain. The suffering has been left behind as the past origin and previous source of today's wellspring. What is poured out here is no longer a present suffering, but a suffering that has been concluded—no longer now a sacrificing love, but a love sacrificed. Only the wound is there: gaping, the great open gate, the chaos, the nothingness out of which the wellspring leaps forth.

Hans Urs von Balthasar, *Heart of the World*

All through his life he thought of the daylight world as a sort of divine debris, the broken remainder of his first vision.

G. K. Chesterton, *The Ball and the Cross*

The General Concept of Sacrament

Since ancient times, the notion of sacrament has been bound up with semiotics (recall Augustine's understanding of a sacrament as a visible sign of an invisible grace).[1] And as divinely instituted signs that make use of creaturely realities for the work of referring to sacred things, they touch on the referentiality of theological anamnesis. In this chapter, I will attempt to clarify the nature of that relation and how the notion of "sacrament" can be enriched by and contribute to our understanding of theological anamnesis.

Sacraments are helpful because it is beneficial for us to encounter the presence of God objectively. Christ in me or Christ in another is Christ as subjectively appropriated: he is always in such cases reflected and refracted. This nourishes, but it is not objective enough to satisfy our christological longing—not with the immediacy we long for. The sacraments (and especially the Eucharist) bring us face to face with God in God's own proper persons. God is, as we have been arguing throughout, objectively encounterable in every creature, thanks to the image each bears. This is sufficient to ground a general sacramental character of all creation, but it is not sufficient to render every creature a sacrament in the truest sense of that word.

The contuition of God in creatures is a double vision in which the creature and its ground are seen, but the creature remains the primary object of vision. God is seen by seeing *the creature* as most truly what it is, and so the vision of God is almost, as it were, a corollary to penetrating vision of the creature. In sacraments the creature recedes to a greater (but, consistent with the necessity of translucency for signification, not entire) extent. Here the vision of the creature must decrease so that the vision of God may increase. A creature called to be a sacrament is one whose obediential potency has been activated. It becomes endowed with a greater humility than even that which it already had: it abjures its demand to be seen, replacing it with a demand that God be seen. Sacramental vision is still contuition, but now God comes to the foreground, and the creature becomes a contingent condition of the possibility of the sacramental moment. As condition of the possibility it remains necessary but only contingently so: God could have used other bread than this bread, or God could have used no bread at all. But the logical accent lies on what it is a condition of possibility for. When I say that the vision of God follows as a quasi-correlate on the true vision of the creature, the intended goal remains the vision of the creature, and the accent falls on that. But when I speak of the vision of the creature as the condition of the

---

1. Cf. Augustine, *City of God*, book 10, chap. 5.

possibility of the vision of God, the goal has become the vision of God, and that is where the accent falls.

The *mysterium rei* is the ground of the suitability of sacramental signification. The creature is summoned according to its *mysterium*, and this is what it looks like to activate its obediential potency. Sacramental imposition is thus an interpretation of the essence of the creature which, because divinely given, always has the character of a revelation.

Nevertheless, suitability is not a necessary condition of sacramental institution: God could use what in no way resembles God as the sign of invisible grace. In this world, that means that even sin could be used by God as a sacramental sign.[2] But it would also seem to follow that even in such a case the sacramental imposition would be revelatory. In the case of sin, it would have to be revealed precisely *as sin*, which can only refer to God through itself negatively: "See, by seeing me, what God is *not*." In this way there is no danger of valorizing the sin; that could only happen if the signification were blasphemous. But sacramental signification unfurls from the *mysterium rei*, and the *mysterium peccati* (mystery of sin) is the truth that the sin should not be, that its existence is an affront and a wrong in the world.

However, God delights in acting according to fittingness, and so sacramental signification ordinarily follows the contours of the *mysterium rei* in such a way as to affirm and elucidate the nature of that *res*. In this way we also learn that sacramental signification is one of the originally coded potential uses of creatures. The particular image of God that each creature is grounds a particular potential sacramental signification, and to be so used would be one of the highest glories of each creature.

Sacraments are not mere signs, however—that is to say, they do not only signify, represent, or remind. They are also efficacious. Specifically, they effect what they signify. Therefore something more must be added for the creature to become a sacrament, and that is divine institution. This is because a sacrament does not merely signify holy things but also makes them present—this is the relevant efficacy. But nothing can compel the grace of God; only God may decide to give it, and this decision is always free, even when it is in response to a creaturely desire or preparation (which is always itself a response to a more primal divine call that is the first grace of each creature).

The sacrament is therefore a question not only of semiotics but also of *presence*. The relation between sign and signified undergoes a transformation under sacramental institution that gives a unique tonality to the character

---

2. Perhaps the saints approach this when their awareness of their sinfulness turns over effortlessly into rejoicing in the grace of God.

of this semiotic moment: it in fact describes a new species of reference in which the success of the sign is not just in causing the signified to be cognized but also in causing the signified (by a divine power that the sign possesses only because this power operates in it according to divine will) to be present.

Because of this requirement for efficacy, not just any divinely imposed creaturely sign is a sacrament but only those that effect what they signify. The sign of the covenant given to Abraham (Gen. 15:8–20) is not a sacrament, for it signifies what would happen to God were the promise to fail—namely, God would be torn in pieces like the animals Abraham slaughtered. But the sign does not effect this punishment; it only signifies it. Further, not just any efficacious, divinely imposed creaturely sign is a sacrament, but only those that cause transcendent realities to be present. When God puts the mark on Cain (Gen. 4:15: "And the LORD put a mark on Cain, lest any who found him should attack him"), this does not turn Cain into a sacrament. For even though it is a sign and a divinely instituted one, and it arguably effects what it signifies (the not-killing of Cain), it does not cause the presence of something holy or transcendent.[3]

In what follows, we are interested in the general dynamics of a divine semiotics, of which sacraments are an especially important and transparent instance. Although I will speak primarily about the Eucharist when discussing Christian sacraments, there are important extensions to be made concerning the sacrament of Baptism, most of which will be left undeveloped here (but will be discussed more in the next chapter).

Secular Quasi-sacraments

In some ways the field of semiotics, especially as practiced by someone like Roland Barthes, is a practice of developing what might be called a secular sacramentology. This secular sacramentology is analogous to Christian sacramentology but with important differences deriving from the one who fills the role of the creator in each instance. This results in a set of semiotic intuitions concerning the nature of sacramentalism that differ greatly from those that underlie a divine sacramental approach to signification.

---

3. I understand transcendence as that which is of non-local provenance metaphysically speaking. This means that the local context is not merely the physical world but the whole creaturely realm, because both physical and spiritual realities are immanent to the physical/spiritual human hybrid. This excludes that the signified be merely of a higher metaphysical order than the putative sacrament: it must be no part of the whole metaphysical system to which the sign belongs (or be united to something that is, as the body of Christ is).

Now, because the intuitions developed from semiotics are fairly wide-spread, even though the reasons for nevertheless electing a divine sacramental set of intuitions can be motivated by the types of claims made to this point, it will be worthwhile to consider the secular sacramentology before teasing out the implications of divine sacraments for the experience of beauty. However, to preserve the great distance that persists in this analogy, I will refer to secular sacraments as quasi-sacraments. For indeed, while they may represent and make present what is most precious and transcendent to us (as the causes and universals set over and against particular humans or readily identifiable particular associations of humans), as the institutions of sinful humans they do not in fact represent and make present holy things and so are not themselves *sacra*.

Quasi-sacramental Elements: Culture and Artifacts

In a proper sense, no one can adopt anything into sacramental or quasi-sacramental signification over which one is not lord: sacramental institution requires lordly authority, because a *res* is made a sacrament by the activation of its obediential potency. Thus the author of the sacrament must be one who has the authority to actualize this potency—that is, the one who institutes must be one to whom the *res* is ordered (*ordinata*) through obedience.

To go further, because a sacramental imposition adds to the signification of a thing at its most fundamental level, sacramental imposition makes an interpretive claim about what the *res* is. But if the imposition is real—that is, if the *res* in fact becomes a sacrament—then the claim is true, and the fact of instituting this *res* to be a sacrament demonstrates this truth. But the freedom of the *res* means that it is bound to submit its *mysterium* to no one other than its lord; and so no one but its lord could confidently claim to know what this *res* is at its most fundamental level with comprehensive specificity. A human could, perhaps, lean on the perception that there is a *mysterium rei* and on an apprehension of what it must be in this particular case and thus make a probable claim about the truth of the *res*. But probabilistic claims are not sufficient for sacramental signification because they lack efficacy. Efficacy requires not merely that one correctly guess the *mysterium rei* but that one be able to engage with it in such a way as to activate or manipulate it. The power required to institute a sacrament is the same as the power required to institute a *res*.

Thus the elements of quasi-sacramental institution are the works of human hands: artifacts rather than natural things. We can make a tree signify by means of metaphor, but we cannot make a tree the element of one of our quasi-sacraments. This inability notwithstanding, we do in fact make the effort to do so: much objectification in the direction of use is an attempt to assert authority over the object in question. The bad reading of Genesis 1:26–28 as giving humanity full authority over the things of the earth is an example of this: we attempt to exercise lordship in such a way that denies that any lordship we may have is subsumed under divine lordship. But this attempt always fails, for we have not been given that right (our lordship has to do with cultivating creatures; it does not extend to the very existence of creatures, and it is limited by the established creaturely kinds), nor do we have the power to wrest such lordship from God.

We begin then with *res artificialis, res* that have been constituted in their being not by a divine creative activity but by human creative activity. These two creative activities (divine and human) are decidedly different. On the one hand, divine creative action is *ex nihilo* and therefore makes things to exist, beginning from no pre-existing matter. All that pre-exists the divine creativity is the divine concept of the thing. Divine creative action thus produces, among other things, *esse*, by which I mean actually existent being that cannot be accounted for by anything that came before. Our current tendency to think that everything can be explained in terms of immanent antecedent causes is just a refusal to ask why there is any antecedent thing at all. It may not be necessary to look outside the system of nature to account for the generation and growth of a new tree (both the principles and the matter involved may be found to be already present in nature), but this is just to take the *esse* that will turn into that of the tree for granted. The root question is also the first metaphysical question: Why is there something rather than nothing? No immanent cause can account for this.

Human creative action, on the other hand, shapes what already exists into something new. This is fundamentally different from the divine activity, for to create from nothing requires infinite power—not primarily in the sense of an infinite amount of power (this is probably a misunderstanding of the nature of non-being, placing it on a scale with being; for even if the space between being and non-being is infinite, if quantitatively infinite power can bridge it, then it is not a non-quantitative difference), but in the sense of a power of infinite quality. Such a power is necessarily authoritative with respect to every finitude and infinitude that falls under its purview. And since only a power that is absolutely infinite could be maximally qualitatively infinite, it is impossible that there be anything, real or possible, that does not fall under its purview. As has been shown over and over again in philosophical and theological argumentation, the existence of a second infinite power would qualify the first infinite power such that even if the first power could still somehow be considered to be infinite, this would not be in the fullest sense because there is another power in existence with the ability to successfully resist the first power.

This difference between divine and human agency in creation is what led Aquinas and Tolkien to wish to use different words for the two. For Aquinas, God creates, while humans only make;[4] for Tolkien, God creates, and humans sub-create.[5] But, without taking away from the rich insights these authors are pointing to (and without claiming that they would object strongly to the current account), it is best to think of the two not as totally different but as analogous. For while human creation is unlike the divine in that it is not *ex nihilo*, does not require infinite power, and is not authoritative, it is nevertheless like divine creation in that it is preceded by a concept in the mind according to which the creation will be executed, and it causes the existence of something that did not exist before.

Human creative activity does cause something new to exist but not in an absolute sense, because no human artifacts are *ex nihilo*; rather, they are always made of material that we find in the world—that is to say, other *res*. The complex ordering and reshaping of this material does not render the original material any less God's creature. And when the human creative activity ends, there is not more being in the world than there was before it began or during the process.[6] This is true not just for human making of *res* but also for human making of concepts and narratives. Thus human creation is like the divine in that something comes to be that was not before. We do not cause existence, but we cause existence of a certain sort: we do not produce being (*esse*), but we do produce things (*res*).

But what are we to say of the things that we invent *to be symbols*? Is an alpha or an infinity symbol a *res*? Indeed, letters are *res* insofar as they have mind-independent existence; and they are signs, for they signify a sound (often in complex ways, as the rules of English phonetics prove). Yet letters of the alphabet are not as such objects of interest for semiotics. Neither is the infinity symbol when it is used to refer to the notion of infinity. Such minimal symbols are about simple concepts (a linguistic concept in the case of a letter; an abstract concept in the case of the infinity symbol) and have a more or less adventitious relationship to what they signify. For example, the relationship of *A* to the sound it signifies is adventitious because nothing

4. Thomas Aquinas, *Summa Theologica* Ia, qu. 45.

5. Tolkien, "On Fairy-Stories," 23.

6. Indeed, one might see the law of conservation of energy as merely an expression of the fact that only God can create and destroy.

about *A* indicates that sound or is especially suited to it.[7] But the same cannot be said for the infinity symbol. Something about it *is* especially suited to the notion of infinity—namely, the way that it returns to itself without end: begin anywhere you like, and you will never find a non-arbitrary stopping point. The same is true of a circle, and for that reason the circle has also been imposed as a symbol of infinity. But the infinity symbol has this advantage: the more meandering path that it takes to return to the starting point references infinity as something more dynamic than the reference made by means of a circle.

But it is not just the case that the circle and the infinity symbol do not reference a concept of infinity that is in every way univocal; they also do not reference whatever concepts they reference with the same degree of distance. For the infinity symbol is imposed to represent infinity in the first instance; the circle, however, is not so imposed but as a geometrical figure is meant to represent a certain relationship occurring in nature (the relationship defined by a set of points equidistant from a common center). The circle is imposed in a secondary sense to reference infinity; and the moment this happens, it becomes an object of semiotics. Likewise, the infinity symbol becomes an object of interest for semiotics when it is imposed to mean something other than infinity—say, a religious concept of eternal life or of reincarnation.

So the type of reference we are concerned with here may employ *res* that are signs but not *nuda signa*; they must be signs that are then imposed to also be signs of something else. This is not surprising, for every *res* has inherent signification, and it is not this innate reference that is of concern but what happens when the *res* is then imposed to mean something else or something further.

Either because of the innate signification that is imported by the *materia* that we employ in manufacturing or because of the external reference for which the signs employed were originally imposed, it happens that even in manufactured signs there is a way they escape our control, and they do so precisely in the direction of some concept we do not author but only discover (e.g., infinity, circularity). In such signs, what is said about *res* of a divine provenance (namely, their *Herrlichkeit*) applies, but less rigorously.

Quasi-sacramental matter is never the outcome of manufacturing as a mere product; it is also a *res culturae*, a cultural item. It is the result of a culture, but it is also the bearer of culture. It is, one might say, a "cultured thing" in the sense of being necessarily marked by its culture. For an ancient Greek

---

7. The Great Vowel Shift in English, when the sounds associated with certain letters changed, proves this point well.

coin held in the palm of a contemporary hand brings with it some sense of the past, some idea of the people who made it and traded with it. This mark abides and is nearly indelible.

I say that it is nearly indelible because even when encountered in archaeological isolation, such that we do not know what culture produced it or even how ancient it is relative to us, it still strikes us with the force of some culture precisely because it is manufactured. This is imaged well in science fiction literature, such as when the characters land on a new planet expecting to find no signs of life and suddenly come on some evidence of intelligent, non-human life. The characters and the readers instantly feel the great import of this, that they have come in contact with the boundaries of deep and important meaning, even if it should be impossible ever to know more about that culture than this set of ruins or this single artifact can convey. And yet perhaps this cultural mark is not entirely indelible, for some artifacts may become unrecognizable by later societies as manufactured without themselves being totally destroyed. In that case, the cultural content is lost to time.

This mark of culture is analogous to the *mysterium rei*: it is the mark that the creator leaves on its creation. Natural things, as creations and signs of the divine, bring with them a *sensus divinitatis* (sense of divinity), if one pays attention; artificial things, as creations and signs of the culture that produces them, bring with them a *sensus culturae*. It is this that forms the basis of suitability for quasi-sacramental signification. The *mysterium* of the cultural artifact grounds its ability to bear additional meaning within the culture and to be instituted as a privileged place where the culture may be transmitted and the one communing incorporated.

Quasi-sacramental Institution: The Assignation of Meaning

Semiotics is faced with the reality of an ever-increasing array of meanings; indeed, it directly contributes to it. These meanings, which go beyond everyday uses, thereby becoming increasingly specialized and arcane, form a sort of excess that the semiotician is bound by professional duty to interpret. But how can one keep up with the accelerating proliferation? Barthes expresses this by pointing to the fact that every object necessarily signifies; he argues that this produces the aforementioned surplus of meaning, a proliferation that we can do nothing about and, increasingly, can do nothing with.[8]

This is the aporia of the proliferation of meaning that is grounded in our inability to make uses of so much meaning: we find it paralyzing and

8. Barthes, *L'aventure sémiologique*, 252–53.

demoralizing, and ultimately we may come to feel, with Jean Baudrillard, that such unbridled proliferation of meaning destroys the possibility of real meaning:

> Properly speaking there is now no law of value, merely a sort of *epidemic of value*, a sort of general metastasis of value, a haphazard proliferation and dispersal of value. Indeed, we should no longer really speak of "value" at all, for this kind of propagation or chain reaction makes all valuation impossible. Once again we are put in mind of microphysics: it is as impossible to make estimations between beautiful and ugly, true and false, or good and evil, as it is simultaneously to calculate a particle's speed and position. Good is no longer the opposite of evil, nothing can now be plotted on a graph or analyzed in terms of abscissas and ordinates. Just as each particle follows its own trajectory, each value or fragment of value shines for a moment in the heavens of simulation, then disappears into the void along a crooked path that only rarely happens to intersect with other such paths.[9]

This leads Baudrillard to the following conclusion: "The glorious march of modernity has not led to the transformation of all values, as we once dreamed it would, but instead to a dispersal and involution of value whose upshot for us is total confusion—the impossibility of apprehending any determining principle, whether of an aesthetic, sexual, or political kind."[10]

But we find that this is not so, not even in quasi-sacraments; for the light of meaningfulness still breaks through the cacophony of signification. Real illumination is still possible and in fact happens. What then is the meaning of this excess of meaning?

It is in fact the attempt to pack the whole of culture into the sign that is the effector of culture. In the Eucharist, Christ is whole in the whole host and whole in the parts of the host. The excess of meaning present in the quasi-sacramental artifact is the analogue of this. The rule of proliferation indicates that no limit can be placed to how much value the symbol can hold. In the lack of any a priori specifiable limit or any a posteriori limit that is of any sort other than accidental (meaning ceases to proliferate, but because the culture collapses and not because the sign achieved maximal saturation), we have no grounds for denying that the artifact can in fact bear the whole. Indeed, the most saturated of cultural symbols do seem to bear the whole of culture.

Yet they are fundamentally distinct from the eucharistic whole because even if the whole culture is present, it is not *integral*; when one has all of it,

9. Baudrillard, *Transparency of Evil*, 5–6.
10. Baudrillard, *Transparency of Evil*, 10.

one has not yet reached anything final or definite. On the one hand, this is because culture is always in flux, and so there is no determinate whole (the body of Christ is not like this, for it has been raised incorruptible and so has stability). On the other hand, this is because no culture is a unity. Indeed, cultures are not the kinds of things that would turn into unities. They are ad hoc assemblages. They are *ad placitum instituta*, but their connection to the world in which they form is very fluid, precisely because it is the virtuosic (subjective) element that dominates in the creation of culture. They are inherently and fundamentally partial and particular expressions of a truth once glimpsed, of a common memory of objectivity. There is therefore distance, partiality (as opposed to totality), and preference at the heart of every cultural expression of anything, whether true or false. Thus cultures have the ability to hold within themselves deep tensions and even contradictions, because they are not wholes that must reconcile the parts. Rather they are containers that may carry within themselves the seeds of their own destruction (like an explosive device that activates when the disparate elements are mixed).

The desire for the sign to say all things may thus lead to contradiction within the sign, and it is this that causes the proliferation of meaning to become an occasion for despair. Baudrillard is driven to a particularly despondent version of this because he has totally excised the objective element from his vision of reference: "The simulation is never what hides the truth—it is the truth that hides the fact that there is none. The simulacrum is true."[11] But we can avoid this despair by keeping in mind that the culture is not arbitrary: it does not develop *ex nihilo* and is not about nothing.

First, culture is not *ex nihilo* because there is pre-existent material that is used in the production of culture. There are two sorts of material: earlier cultural material and *res*.

Earlier cultural material is essential in the production of cultures, and it is this that underscores the power of the theological claim that humanity is all of one family, the family of Adam. For there is then no culture that does not have in its history the original moment of cultural creation that was Adam's imposition of names on the animals and the world. This may be viewed pessimistically as a total lack of objectivity in the realm of human culture, for culture is always built on cultures in a never-ending cycle of self-referentiality from which we cannot escape to refer to anything outside our inherited experience. It is, as they say, turtles all the way down. But we have already shown how this is not the case. At the bottom one finds not just another turtle but a man, Adam, on whose shoulders all the turtles stand. He is not Christ,

11. Baudrillard, *Simulacra and Simulation*, 1.

and so we may not claim divine authority for our cultures; but at the time he hefted his load, he was the truest human apart from Christ, and that gives us ground to stand on. The earlier cultural material therefore forms a tradition that is not best viewed either with pure skepticism or with total acceptance but that must be appropriated creatively. Appropriation of this sort requires constant return to and reevaluation of the source material.

Cultures stand on *res* because the original deposit, the *ur*-culture Adam created, was about *res*. And it is not the case that Adam's was the only culture to have considered *res*: it is the unending preoccupation of culture to return again and again to the *res* in order to try to make sense of them, to try to see more of them and more aspects of them and, in so doing, to better approach a total articulation of the world. That culture cannot accomplish this does not mean that it does not constantly strive to do so.

Second, culture is not about nothing but tends toward something. In this way it is ad hoc in a positive sense, for this means that it is *ad aliquid* (toward something) as opposed to *ad nihil* (toward nothing). The latter is required for nihilism, which is the absurdity to which Baudrillard's analysis of the self-reductive and self-negating dynamics of proliferation tends. But if the result is not *nihil* but *aliquid*, and even a *hoc aliquid* (a particular something as opposed to a universal or abstract something), then self-negation is not annihilation but is merely emptying. Proliferation may be seen as kenotic rather than nihilistic. The kenotic trajectory of the proliferation of meaning is how cultural signs bow to our demand that they carry more and more of our culture (meaning), which they do for us because they are in obediential potency toward us. This is what quasi-sacramental institution looks like.

Confection: Real Presence and the Quasi-sacramental Elements

Given the dynamics of institution just discussed, it becomes clear that what the sacraments of humanity effect is humanity itself—not, indeed, in the sense that they cause the existence of humanity, just as the Eucharist does not cause the existence of divinity or of the body of Christ. Rather, they cause the presence of humanity.

There are two trajectories in sacramental efficacy: one by which something is revealed (and this grounds remembrance, what might be called a noetic spiritual eating) and one by which something is encountered (and this grounds the conferral of grace, what might be called ontological spiritual eating).

According to the first trajectory, the quasi-sacraments of humanity reveal culture. This revelation of culture is not a bare indication of norms and *mores*; it is instead demonstrative of ways of being in the world. What is revealed is not first and foremost a system of manners and artistic tastes but the soul of the people whose culture it is. This soul is specific (it is distinguished from all other collective souls), and it is present in every member of the culture without being identical with any member of the culture. The individual stands to it in a relationship of participation: he or she imperfectly instantiates the collective soul and receives incomplete and variable amounts of nourishment from it.

According to the second trajectory, we encounter culture as an other that has a claim on us and from which we are not excluded. This is making present because in thus coming face to face with the image of our culture, we are forced also to come face to face with ourselves. I encounter myself in the person of culture and am judged by the extent to which I recognize or fail to recognize myself in it. This is not often individualistic, however, precisely because the culture is not individual and I only imperfectly participate in it. Generally I see in the quasi-sacrament not a mirror of the "I" but a mirror of the "we."

Thus in the quasi-sacraments of humanity we become available to ourselves for encounter and analysis in a meaningful and powerful way. This is why the semiotician is above all a cultural critic. We see this especially well demonstrated in Barthes's essays. A few examples from *The Eiffel Tower and Other Mythologies* will suffice to illustrate the point:

> The Tower, almost immediately disengaged from the scientific considerations which had authorized its birth (it matters very little here that the Tower should be in fact useful), has arisen from a great human dream in which movable and infinite meanings are mingled: it has reconquered the basic uselessness which makes it live in men's imagination.

> Why do we visit the Eiffel Tower? No doubt in order to participate in a dream of which it is (and this is its originality) much more the crystallizer than the true object.

> To visit the Tower, then, is to enter into contact not with a historical Sacred, as is the case for the majority of monuments, but rather with a new nature, that of human space.[12]

This presence is mysterious for several reasons: First because, while it lies open to interpretation, it requires interpretation. The presence offers itself without explicating itself, and so the offer is an offer to enter into its depths, not to reduce it to simple uses. Second, because that into which one is invited

---

12. Barthes, *Eiffel Tower and Other Mythologies*, 7–8.

is transcendent to oneself in a broad sense. What I mean is that while it is not supernatural (and so is not transcendent in the absolute sense), it does lie above the sphere of the individual and so is of non-local provenance with respect to the individual. The difference in modality between concrete individual and concrete universal, as well as the difference between that which is *realis* (*res*-like) and that which is conceptual grounds a certain kind of mystery. Third, because the quasi-sacramental presence is infinite in a qualified sense—namely, in that, while it is not truly either qualitatively or quantitatively infinite, yet no end can be fixed to its current state or to its possible future states. This is an infinity of indeterminateness, which is the least excellent infinity; yet it is sufficient to ground the sense of being adrift in a vast sea, which is characteristic of the encounter with mystery.

Quasi-spiritual Eating: Anamnesis and Incorporation

There is traditionally a question of the way in which one eats the Eucharist, which turns on the efficacy of the moment of eating. In realist views of the Eucharist, such as the one presented here, where it is not only a remembrance but also the communication of something (grace as being), this is not a question of the efficacy of the sacrament as sign; for the sign invariably accomplishes the work for which it was instituted—namely, to make the signified present. Rather, this is the question of whether the now present signified has efficacy for the individual who partakes. In the strongest versions of sacramental realism, it necessarily does: whether for the conferral of grace (in those who receive worthily) or for the conferral of condemnation (in those who receive unworthily). More moderate views could allow the former but not the latter: the one who receives unworthily does not receive grace but also does not receive a special condemnation. As a result, the question of eating is typically divided into sacramental eating (receiving the sacramental elements, whether one receives worthily or unworthily) and spiritual eating (receiving the *res sacramenti*, the signified that has been made present, as grace). All that is required for the former is to eat the sacrament knowing that it is the sacrament or that others think it is. For the latter, proper preparation is required. This may also be applied to quasi-sacraments.

To eat quasi-sacramentally will be to recognize the *res* as sign, to stand in the presence of the depth of meaning and have some sense that one *is* in the presence of depth of meaning. Spiritual eating, as previously hinted at, bifurcates into two modes: noetic spiritual eating and ontological spiritual eating. In the Eucharist, this is analogous to Christ entering the mind (the memorial function of the meal) and Christ strengthening the body and soul (the conferral of grace). Noetic spiritual eating of the quasi-sacrament comes with the analysis of the mystery presented by the quasi-sacrament. It is not just to recognize that one is in the presence of mystery but to enter into the mystery (Barthes provides many good examples). Ontological spiritual eating of the quasi-sacrament involves the transmission or communication of the signified to the communicant, and its effect is incorporation.

But, in this instance, incorporation is enculturation. The quasi-sacrament is productive of culture because it initiates the communicant into the culture, causing him or her to participate more fully than was the case before the quasi-sacramental moment.

> Hence, of all the sites visited by the foreigner or the provincial, the Tower is the first obligatory monument; it is a Gateway, it marks the transition to a knowledge: one must sacrifice to the Tower by a rite of inclusion from which, precisely, the Parisian alone can excuse himself; the Tower is indeed the site which allows one to be incorporated into a race, and when it regards Paris, it is the very essence of the capital it gathers up and proffers to the foreigner who has paid to it his initiational tribute.[13]

The Limits of Quasi-sacraments

That to which the communicant is incorporated in the quasi-sacramental moment is a culture. But acculturation lacks ultimacy precisely because cultures themselves lack ultimacy. Mysterious and powerful as it may be, each culture is but one way of organizing intuitions about the world. They are grounded in the objectivity of the world and in the common *ur*-concepts that have sent humanity down one path rather than another of organizing and understanding the world; but they simultaneously are themselves the concretization of the subjectivity principle as a virtuosic appropriation of this world and these *ur*-concepts.

Thus, by terminating at culture, quasi-sacraments terminate at what is itself but a witness to something else. Because of this, if we treat quasi-sacraments as or as expressive of ultimate meaning, we will fall into a sacramentology of semiotic relativism: to elevate culture and its products to the final place is to sever them from their connection to what properly occupies that final place. And once this has been done, the objective ground of culture has also been severed. Each culture will then appear not as the virtuosic appropriation of that to which each culture offers a common witness, but rather as an arbitrary systematization and organization of the world that has no greater

13. Barthes, *Eiffel Tower and Other Mythologies*, 14.

authority than that many people think this way and no greater claim on my allegiance than that it is a viewpoint that accords well with my aesthetic sense. If I should find this fit from a young age with those around me, it will be my mother culture to which I tender my allegiance; but if I feel myself constantly on the outside, seeing things differently, I will expatriate and find the culture that best lines up with my outlook. But it is no less subjective, for there is nothing to ground my outlook and no way to adjudicate among outlooks. Culture reduces to a perspectivalism whose ethics can never be more than purely external: we value difference and multiculturality not because we can give a positive account of why we should but because it is the only way to stop the killing.

Quasi-sacraments as such therefore fall short of the dynamics of beauty, shipwrecking on opacity and relativism. Beauty may be experienced in such times, but it is problematic; it may be a mere shell, the briefest echo of the magnificence that comes when the subjective is an encounter, not with its own subjectivity, but with an unsubduable objectivity. But more likely it comes as an interruption, an in-breaking that cannot be explained and that will not be explained away. It challenges the hegemony of the subjective, and without disrupting the felt contingency of each culture, it teases with a meaning that might offer a different explanation of that contingency. This is why even in a relativist worldview the irruption of beauty comes as a ray of light and shines a light of hope on all it touches. And yet, it is only when the dimension of transparency is realized that beauty can be encountered unproblematically.

Cross as Crux

There is an instance of institution that is not sacramental but that nevertheless forms a bridge between the imposition of a *res* to signify and the peculiarly sacramental instance of that—namely, when a person is sent on a mission. The one who is sent, who is therefore invested with authority or with a message or task that is not one's own, becomes, as sent, a sign. To be sent is to have one's being made semiotic: now one does not simply arrive as other persons arrive; one's arrival is laden with meaning and purpose. The notion of being sent implies one who sends and a purpose for which one is sent. It is the same with investiture with an office: the office converts one's being into a semiotic space that no longer speaks only (or in some cases, primarily) itself.

Nowhere is this more true than it is of the Johannine Jesus, who was sent from the Father into humanity (both into the mass of humanity as a milieu but also into ontological status as a human). Jesus's human nature is therefore a sign, and it is a natural extension of its status to appropriate it for further signification, as when Christ makes his resurrection the supreme sign that the nations seek (the sign of Jonah, the rebuilding of the temple in three days [Matt. 12:38–41; John 2:18–22]). This human nature is a clear sign, for it is not clouded by sin and is clarified by the unwavering obedience Christ demonstrates. His life maximizes transparency, but also it maximizes opacity, for this man, this particular man, cannot be overlooked or passed over: he forces every gaze to stop on him, as declared in the majestic prologue to John's Gospel (1:1–18).

Christ is preceded by John the Baptist as a sign pointing precisely to the inescapability of the man. John is also a translucent sign, and his goal is to force us to the man Jesus. He identifies him publicly and loudly, and in so doing causes two of his disciples to see that, though they cannot answer Jesus's question "What are you seeking?" (John 1:38), they know that they cannot find it anywhere other than with this man. The invitation to come and see, first offered to John's two disciples by Jesus and then to Nathanael by Philip, is grounded in the open (public, and therefore objective) translucency of the sign ("I have spoken openly to the world. I have always taught in synagogues and in the temple, where all Jews come together. I have said nothing in secret," John 18:20).

The wedding at Cana is called the first sign and causes the disciples to believe. And in the cleansing of the temple that immediately follows, Jesus grounds his authority in his coming resurrection. On and on it goes, from the woman at the well who must learn who she speaks with if she is to receive living water (John 4), to the controversy at Capernaum, where Jesus so relentlessly points the crowd to his humanity that they desert him in disgust (John 6).

But because he was sent purposefully, it is the destiny of that flesh to which Christ always points. The sign of Jonah and the sign of the temple both reference the death, burial, triduum, and resurrection. It is here that things get interesting, for being tortured and dying are integral to the sign that Christ's human nature is. But it is just at the same moment that the divinity of Christ also becomes integral to the sign. For it is only because Christ is divine that he rises from the dead, and he presents this as the ultimate proof of his divinity and authority. This is necessary, for it is primarily as divine that Jesus is sent, because the movement of Incarnation does not begin at conception but before, in the moment when he does not consider equality with God something to be grasped (Phil. 2).

The cross then is the crux of the matter, for here one stands before that which does not seem capable of reminding one of God. It is a powerful sign, but what it signifies is the might of Rome, the nature of Roman justice, and, for the Jews, accursedness (Deut. 21:22–23; Gal. 3:13). But in the death of Christ the cross not only is revealed to be capable of reminding us of God but also becomes the ultimate revelation of God's character and the center of God's work in re-creation. The point of extreme distance from God, where the sign cannot be referred to God without the suspicion of blasphemy, becomes the privileged theologically anamnetic moment. From this eruption of beauty where it was not only least expected but indeed thought to be metaphysically impossible the sacramental signs come flowing, as freely as blood and water from the wounded side of Christ.

Divine Sacraments

Sacramental Elements: Promptness and Natural Suitability[14]

We have already seen that the natural suitability on which the sacraments stand is grounded in the *mysterium rei* as the place where the deepest freedom of the creature and its most profound belonging (its obediential potency) coincide. Creatures are therefore prepared for sacramental signification as their highest possibility in the world—not just to be this particular way of imaging God but to be instituted according to one's particular way of imaging God as a place where very God will become personally and specially present.

This preparation for sacramental uses indicates a readiness and even expectation for the purposes of God on the part of creatures. This is possible without anthropomorphism because what we are describing here is not a submission of the will but a disposition of nature. Just as the seed is disposed to the tree it could (but may not) become, so is each creature disposed to divine uses.

Each creature is aimed at God as its goal, and yet it is important to underscore that this directionality lies beyond the creature's ability: to be capable

14. I will speak in what follows of the water of Baptism and the bread and wine of the Eucharist as creatures whose existence continues alongside the real presence of the divine person in the sacramental moment. This is in accordance with my own sacramental views. However, two important expansions are allowed by my comments here with no significant change to the core of the view presented: On the one hand, one could expand the number of elements that enter into the sacramental moment in accordance with a view of the sacrament in which there are more than two sacraments (whether seven or many more). On the other hand, if one's view of sacramental change in the Eucharist entails that the bread and wine no longer exist, one ought still to be committed to the claim that at least the appearances of bread and wine continue to exist. Whether these appearances are called accidents or something else does not matter; ontologically, they are creatures, and so all that I am saying about bread and wine would still hold for the appearances of bread and wine.

of receiving grace confers no ability to seize grace and does not constitute a promise of the eventual conferral of grace. Additionally, because of the sovereign freedom of grace, this disposition does not predetermine the form that the realization of grace must take. This capacity is indeterminate but determinable, and only determinable by a divine power that has at its disposal options that exceed our ability to imagine or foresee. Thus, even were the obediential potency of a creature exhaustively known by a created intellect (whether human or angelic), it would still not be possible to detail the form that grace would take in the appropriation to divine purposes.

Sacramental Institution: Res *Realized*

When a creature is instituted as a sacramental sign, its inner, divinely focused directionality is delimited: now no longer a mere potency that is patient of many possible actualizations, one of the many possible paths becomes actual, and the creature no longer only potentially presents God in a metaphysically thick way, but now does so in a way that may be discussed and reflected on. This is the meaning of the wordplay in *"res* realized": the *res* becomes most *realis*, *res*-like, in its sacramental institution. It comes to be most fully real but also most fully the particular thing that it is. In being activated for sacramental signification, it becomes actual in a way it has never been to this point and could only be by means of divine grace.

One could object in the following way: Is it not strange that this should be the highest capacity of the creature when so few creatures will ever realize it? Only water, bread, and wine of all the natural kinds attain to this excellence. Does this not seem miserly and therefore contrary to the characteristics of divine grace?

This objection fails to take into account the current state of the world, where we have been ejected from God's presence. The surprise is not that so few creatures attain this excellence but that any do at all. But this response also points to another claim—namely, that this paucity is perhaps not to be expected in the coming state of the world. Eschatologically, we may not unrightly expect the fulfillment of the obediential potencies of all creatures. When the Eucharist expands into the marriage supper of the Lamb, there is no creature excluded from this banquet: we will feast on Christ everywhere in his own proper person, assisted by every rational and non-rational creature.

Furthermore, activation for sacramental signification does not exhaust the obediential potency of the creature. It remains as available for divine purposes as ever it was. This means that its Lord may change its sacramental signification, and it means that additional or deeper signification and use may await it at the eschaton. We should not think that because we have seen water, bread, and wine in baptismal and eucharistic signification that we understand the breadth of their obediential potency, on the one hand, and the fullness of the uses to which God will put them, on the other.

Another objection is important here: I have said that I am speaking of *res naturalis*, but the Eucharist is confected in bread and wine, both of which are *artificialis*, the work of human hands. This reveals the importance of the claim that even *res artificialis* are not *ex nihilo*: our creations, because only analogically creations, are never only ours. The material we make them from ties them back to the Lord of all matter. Thus, bread and wine, though human creations, still have obediential potency to God. God is the Lord not just of wheat and grapes but also of bread and wine.

Real Presence: The Union of God and the Sacramental Creature

The moment of confection then becomes, for the particular sacramental elements (this water, this bread), a moment of intimate union with the divine in which the creature is appropriated to the divine. The creature becomes God's in a way that is distinct from its natural belonging to God: it is now God's in such a way that it participates in God's holiness, and so is called by the name of that very holiness (*sacramentum*).

Importantly, however, this intimacy is not directed primarily at the creature so assumed; rather, it is directed at us. God's general presence to creation, as humanly encountered, is mediated because God is not present to creatures primarily for us but for the creatures themselves. God is not present to the tree for me but because of God's great delight in the tree. I may still encounter God there, but I am an outsider, as it were, coming upon a relationship that is open to me but is only for me in a secondary sense, because it is a public relationship and so is patient of many onlookers. God's sacramental presence is not like this. Christ is made present in the bread *for us*. In such instances, God is immediately present but in a veiled fashion. Christ is not mediated to me by bread, but he is veiled (and the veil is for the purpose of teaching me, gradually leading me to where I need to be). Likewise in the Church: the Church is no mediator any more than the place where two people meet is properly called a mediator (*pace Aristotele*). What is the value of a mediator between husband and wife? Incorporation is not mediation; not everything by means of which something is possible is a mediator—otherwise all necessary conditions would be mediatorial causes, which is absurd.

This means that there is a second humility on the part of the sacramental sign in the confection of the sacrament. Not only is it obedient in humility to the divine purposes; it also humbly submits to our needs and receives the divine presence as for another. Again, the suspicion of anthropomorphism is easily averted, for the humility in question is an abnegation, which at its heart is the ability to point away from oneself. This it does by nature, not by will.

By pointing away from itself in two directions, the sign is reduced to its minimum dimensions (without being effaced), and so facilitates a face-to-face encounter. If we were to stop at the bread in the Eucharist, we would say that God is mediated to us in it; but if we eat spiritually, we never stop at the bread. In this case, the bread brings us face to face with Christ himself. It acts as one who makes an introduction and then steps aside to allow the two parties to talk.

Spiritual Eating: Transformation and Conversion

In this way the sacraments model for us what God would communicate to us through the sacraments: a radical availability for the purposes of God that leads to an intimate union with God that is public in such a way that others may be drawn through it into face-to-face encounter with God. This is the economic dimension of sacramental efficacy (where the effecting of the presence of a divine person could be called the immanent dimension of this efficacy): the sacraments effect the confection of realities similar to themselves—namely, the transformed lives of believers.

The sacraments are therefore fruitful and create things like sacraments (sacramentals) that then bear the burden and privilege of carrying this work out into the world. The bread may leave the altar, but it is bound to the places where the faithful can recognize it, for no spiritual eating happens apart from faithful recognition. But the sacramental life of the believer may go into the dark places of the world where no faithful eyes exist and there, as the instruments of conversion, efficaciously make the divine persons present. Sacramental lives are the ordinary means of the creation of the faithful eyes required for the communicative efficacy of the sacrament itself.

The accent here falls on recognition: the sacrament must be recognized as sacrament for there to be sacramental eating, and the body of Christ must be discerned for there to be spiritual eating. Likewise, the sacramental life must be seen as sacramental (it must be known that the believer is a Christian) if the compelling form of life of the believer is to be recognized as a Christian form of life. And Christ must be seen in that Christian life if conviction unto conversion is to occur.

Sacraments versus Quasi-sacraments

The central difference between quasi-sacraments and sacraments has to do with the objectivity of the *res* involved. When one attends to the quasi-sacramental signs, one runs the risk (the more one devotes oneself to the quasi-sacrament) of losing the objective ground of not just the quasi-sacramental sign but also of the *res quasi-sacramenti*, that to which the quasi-sacramental sign points. But because the reality of even artificial *res* lies in a *mysterium* that is not of human manufacture, all things are most truly what they are in relation to the deeper reality of God. Thus, to lose the objective ground of the *res* is also to lose the intelligibility of the *res*. De-tethered *res* are ever diminishing as we move further and further from the ability to see them for what they truly are, and therefore further and further from the ability first to explicate their meaning, then to see their meaning, and finally to even recognize that they are potentially meaningful. Without objectivity, the abnegation required of *res* in order that they be translucent sacramental signs has no fixed boundary, and so there is nothing to keep this abnegation from becoming annihilation.

When one attends to the sacramental sign, by contrast, one is encountered by the presence of the ground of all objectivity. Objectivity is thus inescapable, and the only remaining interesting question is what one will do about it. To see the sacrament *as sacrament* is already to have granted the objectivity of the sacramental sign and the necessary connection it has to something outside itself that secures its meaning and identity. If I were to fail to see the bread as something that bears the presence of Christ and that therefore antecedently had the possibility of bearing this presence (all of which is necessary if I am to de-tether the bread from objectivity), then I have failed to see the bread as sacrament. This objectivity guarantees the sovereignty of the object (annihilation is repugnant to the sacrament of grace) while at the same time demonstrating that this sovereignty exists for the purpose of giving itself away kenotically in obedience to a deeper sovereignty.

As a result of this difference, intuitions built on a sacramental rather than a quasi-sacramental understanding of creatures will better ground beauty and will better prepare us for the experience of beauty. When we have the objective anchor for referentiality that comes from a sacramental understanding, we are more likely to encounter beauty, precisely because we are more likely to allow the sign to point us to its referent; but we are also better prepared to reflect on and ultimately understand the experiences of beauty that we have.

Sacraments and Beauty

The Dynamics of the Sacrament in Relation to Beauty

Here more clearly than in any of the other cases examined so far we see with clarity the relation between the dynamics of reference and the dynamics of theological anamnesis.

1. The natural suitability of the sacramental element for sacramental signification mirrors the capacity of each creature to remind us of God. Indeed, both the natural suitability for sacramental signification and its capacity to remind us of God are grounded in the same thing—namely, its particular way of imaging God.

Here we have a clue to the intuition that beauty and the sacraments have much to do with each other. That there is a beauty of holiness already pointed in this direction, but our general inability to specify what holiness is hinders our ability to explicate the nature of its beauty. But we can say that the condition of the possibility of the creature as broker of the experience of beauty (and, in fact, of the judgment that the creature is beautiful at all) is also the necessary and sufficient condition for any potential sacramental use to which that creature might be put. Sacraments therefore unfold from the particular beauty of each creature; they are in fact explications of the nature of that particular beauty. To institute a creature for sacramental signification is also to explain to some degree how it is beautiful.

2. Sacramental institution mirrors the original divine intention for creatures to be declarative of divine glory. But sacramental institution and the original intention are of different orders, for one belongs to nature and the other belongs to grace.

Nature: To be this particular image of God is natural to the creature; it is, indeed, constitutive of the creature's being, such that it is not first a being and then an image, as if its existence were somehow logically prior to its image-character. Rather, the nature of its being is as this image. In this way, it is perhaps the case not only that being is not univocal between God and creatures but that it is not simply univocal between creatures.

Additionally, the potency of the creature to be the locus of contuition is also natural in the sense that it is a power that can be realized by another natural power (the rational creaturely intellect). This is similar to sacramental institution/confection in that it realizes a potency of the creature that proceeds from the *mysterium rei*; but it is unlike it in that it is based on the part of the *mysterium* that lies on the surface, that is most accessible and that therefore does not require the authority of the Creator to access. In other words, it is not an obediential potency but potency in the normal sense.

Grace: Sacramental signification, in calling on the creature's obediential potency, delves deeper into the *mysterium rei* and reveals what could not have been uncovered by natural means. Thus, the sacrament accomplishes the work of a more transparent theological anamnesis precisely by going deeper into the mystery that grounds the possibility of theological anamnesis at all. The sacrament, viewed *as sacrament*, is an instance of theological anamnesis, and so every sacramental encounter is an especially intense experience of the beautiful.

3. The intimacy of sacramental union mirrors the ontological participation that each creature has in God whereby it is established in being (*esse*), is established as this sort of thing (*quidditas*), and is established as this particular thing (*haecceitas*). The divine intention and action at each level is important: God is no less concerned with individuals than with universals or vice versa (this notwithstanding the difference in the ontological status of things).

The creature's natural being is related to God by participation in such a way that it only *is* (and not merely is only *said* to be) by means of an act of participation in the divine being. This participation is explicable as an image of God that is not merely a dead image—that is, an image cut off from its source, as a photograph is from that of which it is a photograph (no abiding connection remains). Rather, a participation is a live image, one that remains connected to its source, bound to it in fact, such that it is judged by this ongoing relation. This is the highest union naturally possible for a creature, and non-rational creation possesses it merely (that is to say, they possess it automatically and on no further conditions precisely because it is the only state possible for them). Rational creatures may fall away from possession of it to varying degrees and cannot be restored without grace. But sacramental union exists as non-rational creation's highest possibility by grace, just as the human nature reformed by grace is the highest human possibility. In both cases grace is required, but in both cases the conditions required to receive this grace are natural.

In the sacraments this intimate union allows the communication of grace by the self-giving of divine persons; in the experience of beauty, this union allows the anamnesis that is constitutive of that experience.

4. Sacramental eating is mirrored in the experience of the beautiful as implicit contuition; spiritual eating is mirrored in this experience as explicit contuition.

Just as the sacrament, to be eaten sacramentally, requires at least the understanding that one is before what is supposed to be the sacrament (even if one does not believe in sacraments), so the experience of the beautiful requires at least an implicit contuition. The one who has no sense of God whatsoever in that moment no more experiences beauty than one who comes upon a cup of wine and drinks from it while being completely ignorant that it has been consecrated drinks sacramentally.

Consider a person who is in Mass and knows that the sacrament has been confected and understands to some extent what this means, and yet does not have faith and so believes that nothing has happened, not only because this person does not believe in sacramental confection but also because this person does not believe that there is a God who could confect or be represented sacramentally. If this person were to approach and consume, this person would not, on account of his or her unbelief, fail to consume sacramentally. This person would therefore also not be guiltless of the body and blood, for each person is culpable for his or her own blindness. Lack of belief blocks spiritual eating, not sacramental eating. Likewise, it does not matter whether the one experiencing beauty explicitly denies that it is a contuition, for that is not enough to make it true that it is not in fact a contuition. It is only enough to block the spiritual and intellectual benefits of explicit contuition.

Spiritual eating strengthens the soul in grace and may additionally confer spiritual gifts and insight. It transforms the communicant more into the image of Christ and causes Christ in the believer in such a way that the believer can become, as it were, a participation in the sacrament that can go where the sacrament cannot. Explicit contuition has a similar effect, causing the transformation of the individual, making her or him more like the beautiful. And this beautiful is not the nebulous aesthetic ideal of beauty; therefore the one who sees it truly does not become an aesthete. Rather, the beauty glimpsed is either God or an imitation of God, and in either case it is therefore God to whom the perceiver is assimilated. When contuition becomes explicit, beauty becomes a means of sanctification.

Suffering, Darkness, Pain, and Beauty

Our discussion of the semiotic character of mission and the cruciform trajectory of the humanity of Jesus provides the occasion for a few more words here on the ramifications for the beauty of the God-man on the cross.

The cross is beautiful, and this is deepest scandal. Indeed, so deep is the scandal that many have backed away from the claim that the cross is beautiful, fearful of what it might mean for the victims of oppression and torture through the ages and around the world. But we cannot retreat from this claim, for to deny the beauty of the cross is to deny that it has a theologically anamnetic dimension. This is as much as to deny that the cross can be a place of the revelation of God. In this way, what would seem pious (the desire to protect the vulnerable by refusing to valorize suffering) becomes in fact the enemy of divine revelation; for God does not will to become known in a definitively salvific way apart from the cross.

It is further absolutely vital that we not retreat from the cross, for the cross combines with the resurrection to respond to our deepest longing: the hope that in a way that lies beyond what we are able to imagine for ourselves, our deepest suffering can be turned into rejoicing. If the cross is not beautiful, then God cannot make the suffering of the innocent right, and that is no message of hope.

But if we are to embrace the scandal, how are we to articulate the beauty of the cross without calling the ugly beautiful? How are we to honor the economy of grace without descending into blasphemy? Precisely by identifying what is divine about Jesus on the cross, for it is here that anamnesis is grounded. Note what is ruled out: mere pain, mere suffering, mere torture. These are not divine. One need not be divine to undergo them, and they have no power of themselves for the conferral of grace. Jesus's suffering, considered as suffering, is not beautiful. What *is* beautiful are the divine properties that are revealed through his suffering and pain: humility, self-giving, love.

The humility of Christ is the fulfillment of the trait to which all creaturely obediential potency points: it is a self-effacement in order to make maximum space for the purposes of God within one's own life. It is best expressed in the kenotic hymn of Philippians 2. For no greater clearing of space for God within a life exists than the attitude that considers even death a possibility of this clearing: nothing has been withheld in advance or in principle. Here there is surrender without qualification. And this is divine: it is a confidence in self that does not need to hold on to any of what the self has in order to be the self. To be all that exists, to be free of obligations under any number of covenants, to be unbound in love to anyone and therefore to not have to face the possibility of betrayal and death—these were not things God felt were to be grasped, as the entire history of the divine economy shows.

Self-giving is related but distinct. For just as the sacramental element humbles itself before God in obediential potency but also deigns to recede in order that God may be present for us humans, so in Christ there is the kenotic gift of self that is not just making space for the purposes of God but also stepping aside for the good of another, to bring another to face-to-face encounter with God. This too is divine and is grounded in the mysterious life of the Trinity.

These two actions are not love but the results of love. Beyond the willingness to do all for God and neighbor lies the reason for such willingness, a passion for the other so intense that the other replaces the self as the focal point. Christ's humility and kenosis are the signs of love (the first of love to

God, the second of love to both God and creatures), and we cannot become aware of them without also becoming aware of that love to which they point.

This may avoid blasphemy, but it does not indicate what is particularly salient about the revelation of these divine characteristics *from the cross*. How do they shine forth in a particular way in this most horrific of modes? Precisely in accordance with the principle that God's strength is made perfect in weakness (2 Cor. 12:9): the cross shows that the humility and kenosis of God are more powerful than human might. It reveals that our understanding of power is weak, backward, and diseased. As a result, our understanding of the mighty God (God's power is one of the things that Romans 1 says we are responsible for knowing apart from revelation) is weak, backward, and diseased. The cross, in remediating our understanding of what real power is, also corrects an impulse to blasphemy empowered by our false notions of power.

In this way, the cross is not just beautiful, and it is not just (as the fount of sacramental grace) the irruption of beauty into the world; it is also what rehabilitates our notions and knocks the scales from our eyes so that we can see beauty clearly again. In the cross we are brought to the place of absolute darkness in order that we might see how dim the light within us has become. Indeed, our eyes have become so unaccustomed to light that we must be brought to a place where it seems that there is no light at all. There *is* light there; but the lamp has been turned so low that it could be thought to be extinguished. But this little light is the most that we could handle, and it is enough to begin to restore our ability to see. And as we gaze at it ever more intently, it grows brighter until we see that within it is all the light that ever was. Only then, once the little spark of the crucified God has grown to fill our vision, do we become the people walking in darkness who have seen a great light.[15] And so are we brought to the cross that we may be dazzled by the brilliance that shines from there and have our eyes strengthened so that in God's light we may see light.

15. Isa. 9:2; Matt. 4:10; Luke 1:79; Eph. 5:8; 1 Pet. 2:9.

8

Radiant *Res*

Icons and Ecstasy

The uncircumscribed Word of the Father became circumscribed, taking flesh from thee, O Theotokos, and He has restored the sullied image to its ancient glory, filling it with the divine beauty. This our salvation we confess in deed and word, and we depict it in the holy ikons.

Kontakion of the Triumph of Orthodoxy, *The Lenten Triodion*

The icon is an image not only of a living but also of a deified prototype. It does not represent the corruptible flesh, destined for decomposition, but transfigured flesh, illuminated by grace, the flesh of the world to come.

Leonid Ouspensky, *Theology of the Icon*

The Nature of Icons

The final moment of reference we will consider is the case of icons. The use of icons in worship has been contentious through the ages, and even the vindication of their use has, in the West, been continually dogged by those who remain unconvinced that they may be safely or usefully employed. Where they have been used, their distinct way of referencing has often been confused with sacramental forms of signification such that icons seem to be just another type of sacrament.

Icons are important because they reference glorified *res* more properly than the sacraments do, and they have a trans-locational function that grounds powerful moments of spiritual experience. The theotic directionality of icons makes this a fitting place to conclude this study.

Since icons do have an entirely different way of signifying and effecting than sacraments, it will be beneficial to start by distinguishing them from one another.

Distinguishing Icons from Sacraments

It is possible to confuse the logic of sacraments with the logic of icons because both are instances of efficacious referentiality. This is true in spite of the fact that it is generally unlikely that a concrete sacrament be confused with a concrete icon. A comparison of the marks of a sacrament to icons will be instructive.

1. Both sacraments and icons are creaturely signs.

2. Sacraments have a natural suitability for signifying the *res* they are instituted to signify. Icons, however, follow not natural signification but *ad placitum* institution: the visual language of iconology is traditional rather than natural.

3. Both sacraments and icons are efficacious signs—that is to say, they effect what they signify. However, they do so in different ways. The sacrament effects the local presence of the signified *res* (a divine person); an icon does not do this but instead causes the worshipper who gazes upon it to be ecstatically transported to the milieu of the signified *res*. Put differently, the sacrament brings divine things down to us; the icon sends us up in a proleptic and partial fashion to divine things.

4. Both are signs that refer to transcendent, not immanent, realities. The sacrament refers to this grace in a pilgrim sense, however. The grace signified in Baptism, for example, is only ever inchoate: it begins the life of faith, and its fullness still lies ahead. It is the Holy Spirit as comforter and companion through the Vale of Tears that is referenced. Likewise, the Eucharist refers to the glorified Christ, both his eternally glorified divinity and his human nature, now glorified and incorruptibly present in Heaven. But it refers to Christ as *viaticum*, the food that strengthens us lest the journey be too much for us (1 Kings 19:4–8). As such, like Baptism, it references a glorious reality but under the mode of pilgrimage. The icon, by contrast, references glorious

realities as they are *in patria* (in the homeland). It is pointed at the glorified state of things, with the pilgrimage of this life accomplished.[1]

5. The question of institution is a complicated one.

The sacrament stands upon a moment of divine institution. But what is instituted is not any particular instance of the sacrament, but the sacrament as a repeatable rite that will be celebrated throughout the life of the Church: Baptism will be done only once for each believer, but each believer will experience it many times as new members are added to the fold and will return anamnetically to the moment of his or her Baptism on such occasions and at regular intervals. The Eucharist may be done as often as desired, so long as reverence is preserved ("Do this, as often as you drink it, in remembrance of me," 1 Cor. 11:25). The institution of the sacraments is therefore the establishment of an ordinance.

The icon lacks such a moment of institution. The relationship between the general and the particular is likewise less clear. The best iconological analogue for the institution of the sacrament is the establishment of the visual language used in their creation. This language is what fills the role of ordinance. These ordinances are traditionally of apostolic, not divine, origin (Luke is often considered to have made the first icon). As such, while they partake of the highest ecclesial authority (icons were first made by one who also wrote scriptural books), they nevertheless derive from human institution.

While the ordinances governing the creation of icons tend to fossilize (that is to say, icons depicting the same theme tend to be done the same way across all iterations), the relativity of the normative nature of icon writing is revealed by the existence of cultural and geographical differences. As Leonid Ouspensky notes,

> Saint Paul did not imitate Christ by copying His gestures and His words, but by integrating himself into His life, by letting Him live in him. Similarly, to paint icons as they were painted by the ancient iconographers does not mean to copy ancient forms, since each historical period has its own forms. It means to follow the sacred Tradition, to live in the Tradition. But the power of Tradition is the power of the Holy Spirit and of continuity in the spiritual experience of the Church, the power of communion with the spiritual life of all the preceding generations back to the times of the apostles. In Tradition, our experience and understanding are the experience and understanding of the Apostle Paul,

---

1. This is true even when the icon depicts some historical event, such as the Lord's wrath against Sodom and Gomorrah. The icon does not merely or primarily commemorate the historical event but rather, by use of the distinctive visual language of iconography, sets before the worshipper the eternal meaning of such historical events.

of the holy iconographers and of the entire Church: We no longer live separately, individually, but in the body of Christ, in the same total body as all our brothers in Christ. This is in fact the case in all areas of spiritual life, but it is particularly true in that of sacred art. The contemporary iconographer must rediscover the internal outlook of the iconographers of old and be guided by the same living inspiration. He will then find true faithfulness to Tradition, which is not repetition but a new, contemporary revelation of the internal life of the Church. Indeed, an Orthodox iconographer faithful to the Tradition always speaks the language of his time, expressing himself in his own manner, following his own way.[2]

Iconographical language tends to become fixed according to traditional norms, but it need not be: as long as the icon remains readable, it will be able to perform its function, and so room for virtuosity remains.

6. The sacrament grounds an immediate action of grace; for besides the creatures that form the occasion for the presence of Christ (bread, wine), Christ is really present, and so I encounter Christ directly in the sacrament. Indeed, when "sacrament" is taken in its broader sense as referring to the entire mystery on the altar and not just to the part of it that is the sign (its original meaning)—that is to say, as inclusive not just of the *sacramentum* but also of the *res sacramenti*—it is simply true that the sacramental sign has become what it signifies, even while remaining what it is (bread or the appearance of bread). And this is what is most desired in the sacrament (or rather why the sacrament is so desired)—that one be immediately in the presence of the risen Lord in a special way. One may speak of the participation of the sacramental sign in the reality of the sacrament, but this is in fact too weak: it has moved beyond participation into union. Sacramental union is a lesser union than hypostatic union, but it is not immediately clear that sacramental union is not the strongest union after hypostatic union.

Icons, by contrast, are only mediatory: they do not become what they signify. There is no ontological transformation of or within the icon at the time of blessing, and the signified reality does not come to be really present where the icon is. The icon forms a bridge along which the mind may walk. Here one speaks properly of participation. The holiness of the icon is a participation in the holiness of that which is represented. Veneration of the icon is possible only because honor given to the image is transferred to the exemplar.[3]

2. Ouspensky, *Theology of the Icon*, 14.

3. This is an idea that has become hard for the modern West to accept but that is ubiquitous in other societies. We still have some understanding of this fundamental law of reference, as for example when the burning of a national flag is taken to be an attack on the country itself.

The icon is made by one who, for all of the aesthetic qualities the icon possesses, should not be called an artist (at least, not as iconographer). This is not because icons convey a type of meaning that art cannot convey, for that is simply false. Visual art has its visual rules, often as complex as iconography (and certainly not able to be said a priori to be unable to be as complex or more complex), and the way this visual language is used to convey meaning is the same. Indeed, in this sense, the visual language of icons is a species of visual language in general and not a fundamentally different type of thing. Rather, the icon has a different purpose than art, and this is why it is distinct. Art aims to convey meaning, but the icon aims to convey *minds*. It is not fundamentally trying to communicate meaning from the maker to the audience but trying to communicate the audience from itself to the realities depicted.

The icon is composed of common materials, but those materials are sanctified by the prayerful attention of the maker throughout the process of making, culminating in the icon's sojourn upon the altar, a spiritual retreat lasting up to forty days. This sojourn is crucial: it is not the blessing of the finished icon; it is the *finishing* of the icon, though this is true in the realm of signification and not in the realm of ontology. For an icon that has not so sojourned is just as able to accomplish its task, especially if the worshipper is unaware that the icon has not been properly blessed. But the blessing clarifies that the icon belongs among the holy things, that it is a *sacrum* even if it is not a *sacramentum*, and this often aids in its ability to do what it is made to do. This is analogous to the fact that one need not have thought about the natural suitability of water for Baptism in order to receive the baptismal benefit, but reflection on that suitability deepens one's understanding, and potentially awareness, of that benefit.

The key element in icons is the fact that they are ana-logical: they begin below and reach upward toward the divine. Sacraments, by contrast, are kata-logical: they begin with divine condescension that reaches down to us. Icons, therefore, are a human reality that are a response to what we see God doing in the sacraments. God institutes a rite whereby God will come alongside and within us; we in our turn establish an economy of images whereby we will reach up to God. The sacrament begins from human action, for it is we who decide to gather, and our gathering and celebrating the rite becomes the occasion for the divine power to give sacramental grace. Likewise, the icon's deepest power, the power to transport in ecstasy, is in fact an obediential potency: only God can activate it. As ordinary means, the icon reliably works on those who approach it reverently; but as means *of grace* the icon only does this by divine power working through it, and its existence places no claim on the divine power. Like the sacrament, the dependability of the grace received lies not on the part of a creaturely element compelling divine power but on the self-binding commitment of God to work in such ways.

Icons and Thick Signification

OTHERNESS

Though the artistic style of icons owes much to the style of painting at the time Christians first began to beautify their worship spaces (then catacombs outside the city), the continued use of this style despite the fact that it has passed out of secular use and been replaced many times over by different ways of representation gives the icon something the early Christian drawings did not have: otherness.

This otherness may be a barrier to one coming to icons for the first time: they are too strange, too impenetrable. It becomes possible to take offense at the surface and so to stop there and never go on to the depths. The icon is a bad painting, it is thought, so there is no need to deal with its subject matter. This is of course to miss the entire point, for an icon is a sign, and, as we have said repeatedly, to stop at the sign without considering the signified is to not really see the sign properly. This is even more true when the sign was created *to be a sign*, as icons are. Every choice is made with the signification of the icon in mind; to ignore that signification will understandably render those choices arbitrary or inscrutable. The danger of misreading an icon is not primarily the danger of reading it incorrectly (that is, interpreting the symbolism incorrectly), for the icon's language has this trick to it, that the one who does not know it simply does not know how to interpret the symbols, rather than that such a one tends to get the interpretation wrong: we are more likely to be baffled by the icon than to misinterpret it. Rather, the danger of misreading an icon is in failing to see it *as an icon*, seeing it instead as merely a piece of art.

The offense one may take at the otherness of icons has a paradoxical outcome. For the reason for the otherness (the removal of dimension and emotion, the often exaggerated angularity of the figures) is to increase the transparency of the signification: the idea is to make it difficult for us to imagine that we are seeing an image of everyday life or that the things depicted are simply ordinary. But when offense is taken, the opacity increases instead: one fails to note the things depicted, stopping instead at the foreignness of the style.

The icon has to be willing to run this risk in order to do its work, however. Even if the world we live in is flooded with sacred meaning (and it is an implication of my arguments here that it is), we do not penetrate to this meaning most of the time, and so the character of our daily experience is not sacral.

Thus, if the icon is to be true to its subject matter, it must present itself in such a way that it may somehow disrupt our sense of familiarity in order to shift our gaze to something unwonted.[4]

Thus the icon, like the sacrament, must be approached in a certain way if one is to derive any benefit from it. When one looks on an icon and recognizes it as important to others (that is, as a part of religious practice) without understanding the dynamics of reference that ground its existence, something analogous to sacramental eating happens. It is this type of vision of the icon that can lead to the claim that the icon is just an idol: for if the image is severed from its referent, it becomes the object in itself. But if the image, as final object, is part of an economy of worship, then the image is simply being worshiped, and this is against very primal commands of God.

We might call "spiritual vision" that which is analogous to spiritual eating in the Eucharist. This means not just to see the icon as religiously important but also to penetrate to the *res iconis*, which is the spiritual reality referenced by the icon. The *res iconis* is a spiritual reality, even if the subject of the icon is a saint, because the saint referenced by the icon is referenced *as holy*, as a citizen of God's heavenly kingdom and therefore a participant in that heavenly power. Ultimately, then, what is referenced is God's grace but as modulated and particularized by its presence in the life of an individual.

The otherness of the icon is the representation of a world other than ours: the heavenly realm. The world represented in the icon is the divine world, which, it will be recalled, is not the world God inhabits as God's proper and eternal dwelling (there is no such place) but rather the world immediately conditioned by God's overt presence: Heaven.

Heaven is, as previously discussed,[5] the creature created to be the place of greatest intimacy between creatures and God. Heaven is divine in the sense that it is characterized by the qualities of God. Though we cannot specify what this means, we may say that it differs from our world in several ways.

First, God pours out divine grace without measure in Heaven. This is not so here: in this world, under sin and in the time of testing, the divine grace, though lavish beyond our wildest hopes, is qualified. It is for this reason that

> eye has not seen, nor ear heard,
> nor have entered into the heart of man
> the things which God has prepared for those who love Him.
> (1 Cor. 2:9 NKJV)

---

4. "Angels are bright still, though the brightest fell. Though all things foul would wear the brows of grace, yet grace must still look so." Shakespeare, *Macbeth*, IV.3.23–24.

5. Chapter 1, p. 22.

Second, in Heaven, the creature offers no impediment to divine influence. There is no sin or falling short to make the creature less capable of receiving grace. Thus every place in Heaven is as full as it can be of the grace of God.

Third, nothing impedes the intended communication of this grace. Again, lacking sin or any shortcoming, the creature is as capable of communicating grace as it was made to be. So every place in Heaven is not only as full of God as it can be; it also communicates this fullness to the maximal extent possible for it according to its created possibilities.

Finally, this grace does not lie hidden as it often does in this world; it is open for all to see and receive. Heaven is the place where God is met face to face, for it is for this purpose that it was created.

The icon thus represents different types of subjects, each of which is appropriate to Heaven either as one of its denizens or as one who delights to be present there and made clearly known there or as an event that typologically reveals truths about Heaven or its lord. The angels and saints form the first group: as denizens of Heaven, they are made heavenly (divine) by themselves also expressing the aforementioned divine qualities of Heaven. The divine persons form the second group. Events like the destruction of Sodom and Gomorrah and moments from the earthly life of Christ form the third.

The icon's relation to this other world that it represents is complicated. In an important sense, the icon belongs to Heaven. It has one purpose: to represent the heavenly world in an efficacious way. The meaning of the icon is therefore to be found not in the icon itself but outside of itself in the world it represents. And it may be rightly said that an object belongs to the world where the locus of its meaning is, because it is only in light of that world that it can be correctly explicated.

Additionally, a thing may be said to belong to another thing if it is bound to it. The icon is bound to the heavenly realm because it is constrained by it. This is the reason for the many rules governing the language of iconography. Even though the rules could be different, there is a necessity that there be rules, and there is this fundamental rule governing the types of practices that could be used: they must serve the purpose, in the society for which the icon is destined, of inviting the viewer into a contemplation of a world other than the one the viewer inhabits.

Heaven is also what the icon is pointed at. The icon is thus bound to it just like a telescope pointed at a planet is bound to a certain series of orientations if it is to keep that planet in view.

Beyond all this, there is a deeper and harder to explain sense in which the icon belongs to the heavenly realm: it participates in it. It takes on some of the character of what it belongs to (in representing holy things, it *is* holy).

Thus, it is not just a mere pointer to something other, but it becomes itself something other. It is like a little piece of that reality abiding in our own. And yet it is only *like*: it is not actually a part of that reality; it only participates in it. It is important to keep in mind that in another sense, one that is much more readily apparent to the eye, the icon does not belong to Heaven. For it does not belong to Heaven in the sense that it is from there (as if it were hurled here in some primal moment) or properly fits there; it is instead an object of this world that is attached to that world in its creation in such a way that it is on the way to that world. But it can never truly arrive at its destination, for the icons will not make the transition with us to the new earth.

It sits not between the two worlds as external to each but at their juncture. It belongs and does not belong to each world but in different senses, such that it is not caught between the two but properly partakes of each and so is able to mediate. But this mediation is one directional: it is a gateway left here to send us there; it does not, like the sacrament, bring the heavenly realities to us here. The being of the icon is therefore ecstatic: it is situated here, and yet its heart (its meaning) is elsewhere. Its inside is outside of it-self and outside of the world to which it belongs, and it can only be rightly understood when it is seen in its multidimensionality. But as means, the icon is unevenly situated: it belongs much more to this world than to the other world, and its *ekstasis* is of a much paler sort than the one that awaits the one who worships through it.

Depth

The icon is therefore a more totally committed sign than the word, the concept, a simple *res*, or even, in some sense, the sacrament. For in each of them, something is sign and something is not: a part of the reality is reserved for being—that is to say, they do not exist *only* to refer, even if their being is grounded in this referral.

In the case of a word, it is only as a whole that the word has any meaning. The individual phonemes do not reference parts of what the whole word signifies; they only constitute the one reality that as a whole signifies the meaning. In some sense this does not hold for compound words, but it does hold for the words that make up the compounds. Even in monosyllabic words like "cake," the *c* does not reference any part of the confection; it is only as on the way to spelling the word "cake" that it has any discernible relation to the confection.

A concept imposed to signify another concept is not entirely at the service of the signification, for metaphors are founded on analogy, and so there is also dissimilarity. Not all of concept *A* is imposed to signify concept *B*, but only part of it. One could argue that in the case of allegory this fails, for here there is one-to-one correspondence. But the point is not to be granted. For even in a narrative in which the cabin is not a real cabin at all but only stands as a sign for something else, nevertheless a cabin is not inherently a sign for whatever it is imposed to stand for in the allegory. It has its own meaning and being that abide even when they are pushed out of the narrative by strict allegory (and so it matters that a cabin and not a skyscraper was chosen for this representation).

The same will hold true for a *res*, which, as *res*, is only naturally a sign for God. When the *res* is imposed to signify a concept, it cannot be entirely assumed to this purpose with every part of its being because it has its own *mysterium rei* that does not bow to the human will.

But in the case of the sacrament, it does bow, though not to us, for it is now being imposed by God and not by a creature. And the imposition is based on the *mysterium rei*. What remains on the altar after consecration (bread or the appearance of bread) is entirely given over to God, such that the eating of it becomes an act with moral implications in a way that is not true of other instances of eating bread. And yet it remains possible to consume the bread non-sacramentally: if I come upon it in the sacristy and am completely ignorant of Christianity and the claims of the Church and if I consume it thinking it nothing other than bread, I have eaten neither spiritually nor sacramentally. This indicates that what is placed entirely at the service of God is still not entirely given over in every respect: its surrender is kenosis, not annihilation. Indeed, if the sacrament can revert to being bread, as some theologians have allowed, this is even more deeply affirmed.

The icon, by contrast, belongs entirely to the signification because it exists only for this purpose, and every part of it and every aspect of its creation has been subsumed to this purpose. This creates the kind of complex of signification that metaphors tend to grow into. But the fact that the meanings are intended from the beginning and written into the creation process enables them to interact with one another in ways that also come under the creativity and virtuosity of the maker (unlike metaphors, which grow to complexity apart from the guiding hand of the original author). Thus, the complex formed is of a different sort or has a different structure.

The icon has what I would call "thick signification," which is signification in which every part not only is meaningfully on the way to the whole but also contributes its own particular meaning above the meaning of the whole. This adds a dimension of depth to the icon that contributes to its ability to draw the viewer in.

The Efficacy of the Icon

The *res iconis* is not transmitted to the one viewing the icon. I do not receive numerically the same grace that the Virgin Mary received even if I worship properly before an icon of her. Or, if grace is but the gift of God's self as the Holy Spirit, while the *res* is numerically identical, I do not receive the same instance of the communication of that grace (just as the presence of the Holy Spirit in me is not the presence of the Holy Spirit in you, even though it is one and the same Spirit).

Likewise, even when contemplating the Holy Spirit's image in an icon, if I receive spiritual grace, I do not receive what is referenced by the icon *as it is referenced*; for while I receive the Holy Spirit (or have the presence or power of the Spirit increased in me), the Spirit is referenced in the icon not as indwelling me but as the Spirit is in trinitarian eternity or as the Spirit comes in Pentecost or in whatever other way the Spirit may be the subject of icons.

This may seem like splitting hairs, but there is an important principle at work here: I am never the subject of an icon. As such, when I come to the icon, I do not find myself already in it; rather, I must be read into it. The icon, as a depiction of another world, presents a reality from which I am necessarily lacking: for the icon presents that world, and it belongs to it in the sense that it is held to it and bound by it. But it is not in that other world; it is in this one, and this is the place where the icon is properly viewable. Thus, to be looking on the icon at all, I am not yet transferred to that other world but still on my journey there.

And yet the icon is pointed at this other world, belongs to it, and is in some important sense on its way to it. Thus, as I stop to gaze upon the icon, something important happens. Whenever we gaze upon a work of art, we are drawn into the world of the piece. This is not physical, but it is literal: in contemplation I enter the world of the piece, sometimes so deeply that I am minimally or not at all aware of the physical world around me. Indeed, this is common to all the arts: music, drama, and literature all have the ability to take me out of my world and relocate me to another one. This contemplative crossing of worlds is no less real for not being a physical relocation of my body, and this is what grounds its ability to be so life changing. In appreciating art, I am at risk, and I am much more the object than the subject. This is the point of the powerful conclusion to Rilke's "Archaic Torso of Apollo": "For here there is no place / that does not see you. You must change your life."[6]

This same dynamic of drawing the onlooker into another world is active in the icon. It is in fact greater because of the thick signification of the icon. The

6. Rilke, "Archaic Torso of Apollo," in *Selected Poems*, 81–83.

operative difference is that the world the icon draws me to is not an artistic world, and it is not the world of the icon in the same sense in which we might speak of the world of a Beethoven symphony. It differs from these in that it is not a world created by the piece of art, it is not a world created by human ingenuity, and it is not a fictional world or the real world viewed from a human perspective in such a way that one may speak of it as distinct from the world we live in. It is instead the divine world: Heaven, as previously described.

Thus, by drawing me into it in the same way that other art does, the icon is simultaneously sending me, launching me away from itself in the direction that it itself is tending. It is able to do this because in its inception it eschewed the possession of a proper world (a world that would belong to it in a unique and special way) in order instead to belong to another and greater world. The ecstatic being of the icon means that its inside is outside of itself, and so in one effortless motion it may invite me into its depths and point past itself at something greater.

This is the purest form of the kenotic referentiality that we have been developing, surpassing even the transparency of the sacrament. This is in part because the sacrament aims not at the highest signification but at the communication of divine things to us. The icon by contrast aims at the highest signification as a means of drawing us to contemplation of the divine things. It is crucial that in achieving maximal transparency the icon has not sacrificed translucence; it does this not by hiding itself or redirecting the gaze away from itself but by joining the truth of its existence with what it must communicate. For the icon, the *mysterium rei* and the *res iconis* coincide without collapsing into one another: the union of the icon's inner mystery and the reality it points to enables one to see that reality with the greatest clarity *by* seeing the icon rather than *in spite of* or *apart from* seeing the icon.

The icon's ecstatic being thus grounds an efficacy whereby I am caught up (raptured) into the same ecstasy that is the proper space of the icon. The icon communicates divine grace to me by offering proleptic entry into that world in which God's grace is maximally communicated to the denizens and maximally communicable by them. Thus, properly speaking, the icon does not communicate grace; rather, it transports the worshipper to a place where the worshipper is in touch with those who can communicate grace. And these persons are the saints and angels as well as the divine persons because it is God's will to give grace to us both mediately and immediately.

There is therefore an assimilation (divinization, in the sense in which the denizens of Heaven are deified; or better, deiformity) of my being into the reality represented, which is my reconnection to the truest form of my being. As a result, I come to look like the icon in that my *mysterium* and the reality of which I am a sign (*res rei*) are united in such a way that they coincide, just as is the case with the icon. And so, just as the sacrament is fruitful in that it causes the existence of a living sacrament (the graced believer), so the icon is fruitful in that it facilitates the existence of a living icon (again the graced believer).

This transformation is, however, partial and proleptic, precisely because I only belong to the heavenly realm as the icon belongs to it. Through the grace of Baptism I have been called to discipleship ("Go therefore and make disciples of all nations, baptizing them . . ." Matt. 28:19). Thus, like the icon, my purpose becomes to represent the heavenly reality in an efficacious way. My meaning is now found outside myself, as the icon's is. I have also become bound to the heavenly kingdom: I am constrained to be in such a way that the one who looks on me is invited into the contemplation of a world other than the one they inhabit, and I have been ordered to that new reality by having the intention of my life restored to its originally intended location. The divine realm is now where my being is pointed. I also participate in this heavenly reality in that deeper sense in which the icon does: I take on some of the character of that to which I belong, such that Scripture can call even the living holy (e.g., Ps. 116:5; Paul in the salutations of his letters). Like the icon, I am not just a pointer to something other; I have become myself something other: I am the living presence of the heavenly realm in our own ("You are the light of the world," Matt. 5:14).

And yet I am imperfectly assimilated to the heavenly city: I belong to the Church in truth. And yet I am more like a catechumen in some sense: I may have received Baptism and true justifying grace, but I have not yet received the white robe promised to those who overcome (Rev. 3:5); the work of grace has not yet run its course. I remain on the way to the heavenly kingdom, but it is a pilgrim path, and I must stay the course. Thus I belong to Heaven in the same senses in which the icon does, and with similar caveats.

And so, unlike the saints in Heaven, my ability to receive divine grace is limited, and I cannot receive all that my nature, were it not damaged, would be capable of. Until I definitively enter into the world depicted by the icon, my transformation is partial and, in the cases of particularly intense or powerful experiences while worshiping through the icon, temporary. The mystic returns from ecstasy to a world that seems dull in comparison. And yet these glimpses are powerful to inspire, transform, and comfort me as I grow into the reality represented. The taste awakens longing, and that longing drives me forward along the path of sanctification in spite of resistance from this world. The result of the icon's efficacy is that I, like the icon, come to possess an ecstatic being.

Icons and Beauty

Beauty and Thick Signification

OTHERNESS

We said earlier that icons are particularly susceptible not to misinterpretation but rather to misidentification: one fails to see the icon as an icon, and this failure renders the choices made in the making of the icon (perspective, color, the way the figures are rendered) inscrutable. The one who sees in this way sees the icon but fails to see it as icon—that is, as the particular kind of sign that it is. But it has no purpose other than to be a sign of this sort. Thus, an icon seen in this way is seen as superfluous and distracting at best, threatening and idolatrous at worst. But it must always be kept in mind that this position begins from failing to see the icon for what it most essentially is; it has been redefined. No longer a sign of divine *res*, it is simply art whose purpose is ultimately pointed at creaturely realities and references not the Creator but the artist and his or her religious community. They become expressions of human need rather than impressions of divine grace.

This same dynamic is present when the beautiful creature is seen. For like the icon, the creature's being is in the first instance a sign pointing to divine *res*. To not see the creature as such is the same type of failure as the failure to see the icon as such. Note what happens to our understanding of the creature as a result: the language of creatureliness becomes inscrutable. Its features become arbitrary (merely the result of natural selection or the whims of the gods or fate); creatures are superfluous in the sense that they have no fixed place in a putative whole, and so they are available for all sorts of reductive uses; nature becomes threatening as a bar to our human aspirations of immortality, infinite luxury, and an everlasting empire (for it is the express hope of our societies that there should always be such a society: this is played out in our science fiction dreams of endless colonization and exploration so that a society by the humans, of the humans, and for the humans shall not perish from the face of the universe); nature has no meaning but itself, and so if she should eventuate in a species that has the power of self-determination, that species would inherit the right and the responsibility to direct nature according to the dictates of its own needs and desires.

And so, in a world dominated by just such a view of creatures (and such a world is as ancient as it is postmodern), the experience of beauty, which is founded on at least the implicit recognition that the creature is not for itself and is not a mere being but also points to something else, takes the form of an interruption. It is other as the icon is other; it is equally a glimpse of another, transcendent world. The creature belongs to this world as the icon does but in a much more preliminary and veiled way, for it has been subjected to futility (that is, its *mysterium* has been diminished, and so its meaning has become more, but not entirely, vain). But this dim belonging is enough to mediate something of that other world, and this is what appears in the experience of beauty.

Depth

Like the icon, the creature, properly understood, is totally given to the signification of God because it exists only for this purpose: All of a creature's purposes relative to those things that are co-worldly to it are embraced in its fundamental purpose as declarative of a certain view of the Creator. Every part and every aspect of a creature has been subsumed to this purpose.

Creatures thus reference God with thick signification. This is in fact the ontological ground of the complex interrelationality that underlies the possibility and necessity of the growth of metaphorical complexes. This thick signification contributes to the ability of the creature to draw other creatures into itself in a God-directed ecstasy. It is not just a human but body and soul taken individually that reference God; and not just the body but each of its anatomical, chemical, and physical parts; and not just the soul but each of its capacities, experiences, thoughts, and so on. This grounds a certain reduction of the arts to theology precisely because the subject matter of each field of human inquiry is itself a sign pointing back to God and is already enveloped in multiple, overlapping webs of thick signification by virtue of being part of a world.

Beauty and Ecstasy

The Rapturing Power of Beauty

The efficacy of the icon is to snatch the worshipper up into a different world in order that that worshipper may thereby stand exposed to the influence of that world. It is the same for the creature: by presenting its *mysterium* it captivates us, snatches us from the mundane world (which, it may now be said, is a construct; for there *is* no creaturely world but the world in which every being encountered is the bearer of a rich and harmonious *mysterium*) and launches us in the direction in which the creature itself tends: toward God.

The being of creatures is ecstatic: the center of our being, the *mysterium* that gives us meaning, lies not within ourselves but outside ourselves, in God. Thus a creature that is in tune with this ecstatic center, such as a saint, may, by offering him- or herself to us, also be ushering us in, by an internal pathway, to the presence and mystery of God. Like the icon, this requires nothing extrinsic: the saint as such is the very road to be traveled, because the saint, in becoming most truly what he or she *is*, is also now a clear and translucent sign belonging to and pointing to God.

But it is not only the saint that has this function; it is only that in the saint this function is most perfected. The same dynamic whereby creaturely being, understood most authentically and specifically, has the power to launch us to the divine is what we intuit in theologically anamnetic moments. Because what we are reminded of is real, transcendent to us, and immanently relating to us personally, theological anamnesis is ecstatic. We are drawn out of ourselves in the direction of the heavenly realm.

In implicit contuition we do not recognize that this is what is happening. Fueled by our fundamental failure to see the creature properly at a conscious level (though at a deeper level we are seeing it properly, else we would not find it beautiful), we misread what we think is salient in the experience of beauty. We subjectivize it, or we attach it to one or another false transcendent (pleasure of all sorts [sexual, aesthetic, intellectual, athletic, etc.], a cause or ideal, a community [nation, tribe, race, etc.], or whatever). But the fact that our acknowledgment of its beauty can survive the toppling of any of these false transcendents indicates that we know better, that we do not really love beauty for any of these pseudo-transcendent ends.

It is, in fact, irresponsible to speak of rapture without speaking specifically of *whither* one is raptured, as if it were a great thing merely to be seized. If this were so, what is to distinguish rapture from kidnapping? Why is the one desired, and the other deplored? It is to do with the inherent directionality of rapture, which is expressed in both a destination (a place to which) and a purpose (an end for which). The place to which we are raptured is that heavenly realm where it is possible to receive as much of God as one's nature allows. This dovetails with the purpose of rapture, which is precisely this communication of God.

This reveals just how far we have fallen from a right understanding of the divine purposes for creatures in the world. The view we are developing here argues that the divine intent is that every single creature we encounter in the world be a site where God is met and grace is conferred. We were meant to live outside of ourselves in an ecstatic mode—that is, constantly drawn beyond ourselves and our perspective into those of other rational and non-rational creatures alike—and yet we were to be also constantly drawing everything else into ourselves through our own *mysterium*, becoming the occasion for ecstasy for everyone we meet. In this way our two great strivings, expressed by various binaries (to be known and to know, to truly receive and to truly give, to belong and to assimilate, etc.), would be constantly fulfilled in a total reciprocity of mutual sharing that would not threaten the identity of subject and object, but that rather would presuppose and validate the distinction.

The Transformative Power of Beauty

The result of this rapture is transformation.

Beauty transforms even when the contuition remains implicit. Beauty may ennoble, enrage, enliven, mortify, embolden, weaken; it may induce delight or despair, love or hate, devotion or revolution. But all of these are expressions of the fact that it has changed the viewer in a fundamental way. Free will allows us to decide what to do with the glimpse we get in beauty: Rilke does not tell us what to do with our life, only that we must change it. The imperative of beauty does not issue in some one specific action: "You must serve me." It is more humble than that, though no less imperious. The imperative of beauty is: "You must decide. You do not have to serve me, but you must choose this day whom you will serve."

The perception of beauty is therefore a crisis, a decisive moment on which a life turns. There are countless thousands or millions or billions of such moments in a life, to be sure—countless, for they cannot all be noticed because one is distracted by the command itself: one is sometimes too busy responding to the crisis to really take note of it. And yet the decisive nature of such moments is not diminished because of their commonality. Many course corrections are required before a life reaches its end, but none of them are without meaning: each one contributes to make the path taken what it is. Experiences of beauty are moments of testing, for in them God appears and asks us what we will do about the divine presence. And so each of these moments forms part of the larger testing of the human spirit, the central question of whether we will become what we are meant to be or will instead misform and misshape ourselves and follow a different master.

In explicit contuition, the power for transformation is greater precisely because the imperative is louder to the degree that the contuition is more explicit. As transparency increases, so does moral responsibility.

But just as it is irresponsible to speak of rapture without reference to the *whither*, so it is in the case of transformation. Into what are we being transformed? The answer has been given by the nature of the transformative work of the icon: we are being changed into the likeness of him who took on our likeness in order to repair the damaged road between creatures and God.

This is able to be true even where the grace of justification is lacking: unbelievers who encounter beauty may still come to express more of divine qualities as a result of the encounter. This should not be scandalous, or it should not be more scandalous than the Incarnation itself. It is an expression of God's unfailing love for all creation and God's desire for union with every creature. However, the Christian faith is not a matter of works, and so no amount of movement toward God as a result of implicit contuition in theologically anamnetic moments will save; everything turns on the person of Christ, and how one responds when confronted with the creaturely nature that is at the same time hypostatically united to that which appears in the theologically anamnetic moment. The Incarnation is the deepest mystery of beauty, for there the *mysterium rei* is personally joined in the closest possible way (and in a unique way) to that of which it is an image. And yet even here the two do not collapse, for the natures remain unconfused.

But again it is explicit contuition in which we see the dynamics at work in their fullest form. When I come to the experience of beauty with the eyes of faith I make the matter of my soul and life maximally malleable given the conditions of sin in this life. Such a person is most open to the influence that is streaming forth in the theologically anamnetic moment, and so the person becomes most like what is beheld. In such moments the glimpsed beauty takes hold of a life and replicates itself by rapturing the soul to a place where grace is communicated freely and delightfully. This grace repairs and remakes the wounded *mysterium*, rendering the saint more beautiful by rendering the saint more translucently causative of theological anamnesis. The beauty of holiness is the translucence of a saintly life.

Postscript

He that sees the beauty of holiness, or the true moral good, sees
the greatest and most important thing in the world, which is the
fullness of all things, without which the world is empty, no better
than nothing, yea, worse than nothing. Unless this is seen, nothing
is seen, that is worth seeing: for there is no other true excellency or
beauty. Unless this be understood, nothing is understood, that is
worthy of the exercise of the noble faculty of understanding. This
is the beauty of the Godhead, and the divinity of Divinity (if I may
so speak), the good of the infinite Fountain of Good.

Jonathan Edwards, *Religious Affections*

The individual who experiences beauty has come into the discussion of this
volume only obliquely: I have focused on this subject only to the extent that
it is necessary to explicate such beautiful moments. This is in its own way a
response to subjectivism: I wished to show that an account of beauty (and
referentiality in general) could take the subjective elements of the experiences
seriously and give a positive evaluation of them without being reduced to an
account of the subject as such. The general rules of subjectivity hold over any
variety of types of accounts of the nature of possible experiencing subjects.

However, I do not think it right to end the volume without something of a
more direct look at the implications for the individual subject of the account
given here. The implications are legion and range over a wide variety of topics;
but because the interpretive lens is focused on the experience of beauty, it is
above all the question of desire and fulfillment that is in need of attention.

189

Beauty and Desire

Whatever is only one source of fulfillment among others can never be *the* source of fulfillment, for it is partial and therefore only participates in the ultimate source. Relationships, art, meaningful work: these only fulfill even to the partial extent that they do because they mediate the ultimate source to us.

In fact, because each creature is capable of causing theological anamnesis and is itself precisely as this particular sort of reminder, and further because each creature is found beautiful by us to the extent that it in fact succeeds in so reminding us, we confess (often against our will) in the moment of the experience of beauty that it is God who is our soul's delight, it is God who is the object of our truest and deepest longing. This longing does not replace our longing for creatures any more than our delight in God replaces our delight in creatures; rather, the longing for God that is at the heart of all our longing recontextualizes our longing for creatures. The latter is now an instance of the former: without ceasing to desire this particular beauty, my desire for it is itself a longing and desire for the one who is all beauty; without ceasing to take delight in this wonder, doing so becomes itself a way of delighting in the one who is all delight (cf. Song 5:16).

This alone is the love without which we will die, in two senses: First, to be parted from this love is one of the senses of damnation, the true death. Second, we are like other creatures in that our *mysterium rei* is also the place where we most image God, and so we are living images, bound to our original as the locus of our intelligibility. But because we also have been given the power of limited self-determination, our end is not only something toward which we are pointed and to which we can point others; it is also that to which we must cling if we are to be most truly ourselves. Authentic being and life in the truest sense are only possible for us in union with God, the fountain of grace, and so to lack this is a death of loss of self. Union with God is both the deepest desire and the deepest need of the rational creature.

Beauty therefore unfolds from the place where my longing, my need, and what is demanded of me by God coincide. Consider Psalm 37:4:

> Delight yourself in the Lord,
>> and he will give you the desires of your heart.

This does not then mean that if you set aside your desires for everything but the Lord, once you have delighted in God sufficiently or perfectly, you will then also be given the other, non-God things you desire as a sort of bonus. Rather, it means that delight in the Lord by recognition that it is the Lord who is the referent of the excellence of each thing, and the meaning of that excellence, is the only way to truly possess (possess in accordance with the truth) the desires of your heart.

To sharpen the point a little: If I possess the desires of my heart apart from delight in the Lord, then (a) I do not possess the deepest desires of my heart, and (b) even what I do possess will not satisfy, for it will have been evacuated of its mystery and emptied of beauty. I will find that what once delighted me delights me no longer, and I will be powerless to explain why.

This can be pushed further: the phrase "desires of your heart" points to that innermost place where one is most fully oneself. This place is the *mysterium rei*. But the *mysterium rei* is necessarily pointed at God and can only be explained and fulfilled with reference to God. Thus, the desires of our hearts are not just those things we want most but those things we want that make us most ourselves: God and things desired for God's sake. These may not be our most stringent desires, and indeed at least some of the time they are not—our desires are divided. But they are our truest desires in the sense that they come from that place that is most truly us and they aim at a fulfillment that makes us most truly who we are.

It is, then, impossible to possess the desires of my heart in a mode that is in accordance with how I desire them (and therefore in any satisfactory or ultimately meaningful way) apart from delight in the Lord. Note, however, that this delight may be merely implicit, and so it does not follow that only the one who intentionally delights in the Lord ever gains his or her desire. But one who only implicitly and perhaps even against one's conscious will delights in the Lord will always be in danger of losing the desires of that one's heart, because such a person is on a path that is slowly turning the Lord from an object of delight to an object of scorn.

Even for the one who explicitly delights in the Lord, the coincidence of longing, need, and what is demanded by God is hard to achieve because my longing is so often at odds with what I need and with what God desires. Beauty both requires and motivates the rectifying of my desires by calling me to the place of coincidence where alone my heart can find satiety and rest. This leads us to the final consideration: fulfillment.

Beauty and Fulfillment

We are rarely the subjects in experiences of beauty. Rather, beauty surprises us; it addresses us. Generally, we can only describe ourselves as subjects when we describe ourselves as discovering something that lay waiting for us in the world ("I find this beautiful"). The encounter with the beautiful has already taken hold of us when we first become cognizant of it, and so we come to our awareness of beauty as ones already addressed by beauty, as those on whom beauty now waits to see what type of response we will give.

The place from which we can respond authentically to beauty (that is, the place from which we would be most ourselves and most capable of letting beauty be itself) is the place we have just described: the intersection of our desire, need, and duty. What type of response would this be? What response effortlessly meets the appearance of what one longs for and what one needs and what simultaneously allows one to fulfill one's duty? What could this be but joy?

And so in a general sense, we meet the beautiful most properly with rejoicing. And because we are created with a natural capacity for joy, this requires no special action and is common to all observers of beauty. The joy at which we may arrive naturally may be called natural joy. But there is another joy, the joy that it is the fruit of the Holy Spirit. Natural joy is but an analogue to this spiritual joy, which, as a gift of grace, can be given only by God.

Now attention to the beautiful precisely according to what renders it beautiful—namely, its imaging of God—disposes the heart for the reception of grace. Explicit contuition is grounded in faith (at least that mustard seed of faith that does not immediately repudiate what is seen but lets it stand even if it sits in contradiction to the beholder's entire worldview) and is productive of faith (either eliciting the first germination of that tiny seed or causing the increase of a faith that is already underway); thus it stands upon the Holy Spirit as the condition of the possibility of its existence and is itself part of the dynamics of grace and sanctification. Given all this, spiritual joy is not just a possible response to explicit contuition in theological anamnesis: it is its goal.

But we do not stop at joy, for joy is fruitful and productive of gratitude and love. Gratitude is the recognition that the entire blissful economy one is caught up in is one that has been gifted. Gratitude receives the gifts of grace *as gifts*, rather than attempting to dominate them by claiming an antecedent meritorious ground in the self. Gratitude is not blind to merit, but it is aware that even true merit (the faith that is well exercised and deserves to be increased) is itself only the fruit of antecedent grace and so provides no ground for a sense of entitlement (cf. the parable of the talents, Matt. 25:14–30). Gratitude is then deployed in the middle voice: neither entirely active, for one receives rather than takes, nor entirely passive, for one is not simply acted on but must act to receive. It is the stretching out of one's hands to a gift that is offered, or it is a letting be that requires action precisely because the self must be restrained in order to remain receptive.

Where joy and gratitude have arisen there comes the opportunity also for love as a fruit of the Spirit, spiritual love as the highest action of the human will. Just as the highest activity of the intellect (a knowing that is in maximal union with an object that exceeds it and so is inexhaustible) requires grace (because such an object cannot be known unless it offers itself, and such a knowing is not possible unless the intellect is elevated), so the highest action of the will (to cling totally and irrevocably to the object of its most intense desires) requires grace, for the will must be elevated and stabilized to accomplish this.

Beauty then aims at the beatification of the creature: both in the sense that it aims to make the creature *beatus*, blessed in the possession of its deepest longing and need, and in the sense that it aims to render the creature beautiful by maximizing the rational creature's own way of imaging God (by fulfilling the will and elevating it to its highest use). This is not the reason non-rational creatures exist in the world, for their being, in its *mysterium*, is for God, not for rational creatures. But it *is* part of the reason that they are co-worldly with rational creatures, and so when their beauty is recognized it also fulfills something of their own purpose, bringing them to another sort of completion.

In other words, beauty aims at the reproduction of another beauty like itself in another. The image of God in creatures works upon the (broken) image of God in us to restore it or even (in the case of a glorified rational creature) to reaffirm it. But since only God can cause conformity to God, it is the power of the Holy Spirit working through the creature's likeness that is the agent of this transformation. The creature is the occasion for this agency, and that is not to be taken in the sense of "merely"; for it is the greatest honor of creatures to be useful to their Lord by being the means by which the divine power accomplishes the divine plan. In this way it is clear that there is a sacramental character to all of reality that nevertheless does not render every creature a sacrament. It is also worth noting that this sacramentalism is not a response to the fallen state of the world: it is the original intention and will abide even in Heaven.

However, as was said, it is difficult for a sinful creature to arrive at this space where longing, need, and duty correspond. Our sinfulness grounds a suspicion that our duty and our longing cannot line up, and also wrests our longing away from where it should be such that it seems not to line up with either our need or our duty. But this is mere seeming: our ongoing ability to see beauty shows that we have not entirely forgotten what it is we truly long for. But even that we can be deluded by this false appearance is indicative of the fact that sin is the greatest obstacle in the search for beauty and the attaining of fulfillment. And because sin is not simply an inability but a moral problem, we need not only revelation to show us what we have failed to see but also atonement to absolve us of our sins and restore us to a right relationship with both our Lord and the world around us. And because the effects of sin reverberate throughout our entire nature and are not removed but only lightened by Baptism, sanctification and pilgrim grace are required for us to make progress in the way of beauty.

So in the end, beauty is a summons. It begins with the most vulnerable part of ourselves, bypassing our sophistication, training, and habituation to reach that inmost point from which we know ourselves to be creatures and to be under authority. But it touches that place graciously, not in judgment; and so, rather than finding ourselves terrified before a truth we have hidden from for so long, we find ourselves romanced by a desire we can never seem to shake. This is no humble beginning, and so it should be no surprise that from there the summons grows larger and stronger until it encompasses our whole being, our whole way of looking at the world, our whole way of being in the world. Beauty does not demand our allegiance: it reveals that it already holds at least part of our divided allegiance. But it does demand our action: it condemns our continued allegiance to anything else and the lukewarmness of our allegiance to the thing our own hearts confess alone really matters. We shrink from this condemnation because we fear the implications, but this is ignorance and folly. For if we would but bow our heads and accept the sentence, beauty is revealed to be a summons directed not primarily at condemning us but at creating in us another like itself. Beauty comes to teach us that if we endure the divine judgment with patience, humility, and compunction, we will find, through the death and resurrection of Christ and the indwelling Holy Spirit, that all divine judgments are also mercies and that our path to holiness lies through the fire.

Bibliography

Augustine. *City of God*. Translated by Henry Bettenson. London: Penguin, 2003.

———. *Confessions*. Translated by F. J. Sheed. Edited by Michael P. Foley. 2nd ed. Indianapolis: Hackett, 2006.

———. *On Christian Teaching*. Translated by R. P. H. Green. Oxford: Oxford University Press, 1997.

Balthasar, Hans Urs von. *The Glory of the Lord*. Translated by Erasmo Leiva-Merikakis, Andrew Louth, Francis McDonagh, Brian McNeil, John Saward, Martin Simon, Rowan Williams, and Oliver Davies. 7 vols. San Francisco: Ignatius Press, 1982–89.

———. *Theo-Logic*. Translated by Adrian J. Walker and Graham Harrison. 3 vols. San Francisco: Ignatius Press, 2000–2005.

Barthes, Roland. *The Eiffel Tower and Other Mythologies*. Translated by Richard Howard. Berkeley: University of California Press, 1979.

———. *L'aventure sémiologique*. Paris: Éditions de Seuil, 1985.

Baudrillard, Jean. *Simulacra and Simulation*. Translated by Sheila Faria Glaser. Ann Arbor: University of Michigan Press, 1994.

———. *The Transparency of Evil: Essays on Extreme Phenomena*. Translated by James Benedict. London: Verso, 1993.

Begbie, Jeremy S. *Theology, Music and Time*. Cambridge: Cambridge University Press, 2000.

Beowulf. Translated by Seamus Heaney. New York: Norton, 2000.

Bonaventure. *Bonaventure on the Eucharist: Commentary on the Sentences, Book IV, dist. 8–13*. Translated by Junius Johnson. Vol. 23 of Dallas Medieval Texts and Translations. Louvain: Peeters Press, 2017.

———. *Breviloquium*. Translated by Dominic Monti, OFM. Vol. 9 of *Works of St. Bonaventure*. St. Bonaventure, NY: Franciscan Institute Publications, 2005.

————. *Collationes in Hexaemeron*. Vol. 5 of *Opera Omnia*. Edited by PP Collegii a S. Bonaventurae. Florence: Quaracchi, 1882–1902.

————. *Collations on the Hexaemeron: Conferences on the Six Days of Creation; The Illuminations of the Church*. Translated by Jay Hammond. Vol. 18 of *Works of St. Bonaventure*. St. Bonaventure, NY: Franciscan Institute Publications, 2018.

————. *Collations on the Seven Gifts of the Holy Spirit*. Translated by Zachary Hayes. Vol. 14 of *Works of St. Bonaventure*. St. Bonaventure, NY: Franciscan Institute Publications, 2008.

Brecht, Berthold. *The Caucasian Chalk Circle*. Translated by Frank McGuiness. London: Methuen Drama, 2007.

Chesterton, G. K. *The Man Who Was Thursday*. Harmondsworth: Penguin, 1986.

Dante, *The Divine Comedy: Paradiso*. Translated by John D. Sinclair. Oxford: Oxford University Press, 1961.

Edwards, Jonathan. *Religious Affections*. Edited by John E. Smith. New Haven: Yale University Press, 1959.

Gregory the Great. *Dialogues*. Vol. 66 of *Patrologia latina, cursus completus*, edited by J.-P. Migne. Paris: J.-P. Migne, 1866.

Hart, David Bentley. *The Beauty of the Infinite: The Aesthetics of Christian Truth*. Grand Rapids: Eerdmans, 2003.

Hart, Trevor. *Between the Image and the Word*. Surrey: Ashgate, 2013.

Herbert, George. *The Country Parson and the Temple*. Classics of Western Spirituality. Mahwah, NJ: Paulist Press, 1981.

Hopkins, Gerard Manley. "As Kingfishers Catch Fire." In *Gerard Manley Hopkins: Poems and Prose*, edited by W. H. Gardner, 51. New York: Penguin, 1985. First published 1953.

————. *The Major Works including All the Poems and Selected Prose*. Edited by Catherine Phillips. Oxford: Oxford University Press, 2009.

Jeffrey, David Lyle. *In the Beauty of Holiness: Art and the Bible in Western Culture*. Grand Rapids: Eerdmans, 2017.

John Paul II. *Letter to Artists*. Boston: Pauline Books and Media, 1999.

Keble, John. *The Christian Year; Thoughts in Verse for the Sundays and Holy Days throughout the Year*. New York: Dutton, 1891.

Lakoff, George, and Mark Johnson. *Metaphors We Live By*. Chicago: University of Chicago Press, 1980.

The Lenten Triodion. Translated by Mother Mary and Archimandrite Kallistos Ware. London: Faber and Faber, 1977.

Lewis, C. S. *The Lion, the Witch, and the Wardrobe*. New York: Scholastic, 1987.

————. *Surprised by Joy: The Shape of My Early Life*. San Diego: Harcourt, Brace, 1956.

————. *The Weight of Glory and Other Addresses*. Edited by Walter Hooper. New York: Simon & Schuster, 1980.

MacDonald, George. *Phantastes: A Faerie Romance*. Mineola, NY: Dover, 2005.

Ortega y Gasset, José. *"The Dehumanization of Art" and other Essays on Art, Culture, and Literature*. Princeton: Princeton University Press, 1968.

Ouspensky, Leonid. *Theology of the Icon*. Crestwood, NY: St. Vladimir's Seminary Press, 1978.

Rilke, Rainer Maria. *Selected Poems: With Parallel German Text*. Oxford: Oxford University Press, 2011.

Shakespeare, William. *Macbeth*. In *The Riverside Shakespeare*, edited by G. Blakemore Evans and J. J. M. Tobin, 2:1355–90. 2nd ed. Boston: Houghton Mifflin, 1997.

Thomas Aquinas. *Summa Theologica*. Translated by the Fathers of the English Dominican Province. 5 vols. New York: Benziger Brothers, 1948.

Tolkien, J. R. R. "On Fairy-Stories." Brainstorm-services.com. http://brainstorm-services.com/wcu-2005/fairystories-tolkien.html.

————. *Tree and Leaf*. London: HarperCollins, 2001.

William of Ockham. *Summa Totius Logicae*. Translated by Michael J. Loux. 2 vols. South Bend, IN: St. Augustine Press, 1998.

Wolterstorff, Nicholas. *Art in Action*. Grand Rapids: Eerdmans, 1980.

————. *Art Rethought: The Social Practices of Art*. Oxford: Oxford University Press, 2015.

Index